Regulation by Proxy

Regulation by Proxy

How the USDA Relies on Public, Nonprofit, and For-Profit Intermediaries to Oversee Organic Food in the U.S.

David P. Carter

LEXINGTON BOOKS
Lanham • Boulder • New York • London

Published by Lexington Books
An imprint of The Rowman & Littlefield Publishing Group, Inc.
4501 Forbes Boulevard, Suite 200, Lanham, Maryland 20706
www.rowman.com

6 Tinworth Street, London SE11 5AL, United Kingdom

British Library Cataloguing in Publication Information Available

Library of Congress Cataloging-in-Publication Data

ISBN 978-1-4985-7419-8 (cloth)
ISBN 978-1-4985-7420-4 (electronic)

For my dad, Stephen Alonzo Carter, who exhibited an intellectual and spiritual curiosity unrivaled by most. We undoubtedly would have spent hours discussing the ideas in these pages; I hope shadows of those unfulfilled conversations made their way into the words that follow.

Contents

List of Figures

List of Tables

Acknowledgments

This book is the product of a multi-year, multi-institution research effort that I was fortunate to be a part of during my graduate studies at the University of Colorado Denver. Referred to throughout this book as the Organic Regulation Research Project, the effort was supported by the National Science Foundation under Grant No. 1124541. I am especially indebted to Christopher M. Weible, Saba N. Siddiki, Xavier Basurto, and John Brett as project originators and leaders, generous mentors, and gracious colleagues and friends. Thank you for entrusting me with even the most consequential research tasks and showing patience as I found my way through them; I cannot imagine a better scholarly preparation.

I am further indebted to project collaborators Sara Miller-Chonaiew, Alison Kent, and Ainsley Smith. Sara's devotion to the project no doubt bolstered its success and practical relevance considerably. On a personal note, puzzling through various project elements with the benefit of Sara's quick thinking, conviviality, and kind demeanor made the experience that much more enjoyable. Alison's enthusiasm in executing the project's study of organic inspectors filled an important research gap and her ever inquisitive and positive disposition brought levity to the research. Thank you, Sara and Ali.

Of course, the work of the research team would not have been possible without the organic certification professionals and organic agriculture community members that devoted time and attention to our data collection efforts. These include organic certifier personnel, organic inspectors, and organic farmers that responded to survey requests, and the dozens of individuals that picked up a phone or sat down for an interview. Thank you.

I have been unbelievably fortunate to learn from and work with folks that are not only outstanding scholars, but also first-rate humans. I would like to express an immense gratitude to Christopher M. Weible and Tanya Heikkila as co-directors of the University of Colorado Denver's Workshop on Policy Process Research (WOPPR) and my WOPPR colleagues, including Johnathan Pierce, Saba Siddiki, Mark Davis, Sam Gallaher, Kristin Olofsson, Juniper Katz, Daniel Costie, and Jarkko Levänen. The WOPPR provided an unparalleled mentorship and research environment, abundant in challenges, opportunities, and support. Chris and Tanya have created a special space for public policy scholars-in-training—one that is well worth emulating.

A long list of other folks supported me during the research and writing that culminate in this book. In addition to those affiliated with the WOPPER, I am forever grateful to the University of Colorado Denver School of Public Affairs' faculty and staff, who contributed to my graduate education in innumerable ways. I am further grateful to my colleagues at the University of Utah's Department of Political Science and Public Affairs Program. The collegiality and camaraderie I've found at the U are beyond compare. Finally, I am grateful to the guidance, support, and friendship of a number of scholars who helped inform and strengthen (either directly or indirectly) the best parts of this book. These include Jessica Sowa, Edella Schlager, Peter J. May, and Stephanie Moulton, among others.

I extend a final deep and heartfelt appreciation to my family: Kathy Carter-Dulin, Michelle Tucker, and Sandra Carter, and the family I've been fortunate to "pick up" over the years: Larry Dulin, Philip, Lucas, and Dylan Tucker, Camille Shepherd and Keith Fessenden, Conner and Cindy Shepherd, John Owen Shepherd, and John and Cindy Thomas. Thanks for taking the journey with me. Above all, I thank my partner in all things important, Sarah E.E. Shepherd. Your belief in me is an inspiration and gift of the like I never could have imagined. I love you, S.E.E.S.

Abbreviations

ACA	Accredited Certifiers Association
CCOF	California Certified Organic Farmers
CDFA	California Department of Food and Agriculture
CDPH	California Department of Public Health
EPA	Environmental Protection Agency
IFOAM	International Federation of Organic Agriculture Movements
IOIA	International Organic Inspectors Association
ISO	International Organization for Standardization
NASS	National Agricultural Statistics Service
NOSB	National Organic Standards Board
OIG	Office of the Inspector General
OMRI	Organic Materials Review Institute
OTA	Organic Trade Association
USDA	United States Department of Agriculture
WSDA	Washington State Department of Agriculture

Chapter One

Regulation by Proxy

On May 1, 2017, under the headline "Why your 'organic' milk might not be organic," *Washington Post* investigative journalist Peter Whoriskey used a combination of site visits, satellite imagery, and product analyses to show that Aurora Organic Dairy's largest facility failed to comply with U.S. organic regulations. At issue were United Stated Department of Agriculture (USDA) requirements that organic livestock operators feed cattle on open pasture for at least 120 days during the grazing season. Because Aurora's northern Colorado High Plains complex was home to over 15,000 cows, reporters should have seen thousands of grazing cattle. Instead, drone footage revealed near-empty fields alongside cows confined to feedlots. A high-resolution satellite photo from earlier in the 2016 season similarly showed hundreds, rather than thousands, of pasture-grazing cattle.

Product analyses conducted by Virginia Tech dairy science professor Benjamin Corl confirmed reporters' observations. Milk produced by grass-fed cows exhibits higher levels of certain fats, such as conjugated linoleic acid and alpha-linoleic acid, and lower levels of others, such as linoleic acid. Corl's blind comparison of milk from eight companies found that Aurora milk exhibited characteristics more in line with conventional milk than organic: relatively *low* levels of conjugated linoleic and alpha-linoleic acids and relatively *high* levels of linoleic acid. The findings mirrored those of a 2008 analysis by Milkweed, a dairy economics report, which found Aurora's milk ranked last out of ten organic milks tested for the presence of grass feeding-associated fats.

The *Washington Post* investigation was not the first time Aurora Organic Dairy was caught skirting the regulations. *The Chicago Tribune* published similar reports as early as 2005. In a subsequent 2007 investigation, the

USDA found Aurora responsible for 14 "willful violations" of the organic standards. Although the USDA proposed revoking Aurora's organic certification, it ultimately resolved the issue through a consent agreement in which Aurora agreed to undergo a one-year probationary period and make major operational changes. Two years later, self-proclaimed organic industry watchdog the Cornucopia Institute filed a formal complaint with the USDA that the High Plains complex continued to ignore the organic livestock grazing requirements. Reflecting on Aurora's track record, Whorikey's 2017 article quoted Milkweed's editor Pete Hardin as stating: "There has been an obvious failure by USDA to enforce the organic pasture standard."

But, according to the *Washington Post* investigation, the failure was not the USDA's alone. Whoriskey found that the Colorado Department of Agriculture, the certifying agent that Aurora Organic Dairy paid $13,000 a year to administer its organic certification, failed to follow USDA guidelines for conducting organic livestock inspections. The Colorado Department of Agriculture held its 2016 annual inspection of the High Plains complex in November, well outside of the grazing season, thereby making it impossible to verify Aurora's pasture rule compliance. Although the USDA allows certifiers to conduct additional site visits outside of an operation's annual inspection, an Aurora representative confirmed that the November inspection was the only one held at the High Plains complex in 2016. "We do expect that inspections occur during the grazing season for a livestock operation . . ." stated National Organic Program Deputy Administrator Miles McEvoy in an interview with Whoriskey ". . . so if that was a pattern, that a certifier was not doing that, that would certainly be a big problem."

Assigning responsibility for the apparent regulatory breakdown at the heart of the Aurora Organic Dairy case is straightforward: it arguably falls on the USDA's National Organic Program, the regulatory body charged with ensuring what industry members refer to as "organic integrity." Determining what *caused* the breakdown is more challenging, complicated by what Whoriskey calls the USDA's "unusual system" for regulating organic food. Under this system, the National Organic Program oversees organic certification in the U.S. but relies on independent certification organizations, like the Colorado Department of Agriculture, to monitor organic food producers and handlers for organic standards compliance. As such, several factors help explain the Aurora Organic case, including monitoring inadequacies at the Colorado Department of Agriculture, lapses on the part of the National Organic Program in overseeing the Colorado Department of Agriculture's regulatory practices, and the competing mandates the Program juggles—not to mention the fact that the organic industry's growth has arguably eclipsed the Program's regulatory capacity since its implementation in 2002.

For organic policy stakeholders and consumers, alike, the compound explanation of regulatory failure is sure to raise broader questions about how organic food is regulated. Is the Aurora Organic case an exception to an otherwise robust regulatory arrangement or does it represent systematic flaws in organic food oversight under the USDA? How is organic integrity upheld when the causes of regulatory failures are diffuse and varied? What unseen vulnerabilities arise from the USDA's "unusual" regulatory system and are they justified by its benefits? Such questions, in turn, arouse perennial scholarly debates over the strengths and liabilities of administrative complexity, the tradeoffs involved in program decentralization, and accountability challenges when governmental authority is bestowed upon independent, sometimes nongovernmental actors (Stoker 1998). Indeed, the administration USDA organic standards offers a timely context in which to better understand the implications of decentralized regulatory administration, or, put another way—regulation by proxy.

ORGANIC CERTIFICATION AS DECENTRALIZED REGULATION

Although the term organic food often conjures images of bucolic family farms, Aurora Organic Dairy—a mega-dairy that supplies milk for the house brands of major retailers, such as Walmart and Costco—is in many respects a more accurate representation of most organic farming today. Organic food has gone mainstream. What was once a niche market spurred by fringe social movements reached a $47 billion a year global industry in 2016 (OTA 2017c). Fifteen years ago most organic products in the U.S. were sold at local farmers' markets or high-end specialty outlets (Raynolds 2004). Today, organic products are found across the shelves of just about every major retail grocery store. The Organic Trade Association (2017c) estimates that as many as 82 percent of U.S. households purchased organic food products in 2016.

Much of the growth in demand for organic products stems from consumers' desire for credible information over how their food is grown and produced. As agricultural practices advance in sophistication, food markets continue to consolidate, and global agri-food systems become progressively interconnected, consumers are evermore disconnected from their food sources (Kneafsey et al. 2008). Shoppers seem increasingly concerned by the chemicals and industrial processes that characterize conventional agricultural practices and strive to avoid them in their purchasing decisions (Yiridoe, Bonti-Ankomah, and Martin 2005). Suspicion is growing among many consumers over the role of technology, such as genetic engineering, in agricultural production, and what unknown risks such technology might pose to human and environmental health (Eiser, Miles, and Frewer 2002).

Food companies have been quick to cater to consumers' desires for healthy and environmentally friendly food, resulting in an array of marking claims and confusion over terms such as "natural" and "sustainable." In the search for alternatives to conventionally produced foods, certified organic products are meant to inspire consumers' confidence in their understanding of the ingredients and processes that products reflect. Certification acts as a signal—indicating that a food product and the processes used to create it have met certain verified standards (Bartley 2011, Levi-Faur 2011). In the U.S. this signal takes the form of USDA organic certification. Although most consumers recognize the USDA organic label and associate organic certification with minimal-input or synthetic-free agricultural practices, few understand the regulatory standards that define organic in the U.S. (Yiridoe, Bonti-Ankomah, and Martin 2005), much less how they are determined, administered, and enforced.

What most shoppers know about organic food policy likely does little to increase their understanding of (much less confidence in) the USDA organic label. The media tends to limit its coverage to provocative investigative reports that highlight what appear to be regulatory failures, such as how hens raised to lay organic eggs live in conditions surprisingly similar to their conventional counterparts (Warner 2010b) and accounts of "big ag" dairy producers flouting organic rules. While most of such investigative reports appear credible, they often fail to couch the findings in their wider contexts, such as whether the treatment of organic poultry violates traditional principles of organic agriculture. Perhaps more importantly, they typically stop short of examining the extent to which there are systemic flaws in the USDA's oversight of organic food, such as whether regulatory violations like those seen in the case of Aurora Organic Dairy are exceptions or widespread.

This book offers a window into the decentralized regulatory landscape that makes up USDA organic certification—a landscape populated by an assortment of actors from both within and outside of government. The book describes how organic certification was born from a mix of competition, informal associations, and collective action, and only more recently codified in federally mandated regulations. It shows the many ways in which USDA organic certification is reliant on a host of governmental and nongovernmental entities to ensure regulatory effectiveness and credibility, and the interdependent relationships that exist between public, nonprofit, and for-profit organizations in determining, administering, and enforcing organic standards. In the process, it examines the strengths and vulnerabilities of such a decentralized and organizationally diverse regulatory arrangement.

My analysis does not present USDA organic certification as a regulatory anomaly. Rather, it considers the administratively decentralized landscape of organic regulation as an illustrative example of the complexity found across many regulatory settings. A renewed interest among contemporary regulatory scholars grapples with the structural variation observed in empirical regulatory contexts and the manners in which regulation depends on the engagement, both formal and informal, of actors that are legally and functionally independent of regulatory authorities. Embracing such complexity casts fresh light on routine questions regarding how regulations are administered. It also raises new questions regarding the appropriate roles and functions of de facto regulatory actors.

The USDA organic certification case shows that there are undeniable strengths to an administratively decentralized and organizationally diverse program design. By drawing on entities from outside of the regulatory agency, the system leverages the expertise, capacity, and innovation of the nonprofit and for-profit sectors towards more informed and responsive regulatory administration. It further incorporates choice for the targets of organic food regulations by allowing food producers and handlers to choose the agent that provides them organic certification. Recognizing the immense variation within the U.S. agricultural industry, this choice allows organic businesses to tailor their certification services to better align with their business needs and constraints.

The analysis also illuminates the vulnerabilities that are created by the way that organic food is regulated. Organizational diversity in the administration of regulatory standards equates to differences in organizational capacity and competence, threatening inconsistent application of standards and disparities in the monitoring and enforcement of regulatee behavior. Each layer of decentralization introduces a new potential for "agency problems" (Coglianese and Lazer 2003, 718) in which the actors to whom regulatory authority is delegated face their own incentives; incentives which may or may not align with regulatory program objectives. For example, the choice that benefits organic businesses creates competition between organic certifiers—the agents charged with monitoring USDA organic standards compliance. Competition between certifiers, in turn, can undermine the integrity with which those standards are administered if it drives certifiers to loosen their regulatory stringency to attract and retain certification clients.

Examining a regulatory arrangement as complex as USDA organic certification requires assembling several theoretical traditions from the fields of regulation, public policy, and public administration; an exercise in "theory-pluralism" to address questions "[for] which no one theory or set of theories will be able to cope with in isolation" (Whetsell 2013). My analysis is grounded in a framework for understanding decentralized regulatory governance (Abbott, Levi-Faur, and Snidal 2017b). Within this framework, the analysis deploys insights from relevant literatures, including literature on regulatory enforcement approaches and inspection styles (May and Burby 1998, May and Winter 1999, May and Wood 2003), public administration literature on public, nonprofit, and private sector differences (Bozeman 2004, Boyne 2002, Dahl and Lindblom 1953), organization theory literature on organizational responses to competitive service environments (Andrews, Boyne, and Walker 2006, Walker and Jeanes 2001), and public management literature on street-level bureaucracy (Dias and Maynard-Moody 2006, Hupe, Hill, and Buffat 2015), among others.

The benefits of the exercise extend beyond a more complete understanding of the organic certification case. U.S. organic regulation offers a context in which to examine the theoretical implications of a decentralized regulatory system that depends on public, nonprofit, and private action. In doing so, it offers scholars empirically informed insights into how such a system functions and the implications of such a program design on key program outcomes. It further takes seriously a lesson long noted by public administration scholars but often overlooked in regulatory studies: that organizations and the administrators that run them have profound impacts on how public programs are implemented (Bozeman 2007, Robichau and Lynn Jr. 2009). As stated by Rinquist, Worsham, and Eisner (2000, ix, see also Selznick 1985):

> If public policy is, in essence, a pattern of goal-driven actions, the way in which it is implemented by regulatory agencies must be of central concern . . . [y]et much of the existing work in regulation adopts simplifying assumptions that remove organizations from the picture.

This book presents an organizationally focused analysis of USDA organic certification. It maps the actors that play critical roles in the administration of organic regulations, examines the relationships between them, and considers the incentives and constraints they face. Finally, it assesses how they approach and execute their regulatory responsibilities and offers conclusions regarding how these regulatory behaviors impact the consistency and integrity of organic certification in the U.S. In doing so, it demonstrates that the benefits of engaging program complexity extend beyond a better understanding of regulatory processes and outputs—it can also help identify the program aspects that may hinder or promote policy goals.

USDA ORGANIC CERTIFICATION: AN OVERVIEW

Organic food regulation in the U.S. is mandated by the Organic Foods Production Act, passed as part of the 1990 Farm Bill. The Act outlined three explicit goals: (i) to establish national standards regulating the marketing of organically produced foods, (ii) to assure consumers that organically produced foods meet a consistent standard, and (iii) to facilitate interstate commerce in organic food products. To accomplish these goals, the Act authorized the creation of the National Organic Program. The National Organic Program, a regulatory entity housed under the USDA's Agriculture Marketing Service, is charged with developing and enforcing standards by which organic food is produced, handled, and marketed in the U.S.

A key attribute of USDA organic certification, and a central focus of this book, is that the regulatory arrangement is not as simple as a regulator (the National Organic Program) regulating industry activity (organic food production). Rather, the assortment of government and nongovernmental entities that gave rise to USDA organic certification were codified in it. Still others have emerged since the National Organic Program's implementation to fill key gaps in the Program's design. As such, the National Organic Program relies on a range of organizations and individuals from both within and outside of government to fulfill its mission. In the terminology used in this book, the Program is dependent on an assortment of "regulatory intermediaries"—organizations that are legally independent of the National Organic Program, yet nonetheless play crucial roles in contributing to USDA organic certification failures and successes.

First, the National Organic Program relies on a fifteen-member panel of experts known as the National Organic Standards Board (NOSB) to advise the development of organic standards and National Organic Program implementation. Composed of representatives from across stakeholder groups, the NOSB strives to reconcile the divergent understandings and goals that are reflected in the contemporary organic agriculture industry and market. The NOSB has an important but limited role: the Board has the *potential* to shape the manner in which organic food is both produced and regulated—but only to the extent that the National Organic Program values and incorporates NOSB recommendations.

Furthermore, rather than carry out inspections of every operation that wishes to be certified USDA organic, the National Organic Program accredits independent organizations known as accredited certifying agents, or simply certifiers, to certify agricultural producers and processors and monitor them for compliance with Program regulations. Certifiers make up a diverse organizational cohort. For example, some are governmental, such as state or county departments of agriculture, others are 501(c)(3) nonprofits, and still others are private, for-profit businesses. Organic certifiers, in turn, employ inspector personnel to conduct on-site inspections of certified operations. Some inspectors are in-house employees, while others are contracted on an inspection-by-inspection basis, working for many certifiers in a given year.

Organic certifiers play an essential role in USDA organic standards enforcement by monitoring for National Organic Program regulation compliance and initiating enforcement actions in response to regulatory violations. The enforcement actions available to certifiers are limited to those pertaining to certification—such as the proposed suspension or revocation of an operation's USDA organic certificate. Throughout most of the country, the National Organic Program, alone, holds the authority to enforce Program regulations through legal action, such as when fines or imprisonment are called for in response to fraudulent organic product claims by non-certified operations. Not so in California. Under National Organic Program oversight, the California State Organic Program is responsible for enforcing USDA organic standards by taking the legal actions that the National Organic Program is responsible for in other states.

Finally, although the National Organic Program's reliance on the NOSB, accredited certifiers, organic inspectors, and the California State Organic Program reflects the formal structure of USDA organic certification authority delegation, the regulatory arrangement informally relies on yet other organizations outsight of its direct authority. Organic certifier and inspector cohorts organize through professional associations—the Accredited Certifiers Association (ACA) in the case of certifiers, and the International Organic Inspectors Association (IOIA) in the case of inspectors—which play critical education and coordination roles both within the cohorts and with external entities. Furthermore, "materials review organizations," such as the Organic Materials Review Institute (OMRI) and Washington State Department of Agriculture's (WSDA) material review program, serve as credible brokers of information related to the input materials used in organic food production.

The chapters that follow, I investigate the layers of regulatory action created by USDA organic certifications' reliance on regulatory intermediaries, the authority and functions delegated to these intermediaries, and the authorized and informal relationships between the USDA and its intermediaries. I also delve into the regulatory implications that arise from USDA organic certifications' administratively decentralized design. For example, earlier in this chapter I referenced how organic producers chose their organic certifier and pay them a fee for certification services—an arrangement which creates opens the door for "certifier shopping" in which some producers search for a certifier that lets them get away with practices that more stringent certifiers won't (Miars 2012). Certifier shopping is just one of several implications that I explore in this book's analysis. The following section offers an overview of the research that informs the analysis. A chapter-by-chapter sketch then outlines the remainder of the book.

THE RESEARCH APPROACH

I assembled a variety of data and evidence in the analysis that follows, drawing from sources pragmatically and according to how well they spoke to the topic at hand. Primary or secondary data make up the foundation for analysis wherever possible, however, I also rely on synthesis of existing documents and scholarly literature to examine aspects of USDA organic certification that primary and secondary data fail to speak to. This section summarizes the various evidence sources; a more detailed description can be found in the Methodological Appendix.

Primary data were collected in a three-year long research project carried out by a research team spanning multiple universities (hereafter referred to as the Organic Regulation Research Project; see the Acknowledgments). These include quantitative data from surveys of three populations: accredited certifier representatives, organic inspectors, and certified organic farmers. They also include qualitative data from interviews with certifier personnel, inspectors, a National Organic Program representative, and other key informants. Many of these findings can be found across a number of journal publications (Carter et al. 2015, Carter et al. 2016, Carter 2016, Carter, Scott, and Mahallati 2017, Carter and Mahallati 2017, Carter 2017a, b, c, d, Carter, Heikkila, and Weible 2018), however, they have been reframed and reinterpreted within the framework of this book. Previously unreleased data accompany published findings in select chapters.

I compiled secondary data and evidence from several sources. The USDA's Organic Integrity Database (USDA 2018) was particularly valuable, as it lists all USDA certified organic operations, their locations and certification statuses (active, surrendered, suspended, or revoked), as well as their certifiers. Several administrative reports from entities such as the USDA, the U.S. Office of the Inspector General (OIG), and state government agencies were also very useful. Such secondary materials are incorporated throughout various chapters and are referenced directly where relevant.

Finally, the efforts of many scholars and practitioners contribute to the analysis. Of note are the works of Brian Obach, Julie Guthman, and Samantha Mosier, which feature heavily in my account of the evolution of U.S. organic food governance. Publications authored by CCOF's Kelly Damewood also deserve highlighting, as they form the basis of my examination of the California State Organic Program. To the extent this book succeeds in offering a comprehensive analysis of organic food regulation in the U.S., it is enabled in no small part by the work of these, and other, authors.

PREVIEWING THE BOOK

This book presents an organizationally focused analysis of USDA organic certification in twelve chapters. The second chapter draws on developments in regulatory design and administration theory to present a framework for examining the processes and implications of a decentralized regulatory design. The framework identifies broad categories of interest for analyzing regulation through diverse intermediaries, including regulatory arrangement institutional design, regulatory actor attributes, and regulatory actor interests and objectives. The framework also offers a structure for examining the policy implications raised by administrative decentralization, considered along four dimensions: regulatory fidelity, regulatory integrity, program feedback, and policy durability. The chapter concludes with a brief discussion of how the framework guides the book's analysis.

The third chapter paints the history of organic food governance in the U.S. It traces the evolution of organic regulation from early nongovernmental certification schemes in which farmers inspected farmers, through the emergence of third-party certification and state organic legislation, and finally to the passage of the Organic Foods Production Act. It recounts the controversy entailed in National Organic Program implementation and development of national organic standards. Drawing on this history, I depict how no single theory of institutional emergence explains the evolution of organic food governance in the U.S. Rather, it is a story of both market forces and political construction that continues today.

Chapters 4 through 10 each examine a different category of organic certification actors. The fourth chapter introduces the USDA organic standards, describing their substantive contours and the tensions created by their systems-based nature. The chapter then turns to the NOSB as the stakeholder advisory committee charged with making organic standards recommendations. The NOSB has come under considerable criticism from some stakeholders who charge the conventional agricultural sector holds disproportionate influence over Board processes and decisions. I discuss the resulting decreased legitimacy with which the NOSB and National Organic Program are held by such corners of the organic community and what decreased legitimacy could mean for the long-run viability of organic food policy.

The fifth chapter focuses on the National Organic Program as the regulatory authority charged with overseeing the decentralized organic certification landscape. By tracing the evolution of Program initiatives over time, I show how the Program pursues the parallel—and somewhat conflicting—core mandates of supporting a robust organic industry and ensuring rigorous organic standards enforcement. The chapter then zooms in on one of the Program's central functions: overseeing the competitive administration of USDA organic standards through a cadre of certifying agents. Synthesizing available records of the National Organic Program's accreditation oversight actions, I show that the Program has a track record of active accreditation enforcement. The Program's oversight suffers from a blind spot, however, as the Program fails to closely track the enforcement actions that certifiers take on its behalf. The chapter closes by discussing what the findings suggest for the consistency and integrity with which organic regulations are administered.

The sixth chapter engages the first "link" in the regulatory chain that extends from the National Organic Program, with an examination of accredited organic certifying agents. The chapter first offers a descriptive snapshot of the U.S. organic certifier cohort. Then, leveraging USDA organic certification status records, the first of two analyses finds evidence that certifiers vary considerable in either their willingness or capacity to take the more consequential actions available to them. Drawing data from the nation-wide survey of certified organic producers, a second analysis seeks to explain differences in certifiers' regulatory behaviors and services on the basis of organizational attributes and the competitiveness of regional markets for organic certification. I find a link between certifiers' sectors and the services they offer and no relationship between certification market competitiveness and certifiers' regulatory approaches. The findings are encouraging when it comes to the integrity of organic standards administration, but less so regarding regulatory consistency.

The seventh chapter turns to the second link in the National Organic Program's chain of authority, with an examination of organic inspectors. It, too, begins with a descriptive overview of inspector personnel—including who they work for and under what arrangements—before examining the relationship between inspectors and their employing certifying agents. Leveraging survey and interview data, I then investigate how organic inspectors navigate multiple obligations—including their commitment to the National Organic Program, their duty to their employing certifiers, and their sense of responsibility to organic operations—as well as inspectors' attitudes towards discretion. The findings show that inspectors tend to see themselves first and foremost as regulatory officials and generally favor strict adherence to the National Organic Program regulations, suggest that organic inspectors constitute a robust facet of organic certification.

The eighth chapter examines the somewhat unusual regulatory arrangement governing organic food production in the only state that hosts a state-level organic program: California. I cull the limited available evidence compiled to date regarding the California State Organic Program to outline potential the drawbacks and strengths of state-level organic standards enforcement. The State Program has historically compounded the administrative burdens facing California organic producers and processors, although the state has sought to reduce this burden through legislation. Meanwhile, proponents argue that the limitations are outweighed by State Program benefits. The discussion identifies the ways in which state organic programs *may* promote greater organic regulation fidelity, should they be implemented in other U.S. states.

The ninth chapter steps out of the authorized chain of National Organic Program authority to examine the manners in which informal actors, while operating outside of the formal regulatory structure, nonetheless contribute to organic standards administration. The chapter first examines how accredited certifiers and organic inspectors coordinate through professional associations—the ACA and IOIA—and the role these associations play in generating shared organic standards interpretations, offering important organic monitoring and enforcement education and training, and providing feedback to the National Organic Program. The chapter then describes how materials review organizations have emerged to address a critical gap in the National Organic Program's institutional authority—an inability to regulate organic input material. Collectively, these informal actors contribute to the consistency of organic standards administration, although incorporating them in the formal institutional structure of organic certification has proven a challenge, as I discuss at the end of the chapter.

The tenth chapter shifts the analysis from actors involved in organic standards administration to the regulatory targets that constitute the foundation of the organic food supply chain: certified organic producers. The chapter looks at the motivations that drive organic producers to practice organic methods and pursue organic certification, their perceptions of the USDA organic standards and National Organic Program impacts, and their experiences maintaining organic standards compliance. My analysis paints a favorable picture of some organic regulation impacts, while confirming the concerns critics claim regarding the Program's facilitation of "Big Ag" cooptation of the organic market and the burden that organic regulations impose on organic farmers. It also suggests organic producers' compliance motivations may constitute a net strength for USDA organic certification's regulatory integrity.

Finally, two concluding chapters reflect on the analysis to draw out the empirical and theoretical implications of USDA organic certification's decentralized regulatory design. The eleventh chapter reflects on the book's empirical findings. It recaps the analysis, considers USDA organic certification strengths and liabilities as they pertain to organic regulation fidelity and integrity, National Organic Program feedback, and U.S. organic policy durability, and discusses avenues for extending the analysis. The final chapter steps back to consider the study's theoretical implications. Beyond an understanding of organic food regulation in the U.S., the analysis offers timely insights into the consequences of institutional design and administrative decentralization, in the realms of regulatory policy and beyond.

Chapter Two

A Framework for Examining Decentralized Regulation

Traditional regulatory programs rely on an agency's control over specified activities through the development and direct application of regulations (May 2002, Selznick 1985). As a result, the conventional view of regulation focuses on two central actors: a regulator and a regulatory target. The regulator is an organization with authority—often, but not always, a government agency—that sets regulatory standards and is responsible for enforcing them within a specified industry or population. The industry or population that is expected to comply with those rules is the regulatory target (aka regulatees).

This book examines an administratively decentralized and organizationally diverse regulatory program—a task for which this conventional conceptualization of regulation is not well suited. My analysis therefore relies on a framework developed out of Abbott, Levi-Faur, and Snidal's (2017b) more nuanced model of regulatory activity. The model hinges on recognition of another actor category, known as regulatory intermediaries, which are defined as any entity that acts on behalf of a regulatory authority, or in conjunction with it, to achieve regulatory goals. Identification of regulatory intermediaries depends on their roles and behaviors, rather than their forms. This allows for the recognition of the diverse array of individuals and organizations that are found in empirical regulatory settings, including nonprofit and for-profit organizations, associations, and government levels and organizations outside of the regulatory authority in question (Abbott, Levi-Faur, and Snidal 2017b, Black 2008).

Situating intermediaries as a central concern for regulatory research expands the conceptualization of regulatory administration from a two-way to a three- (or more) way relationship. The basic resulting model assumes unidirectional linkages between a regulator (R), intermediaries (I), and regulatory targets (T): R → I → T (Abbott and Snidal 2009), in which linkages represent the exercise of authority between the regulator and the intermediary, and between the intermediary and the regulatory target. As the case of USDA organic certification makes clear, a variety of intermediaries may be engaged in regulatory activities, both under the authority of a regulator and outside of it. This chapter discusses the types of intermediaries that are relevant to USDA organic certification and constructs a framework for analyzing such cases of decentralized regulation.

INCORPORATING REGULATORY INTERMEDIARY DIVERSITY

Making sense of intermediary diversity is facilitated by identifying their relative positions in the regulator-intermediary-target model. Abbott, Levi-Faur, and Snidal (2017b) suggest that intermediary classification should follow the roles that intermediaries play in different stages of the regulatory process (agenda-setting, negotiation, implementation, monitoring, and enforcement). I take a slightly different approach. Recognizing that a stages conception of public policy imposes an unnecessarily simplistic depiction of what are, in reality, dynamic processes (Weible and Carter 2017), I use two factors to understand the roles of regulatory intermediaries in organic regulation: their relationships with other entities in the regulatory system and the functions that they perform relative to those other actors (see also Kourula et al. 2019).

The aforementioned three-party regulator-intermediary-target model depicts relationships among regulatory actors that are authoritatively sequential, representing a serial chain of authorized action. In decentralized regulatory arrangements, a serial chain involves more than one intermediary "link," particularly when an intermediary employs or empowers a second intermediary to perform some aspect of regulatory administration, such as compliance inspections (Abbott, Levi-Faur, and Snidal 2017b, Loconto 2017, Lyton 2017, van der Heijden 2017). Other intermediaries operate outside of authority chains, sometimes serving as a "go-between" connecting the regulator and another intermediary, the regulator and the regulatory target, or acting as a link between intermediaries. Because they operate independent of the authorized chain of action, such intermediaries can be considered parallel intermediaries (Abbott, Levi-Faur, and Snidal 2017b, Black 2008).

The functions that regulatory intermediaries perform vary widely depending on the regulatory context, goals, and design in question. Regulatory arrangements that incorporate expert counsel in the development of regulatory standards can be thought of as relying on rule-making intermediaries (Auld and Renckens 2017). In programs composed of serial intermediary chains, intermediaries perform vital oversight responsibilities; for example, third-party intermediaries can administer regulations and may employ inspection intermediaries to discharge monitoring functions (Lyton 2017, De Silva 2017). Where an intermediary group, itself, is composed of diverse organizational entities, they may seek to organize through coordinating bodies outside of the chain of authority (Carter and Mahallati 2017). Finally, where regulatory arrangements exhibit information "gaps," information intermediaries can emerge to serve as credible information suppliers and brokers (Lee 2010).

Figure 2.1 provides a visual representation of the intermediary functions reflected in USDA organic certification. The NOSB serves as a USDA organic standards rule-making intermediary, informing national organic standards development and the resulting National Organic Program regulations. The National Organic Program heads a serial chain of regulatory activity in which the Program accredits certifying agents to serve as third-party administrators (Carter 2016). Certifiers, in turn, employ inspectors to inspect certified operations for compliance with USDA organic standards (Carter 2017c). The California State Organic Program acts as enforcement intermediary within the state's geographic jurisdiction. The ACA and IOIA serve as coordinating bodies within certifier and inspector cohorts, and between the cohorts and the Program (Carter and Mahallati 2017). Finally, organic materials review organizations serve as information intermediaries, supplying credible organic input information to the NOSB, accredited certifiers, and organic operations, alike.

The diagram brings the administrative decentralization of USDA organic certification into greater focus and raises a number of questions regarding the implications of decentralized regulatory oversight. Of course, mapping the actors and relationships reflected in a program's design is only a first step in understanding how a regulatory arrangement functions and to what ends. The remainder of this section identifies the factors of interest incorporated in this book's analysis and outlines the resulting implications for regulatory administration, which I conceptualize through four interrelated constructs: regulatory fidelity, regulatory integrity, program feedback, and policy durability.

ANALYZING DECENTRALIZED REGULATORY ADMINISTRATION

Synthesizing lessons from the regulator-intermediary-target model and parallel literature on regulatory regimes (May and Jochim 2013, May 2007), three broad categories of interest guide my analysis of decentralized regulatory administration: regulatory arrangement institutional design, regulatory actor attributes, and regulatory actor interests and objectives (see Table 2.1).

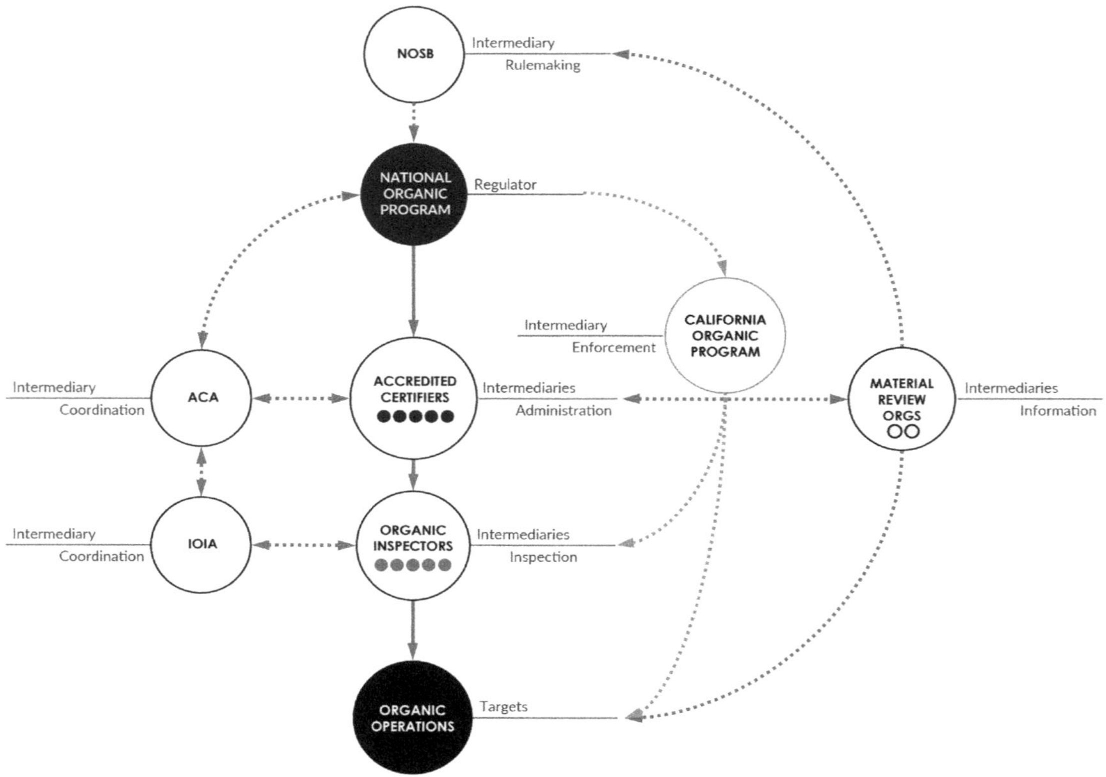

Figure 2.1. A regulator-intermediary-target model of USDA organic certification
Source: Author

Regulatory Arrangement Institutional Design

Regulatory actors operate in institutional contexts established by the regulatory arrangement in question and institutional contexts (in part) define the incentives and constraints that actors face (Abbott, Levi-Faur, and Snidal 2017b, May 2007). Institutions are the rules and norms that govern individual and collective behavior (Ostrom 2005). At a general level, a regulatory arrangement's institutional design is reflected by its overall structure, such as the decentralized nature of USDA organic certification. Within this structure, however, are more nuanced institutional considerations. For example, a regulatory arrangement's institutional design shapes "the nature of the [arrangement's] rules and standards and the means for gauging adherence to them" (May 2007, 9). Among the most important USDA organic certification design features are rulemaking under advisory board counsel, systems-based regulatory standards, and the quasi-voluntary nature of program participation.

Institutional design also determines the authoritative scope of a program's regulatory standards. For example, National Organic Program regulations outline standards for organic crop production and livestock, including poultry and ruminant animals (e.g., cattle, pigs, etc.), but say nothing about organic standards for seafood. Consequently, as of 2019, fisheries cannot obtain USDA organic certification. Less obvious institutional limitations create regulatory "gaps" where the inability of a regulator to address key activities creates barriers in interconnected markets and production systems. As shown in this book, this is the case for organic input materials, such as commercial fertilizers and crop treatments, which fall outside of the National Organic Program's authority to regulate.

Finally, a regulatory arrangement's institutional design sets the authority and discretion afforded to regulatory actors, the information that they can access, and the benefits that they derive from regulatory functions (May and Jochim 2013, Ostrom 2005). Institutional design interacts with regulatory actor attributes, interests, and objectives, to create strengths and vulnerabilities in a regulatory arrangement's performance and effectiveness. A key interaction of this sort exhibited in the case of USDA organic certification is the competitive pressures that are generated by certifiers that rely on certification fees for revenue and regulatee-clients' choice from among certifier alternatives—a point that is expanded on later in this section.

Regulatory Actor Attributes

A key characteristic of USDA organic certification is regulatory actor diversity. Diversity is particularly pertinent in this context, as it extends beyond variation in intermediary functions: in organic certification, layers of administrative decentralization are populated with an assortment of organizations and individuals. For example, the accredited certifiers charged with administering organic regulations come from across the public, nonprofit, and for-profit sectors, are varied in size and sophistication, and operate in different regions across the U.S. Similarly, the individuals deployed by certifiers to inspect organic operations vary in their employment statuses and affiliations: some are full or part-time personnel at a single a certifier, while others work on a contract basis for many certifiers.

Often related to such attributes, regulatory actors can vary in other important manners. Among these is operational capacity: the resources that actors bring to bear on regulatory responsibilities and which influence their ability to effectively perform regulatory functions (Abbott, Levi-Faur, and Snidal 2017b). A particularly important capacity dimension in the context of regulatory administration is expertise, as an information asymmetry often exists between regulatory agents and the firms that they are responsible for monitoring. Assumed specialized knowledge is a primary rational for incorporating intermediaries in the delivery of regulatory standards—but there is no guarantee that diverse intermediaries possess sufficient expertise to execute the regulatory duties for which they are responsible.

Furthermore, regulatory actors are shaped by organizational histories and cultures. In organic regulation, for example, some certifiers predate the enactment of federal organic standards and even helped to develop them, while others are more recent additions to the organic certification landscape. Histories and cultures have a profound influence on organizations and the individuals that work in them—from the manners in which they interpret regulatory policy intents to how they prioritize potentially conflicting responsibilities and pressures.

Regulatory Actor Interests and Objectives

As with actor attributes, regulatory actors' interests and objectives vary widely. Diversity in interests and objectives is a noteworthy consideration in the administration of regulatory standards for two reasons. First, actor interests and objectives sometimes align with program goals and other times they do not. Obvious disparities between actor objectives and program goals constitute clear vulnerabilities to regulatory program effectiveness, to the extent that they lead to regulatory actions that conflict with program aims.

Perhaps less apparent, however, are the opportunities regulatory administration represents for actors to legitimately pursue, and even institutionalize, their interests and objectives. With the delegation of authority comes a level of discretion—discretion that regulatory intermediaries exercise, for example, in how they interpret program directives. Here, differences in actor attributes

Table 2.1. Factors of interest for examining decentralized regulation

Factor	*Description*
Regulatory program institutional design	Rules, procedures, and norms established by the program in question that shape the incentives, opportunities, and constraints of regulatory actors
Regulatory actor attributes	Organizational characteristics, such as organization form (e.g., public, nonprofit, private), size, capacity, history, and culture; individual characteristics, such as organizational affiliation and employment status
Regulatory actor interests and objectives	The organizational and individual values and goals that motivate regulatory actor decision making and actions

can correspond with actor interest and objectives. For example, if the revenue generation imperative of for-profit accredited certifying agents results in organizational objectives that diverge from those of their governmental or nonprofit counterparts, the result could be greater flexibility in some certifiers' interpretations of regulatory "gray areas" (Carter 2016, 2017b).

Finally, regulations do more than outline rules for behavior; they also codify select values and aims in regulatory standards (May and Jochim 2013). As discussed further in this chapter, the delivery of regulatory standards generates experiences and information that authorities rely on to adapt regulations (May 1992). Where program administration is carried out by intermediary organizations, the lessons that are garnered in the delivery of regulatory standards—and more importantly, the lessons that are communicated back to authorities—are shaped by intermediary interests and objectives.

CONCEPTUALIZING THE POLICY IMPLICATIONS OF DECENTRALIZED REGULATORY DESIGN

As described above, USDA organic certification can be usefully thought of as organizationally diverse, both generally speaking and in terms of pertinent actors' attributes, interests, and objectives, and decentralized; it relies on the devolution of authority from central authorities to independent intermediary organizations (Black 2008, Pollitt 2005). These characteristics have notable strengths, which are described throughout this book. They also raise concerning implications for regulatory administration qualities and outcomes. These implications are outlined here according to four dimensions of regulatory administration: regulatory fidelity, regulatory integrity, program feedback, and policy durability (see Table 2.2).

Implications for Regulatory Fidelity

A central concern of any regulatory program is the extent to which regulatory standards and their administration conform to the intents of policy designers and program administrators. Following policy analysis and program evaluation literature (Century, Rudnick, and Freeman 2010), I refer to this dimension of regulatory administration as regulatory fidelity, although the concept is analogous to what May (2007) refers to as consistency and captures aspects of May and Jochim's (2013) concept of policy coherence. While fidelity is desirable in any regulatory context, an administratively decentralized and organizationally diverse arrangement raises concerns that might not be found under more traditional regulatory designs; concerns which stem from both institutional design and the intermediaries that contribute to regulatory standards administration.

The most evident threat to regulatory fidelity in the case of USDA organic certification is its dependence on intermediaries. A central rationale for engaging intermediaries is grounded in the particular competencies they possess, for example, industry expertise that an agency may lack (Abbott, Levi-Faur, and Snidal 2017b). Yet, intermediary capacities vary in ways that can lead to unwanted variation in regulatory activity. Disparities in organizational resources and expertise are a baseline cause of imbalanced intermediary capacities. In the simplest example, adequately resourced monitors with highly competent personnel are more likely to effectively monitor regulatee behavior than their under-resourced or less competent peers. Furthermore, where regulatory directives must be interpreted by intermediary organizations, regulatory fidelity is vulnerable to the filter of the histories and values held by intermediary organizations (Hill 2003). Because regulatory administration is always an interpretive exercise on some level, the manner in which regulations are monitored and enforced is shaped by the priorities emphasized by organizational cultures.

Regulatory fidelity can also be undermined by more subtle aspects of institutional design. Limits or gaps in program authority, for example, may create vulnerabilities in an otherwise robust regulatory framework. In particular, where interconnected systems (such as those of agricultural supply chains) rely on uniform standards across system elements, requirements which do not apply to all relevant elements can cause complications or barriers that impair operations of the system as a whole. Furthermore, differences in intermediary interpretations may impair the consistency of regulatory administration as intermediaries devise their own guidelines absent authoritative standards.

Implications for Regulatory Integrity

A second concern that stems from an administratively decentralized and organizationally diverse regulatory arrangement is the influence that intermediaries exercise over the content and administration of regulatory standards when intermediary interests and objectives do not align with program goals. In some instances, this influence may constitute regulatory capture, or "the domination of one regulatory actor by another, restricting the autonomy of the captured actor in performing its regulatory functions" (Abbott, Levi-Faur, and Snidal 2017b, 28, Carpenter and Moss 2013). Other forms of intermediary influence may not raise to the level of capture, but nonetheless pose a threat to regulatory effectiveness, and undermine the integrity of the system as a whole.

A design that creates competition in the administration of regulatory standards fosters a context particularly vulnerable to regulatory target influence over intermediaries, as "third-party [intermediaries] probably face incentives to satisfy their clients through at least marginally more lax enforcement" (Coglianese and Lazer 2003, 718, Levi-Faur and Starobin 2014). Similarly, where monitoring and enforcement intermediaries employ additional intermediaries to assess regulatee compliance with standards, there is a risk that the employing intermediaries emphasize "customer service" over stringency in the expectations and incentives they establish for inspector personnel (Carter 2017c). Where intermediaries are unwilling to bend to regulatee expectations, regulatees may engage in "intermediary shopping," looking for an intermediary that will (Abbott, Levi-Faur, and Snidal 2017b, 30); as is discussing in this book, anecdotal evidence suggests that "certifier shopping" occurs in the organic certification context—to some degree.

Furthermore, in a decentralized regulatory structure, each interaction between regulatory actors represents an opportunity for one actor's influence over another. For example, and as discussed further below, intermediaries that serve as feedback channels for regulatory authorities can attempt to shape regulatory standards and program administration through the information that they chose to share or highlight. They may do so on an individual basis or may band together to leverage a unified voice towards affecting regulatory changes. Collective representation can buttress regulatory integrity if it is used to draw an authority's attention to problems that threaten regulatory effectiveness. It can also undermine regulatory integrity if a collective voice is used to push political or self-interested agendas, resulting in authority capture by serial or parallel intermediary organizations.

Implications for Program Feedback

A third concern that stems from an administratively decentralized regulatory arrangement is the operational distance that is created between regulatory authorities responsible for rulemaking and the realities of regulatory administration. Literature on policy learning (Heikkila and Gerlak 2013, May 1992) makes clear that program administration provides a critical opportunity for authorities to assess the appropriateness of regulatory standards and the extent to which directives can be effectively administered as outlined. Regulations may be amended, or guidance on how they are to be applied may be modified, as a result of learning that occurs during administration—resulting not only in more effective regulatory administration, but also more durable regulatory policy over time (May and Jochim 2013).

When the delivery of regulatory standards is delegated to intermediary organizations, it inhibits the program feedback function that regulatory ad-

Table 2.2. Policy implications of decentralized regulation

Relevant dimension of regulatory administration	*Description of implication*	*Likely causes*
Regulatory fidelity	Regulatory "gaps" and/or inconsistent application of regulatory standards	Disparities in regulatory intermediary capacities Differences in intermediary histories, cultures, and objectives Gaps in program authority or the scope of regulatory standards
Regulatory integrity	Intermediary influence over regulatory standards or regulatee influence over standards administration	Intermediary incentives Regulatee expectations and intermediary shopping
Program feedback	Incomplete information regarding regulatory standards administration and performance	Operational distance between regulator and regulatory administration Withholding of information by regulatory intermediaries
Policy durability	Threats to the sustainability of political commitments represented by a public policy	Decreased perceived legitimacy in program standards and/or standards administration Stakeholder opposition to the program

ministration otherwise fulfills, impeding learning through the administrative process and subsequent regulatory changes that can improve regulations' appropriateness and effectiveness.[1] Of course, given appropriate institutional mechanisms, feedback and learning can be facilitated by intermediaries and may even contribute to dynamic rule adaptation over time (Auld and Renckens 2017). Such arrangements, however, rely on intermediaries for program information in a manner that can afford them a privileged position in shaping regulatory action—a position that can be used to bend administration to serve intermediary interests—contributing to concerns over regulatory integrity, as referenced in the preceding section.

Implications for Policy Durability

A fourth concern that may be exacerbated by an administratively decentralized and organizationally diverse regulatory arrangement emerges from threats to a program's long-run viability—what May and Jochim (2013, 433) dub "policy durability" and define as "the sustainability of political commitments over time." Although a program is expected to be amended as a result of program feedback and learning (as indicated in the preceding discussion), an expectation of durability assumes that the program's basic objectives remain unaltered. Program objectives that are undermined or abandoned, in contrast, signal a lack of durability.

Policy durability relies in part on an adequate supply of the basic resources needed to pursue a regulatory arrangement's objectives, such as program funding, personnel, and support from political officials. Policy durability further hinges on in the relative legitimacy with which a regulatory arrangement is perceived. In other words, durability is fostered when stakeholders see a program as appropriately and justly implementing policy goals. Durability is undermined, however, where stakeholders perceive a program as failing to achieve its purpose or otherwise generating unintended side effects, thereby "turning supporters into opponents" (May and Jochim 2013, 433). Similarly, program legitimacy can be eroded, and durability threatened, if stakeholders perceive a regulatory arrangement to be unduly influenced by political opponents.

Although policy durability concerns are not unique to decentralized program contexts, decentralized designs may be more vulnerable to them. For example, rulemaking with advisory board counsel opens the door to perceived program legitimacy threats if a program is seen as ignoring the recommendations of a rulemaking intermediary or if the intermediary, itself, is seen as biased in favor of select or narrow interests. Policy durability concerns also highlight the interdependence of the different regulatory administration dimensions raised in this section, as threats to regulatory fidelity, regulatory integrity, and program feedback can precipitate or contribute to declines in durability. For example, if organic certifier shopping concerns lead to decreased USDA organic certification legitimacy in the eyes of organic consumers, the result is likely an impediment to organic food market growth and a lower return-on-investment for producers and processors pursuing organic certification—trends that would arguably threaten the National Organic Program's long-run viability.

THE FRAMEWORK IN REVIEW

The preceding discussion highlights key categories of interest for analyzing decentralized regulatory administration alongside a set of theoretically and practically important implications for regulatory processes and outcomes. It's worth noting that the discussion in this chapter, while positing theoretical relationships, is not meant to specify a discrete *theory* of decentralized regulatory administration. Rather, this chapter outlines a conceptual *framework*. The distinction is best made by Elinor Ostrom (2011, 8):

> Frameworks identify the elements and general relationships among these elements that one needs to consider . . . and they organize diagnostic and prescriptive inquiry. They provide a general set of variables . . . a metatheoretical language . . . [and they] help analysts generate the questions that need to be addressed when they conduct an analysis.

The framework is designed for analysis of regulatory arrangements that are administratively decentralized. Thus, reliance on regulatory intermediaries as consequential regulatory actors is assumed, although an alignment between intermediaries' objectives and regulatory program goals is not. In application, the types of intermediaries and their associated roles in regulatory administration is best determined by the empirical context at hand. Regardless of intermediary types and roles, however, the framework suggests three general sets of variables that one ought to consider when analyzing such regulatory arrangements: the arrangement's institutional design (at both general and more nuanced levels), regulatory actor attributes, and regulatory actor objectives and incentives.

The framework highlights four dimensions through which a decentralized regulation's processes and outcomes can be understood and assessed: regulatory fidelity and integrity, program feedback, and policy durability. Absent from the list are more traditional performance measures, such as impact on a target group's behavior, cost-effectiveness, efficiency, and distributional fairness (Coglianese 2012). The rationale is twofold. My intent with this book's analysis is to understand how regulatory design and regulatory actors interact to shape USDA organic certification's administration, rather than the societal impacts of U.S. organic policy. Dimensions such as fidelity and integrity are thus more appropriate gauges of regulatory administration than other performance indicators.

Second, following Peter May (2007, 9), I assume that reliance on independent nongovernmental intermediaries for the realization of critical program functions "raises fundamental issues concerning regulatory accountability . . . [and] how that accountability is achieved when nongovernmental actors assume important roles in regulatory regimes." As outlined throughout the first two chapters of this book, USDA organic certification depends on intermediaries for a range of National Organic Program functions, from the development of regulatory standards to compliance enforcement. By drawing attention to regulatory fidelity and integrity, program feedback, and policy durability, the framework identifies key manners in which intermediaries may either support or undermine regulatory standards administration, and the extent to which the National Organic Program adequately ensures the accountability of USDA organic certification intermediaries.

THE FRAMEWORK'S APPLICATION IN THIS BOOK

The framework presented in this chapter guides my analysis of USDA organic certification. In the chapters that follows, I apply the framework to present a descriptive examination of how the USDA organic standards are approached, experienced, and engaged by each set of actors identified in Figure 2.1's regulator-intermediary-target model. In other words, my primary objectives are to apply the scholarly lessons synthesized in the framework to: (i) describe the intermediaries upon which the National Organic Program relies and the functions that they perform in USDA organic standards administration, (ii) understand how the attributes, objectives, and interests of organic certification intermediaries interact with their institutional context, and (iii) identify the resulting implications for U.S. organic certification regulatory fidelity and integrity, program feedback, and policy durability.

Although my primary objectives are thus empirical, the analysis should not be construed as without theoretical insights. The chapters that follow hold a number of contributions to regulatory theory. For example, the following chapter details how an institutional legacy of industry collective action and self-governance may give rise to decentralized regulatory designs reliant on diverse actors as consequential regulatory intermediaries. Examination of the National Organic Program illustrates the dual mandate inherent in quasi-voluntary programs and the administrative challenge of balancing parallel program goals. Analyses of accredited certifiers and organic inspectors suggest that the behaviors of third-party administrators and inspection intermediaries may generally lean in the favor of regulatory fidelity and integrity *despite* the perverse incentives established by a competitive third-party environment. These and other insights are identified in the examinations that follow and discussed in the book's concluding chapters.

Arguably, the greatest theoretical contribution this book offers is a catalogue of various intermediary types—including rulemaking intermediaries, third-party administrators, inspector intermediaries, coordinating intermediaries, and information intermediaries—alongside descriptions of their roles in regulatory standards administration and assessments of their impacts relative to one or more of the highlighted implications. In the process, the analysis highlights the interconnectedness of regulatory arrangement institutional design, regulatory actors, and regulatory administration. Similarly, the analysis demonstrates the interdependence of key regulatory concerns; regulatory integrity depends in part on regulatory fidelity, for instance, and policy durability is unlikely without regulatory integrity.

Finally, the framework outlined in this chapter constitutes its own contribution to regulatory theory. The study of regulation intersects a daunting range of scholarly literatures and theoretical approaches, including: regulation and regulatory governance, broadly conceptualized (e.g., Coglianese and Lazer 2003, Coglianese, Nash, and Olmstead 2003, Levi-Faur 2011); narrower perspectives such as club theory (Potoski and Prakash 2009, Prakash and Potoski 2007), certification (Auld 2014, Bartley 2011, Cashore, Auld, and Newsom 2003), regulatory enforcement and inspection styles (May and Winter 1999, 2000, 2007, May and Wood 2003, Winter and May 2001), and street-level bureaucracy (Nielsen 2015, Pautz 2009, Pires 2011); and more recent developments, such as the regulator-intermediary-target model (Abbott, Levi-Faur, and Snidal 2017b, Abbott and Snidal 2009), among others. This book's framework offers a step towards theoretical synthesis of such literatures' insights for the purposes of analyzing regulation by proxy.

NOTE

1. It is worth noting that a similar term—policy feedback—is found widely across the political science and policy process literatures. Where these literatures use policy feedback in reference to when the consequences of policy decisions drive future policy change (Pierson 1993), this analysis uses "program feedback" in reference to the learning that occurs during the administration of a policy or program. This may result in policy change, but the mechanisms and scope of change are different.

Chapter Three

Institutional Emergence and Evolution

The History of Organic Food Governance in the U.S.

In March of 1971, a small group of California farmers gathered to discuss a growing problem: the low-input, soil-focused farming methods that they'd come to celebrate were under threat. The threat was not weather-related, as many agricultural hardships are. Nor was it biological; no insect swarm or crop blight loomed on the horizon. The farmers gathered in response to organic pioneer J.I. Rodale's (1971) call to "join the fight against organic phonies"—to address the problem of other farmers misusing the term "organic." Out of this and subsequent meetings emerged the first organic certification program, sponsored by the Rodale Press, which issued labels to qualifying farmers that read "Organic Farmer: Certified by Organic Gardening and Farming Magazine." Rodale would go on to help establish similar famer self-regulation schemes in other regions, sparking the proliferation of organic certification across the U.S. To this day CCOF, the organizational descendent of Rodale Press program, continues to wield considerable influence within the organic community. As the largest domestic administrator of USDA organic standards, it certifies over 35,000 farmers and facilities within and beyond U.S. borders.[1]

This evolution, from an informal gathering of organic farmers in 1971 to the formidable CCOF, is one example how the governance of organic agriculture in the U.S. transformed alongside consumer demand for organic foods (Guthman 2014). Governing institutions—the rules and norms that societies use to coordinate human behavior—are rarely the product of intentional design. Rather, they emerge out of collective "tinkering" with different ways to solve a common problem (Ostrom 2014) and are the by-products of political conflict, bargaining, and settlement (Bartley 2007). Such is the case for institutions of organic food governance, the history of which reflects a dynamic institutional emergence and evolution from grassroots industry self-regulation, to a patchwork of more formal yet incongruous certification programs, and finally to a federally established set uniform of national organic standards enforced under the USDA's National Organic Program.

Institutions perform two basic functions (Ostrom 2005).[2] The first is in providing shared understandings, or definitions, for key phenomena of interest. The second is in prescribing appropriate behaviors relative to those phenomena—actions that are required, allowed, or prohibited within specified contexts. Throughout the evolution of organic food governance, both dimensions have been the source of contestation, conflict, and adaptation. A perennial tension throughout the emergence and growth of the organic industry is whether "organic" represents a philosophy that extends beyond agricultural production to include social and political relations, or if it should be more narrowly considered a production method limited to agricultural practices (Obach 2015). Within this broader philosophical tension, organic proponents have disagreed over the principles and practices that constitute appropriate organic food production standards, ranging from the acceptability of synthetic fertilizers to adequate husbandry requirements for livestock producers.

This chapter outlines the evolution of U.S. organic food governance in five sections. It begins with the origins of what is now recognized as organic agriculture, found in the efforts of organic pioneers such as Sir Albert Howard and J.I. Rodale. It then turns to the counterculture and environmentalism of the 1960s and '70s. The third section describes the emergence and proliferation of both nongovernmental and governmental organic certification programs. The fourth section chronicles the implementation of federal organic agriculture policy with the 1990 Organic Foods Production Act and the fifth section continues with an account of the subsequent national organic standards rulemaking. A sixth section positions the institutional evolution of organic food governance relative to theories of certification as institutional emergence. A conclusion summarizes the chapter.

THE ROOTS OF ORGANIC AGRICULTURE

Scholarship traces the origins of organic food production, as a method and an ideal, to the early twentieth century (Conford 2001, Guthman 2004a, Kuepper 2010). Although the practices of organic farming date back to much earlier agricultural systems of Europe and Asia, organic production coalesced into a distinct movement in opposition to the industrial practices that became widespread after World War II (Obach 2015). During the period in which many turned to technological innovation in the form of chemicals and mechanization, small cadres of farmers eschewed the "industrial" turn of food production, favoring methods that emphasized "natural" processes and ecological harmony.

Many credit the work of British agricultural scientist Albert Howard as establishing the early foundations for an organic philosophy (Heckman 2006, Kuepper 2010, Obach 2015).[3] From extensive field research observing the practices of Indian farmers Howard became a proponent of the "rule of return"—the idea that healthy soil is paramount and best achieved by returning the nutrients that are drawn from soil by plants during food production. Of particular concern was humus, a biologically rich soil subtype. Howard went on to develop the idea in his 1943 book *An Agricultural Testament,* in which he advocated the recycling of all organic waste materials, including sewage sludge, to support soil fertility and humus content (Heckman 2006).

The ideas and writings of several other agricultural scholars and practitioners of the time contributed to what became known as organic farming. Among the most widely recognized are British farmer and educator Lady Eve Balfour, American agricultural scientist Franklin H. King, and American conservationist Louis Bromfield (Heckman 2006, Mosier 2017). Austrian philosopher Rudolf Steiner stands out among these as a proponent of an alternative farming method that combined elements of scientific research and esoteric spiritual beliefs regarding the nature of the earth and cosmos (Obach 2015). Steiner's philosophy is notable as the foundation for what is now known as biodynamic farming. His biodynamic methods were codified as biodynamic production standards in 1928 by the Demeter organization, thereby establishing the first explicit sustainable agriculture standards, predating formal organic standards by several decades.

The foundation of what many today refer to as organic farming is a combination of Steiner's biodynamic method and the soil-focused humus farming that extends from the work of Howard and his contemporaries. These terms were reportedly supplanted for the now-recognizable label "organic farming" as a result of English agriculturalist Walter Northbourne's 1940 publication *Look to the Land* (although biodynamic farming continued to be practiced as an alternative to organic by some agricultural producers). In the book, Northbourne developed a concept of a farm as an "organic whole," with "organic" referring to a farm as composed of many interrelated parts analogous to the biological components that make up living organisms (Heckman 2006, Scofield 1986). In line with biodynamic practices, Northbourne's organic method called for a recycling of all farm materials and by-products through the production system (Obach 2015).

These contributions notwithstanding, perhaps the most recognizable American organic agriculture pioneer is J.I. Rodale. Rodale was an entrepreneur with a deep interest in the connections between health and the environment, likely due to his own history of health complications. Apparently moved by the writings of Howard, Rodale migrated to a Pennsylvania farm in 1942 and launched *Organic Farming and Gardening,* with Howard serving as the associate editor. Over time, *Organic Farming and Gardening* came to be an important platform for the dissemination of organic philosophy and methods in the U.S., reaching a readership of 100,000 in 1950, 260,000 in 1960, and 1,300,000 by 1980 (Heckman 2006, Obach 2015).

Rodale's role in the diffusion of organic practices extended beyond *Organic Farming and Gardening.* In 1945 he published the book *Pay Dirt* (Rodale 1945), with an introduction from Howard, introducing and outlining organic farming concepts for a wider lay audience. A couple of years later, Rodale started the Soil and Health Foundation to support research into understanding and improving organic practices. The Foundation later became the Rodale Institute, which remains in operation today. In the meantime, community-supported organic gardening clubs began emerging around the U.S. and Canada, which Rodale supported through networking and education, and later through a community gardening organization directory (Obach 2015).

The principles and practices of organic agriculture spread at a steady pace during the 1950s, but the growth was modest. Commercialization of organic food remained limited, although moves towards an identifiable organic food market can be seen. For example, Rodale's magazines provided advertising space for organic businesses (including mail-order organic product services) and the first organic market appeared in New York in 1951 (Obach 2015). A likely contributing factor to the sector's relatively slow commercial growth was many organic practitioners' aversion to a marketplace dominated by industrial agriculture and conventional agribusiness, as expressed in Howard's *The War in the Soil* (1994). The sentiment is one that appealed to the counterculture turn of the 1960s, which ultimately (and perhaps ironically) helped to propel organic into mainstream consciousness.

THE COUNTERCULTURE AND ENVIRONMENTAL MOVEMENTS

Although many consider organic agriculture to be a product of the 1960s counterculture, it is more accurate to say that the 1960s and early '70s transformed the then-obscure movement. The 1960s mark a period during which fringe movement's politically and socially conservative leaning was redirected to a leftist cause (Belasco 2014, Kuepper 2010). Furthermore, and as part of this shift, it is during the 1960s and ’70s that organic agriculture became associated with the broader environmental and “pure food” consumer movements, setting the fringe organic movement on the trajectory to become a widely recognized industry.

According to Michael Pollan (2006), the 1960s counterculture vision for organic agriculture was composed of three main pillars: (i) environmentally sound production without synthetic inputs, generating high quality and safe foods; (ii) an alternative food distribution system that relies on few “middlemen” and is instead composed of consumers purchasing directly from producers or cooperatives, and; (iii) whole, fresh food that undergoes minimal processing and is devoid of artificial ingredients. Sub-movements within the broader counterculture emphasized distinct aspects of this vision though various strategies (Belasco 2014, Guthman 2014, Obach 2015). Some of the more ideologically moderate included farms, often associated with food-cooperatives, which emphasized organic practices and principles. Among the more radical were farm-based communes inspired by back-to-the-land ideals (Guthman 2014).

Such counterculture experiments helped to distinguish organic agriculture from conventional alternatives, to a degree, but it is an alignment with broader environmental and consumer movements that increased organic food’s recognition among consumers. Publications such as Rachel Carson’s *Silent Spring* (1962) focused attention on the detrimental impacts of synthetic chemicals and the risks that they posed to environmental and human health. Agricultural pesticides, like DDT, received particular scrutiny, spurring a study by President John F. Kennedy’s Science Advisory Committee that validated many of the human health and safety concerns raised by Carson (Beyl 1992). As the 1960s progressed, the counterculture social justice elements associated with organic agriculture receded, while environmental and human health took on greater prominence (Obach 2007, 2015).

Consumer demand for organic produce built momentum towards the end of the 1960s and organic food markets matured. Supply chains became longer and the figurative and literal distance grew between organic producers and consumers (Kuepper 2010). A threat to the viability of an organic foods market emerged—the difficulty of identifying truly “organic” produce. Some concerns stemmed from producers not properly trained in organic principles; others originated from what was perceived as fraudulent misappropriation of the term organic—“organic phonies” in the words of Rodale (1971). In an effort to protect the identity and integrity of the organic movement, producers turned to institutional remedies for verifying organic claims, developing the first organized organic food governing institutions in the process.

ORGANIC INSTITUTIONS: FROM SELF-REGULATION TO THIRD-PARTY CERTIFICATION

In 1971, Rodale initiated several gatherings of California organic producers to explore the idea of a certification program, out of which the first organic certification program in the U.S. was initiated. The program (which later became CCOF) was sponsored by the Rodale Press and provided labels for products of qualifying farms that read "Organic Farmer: Certified by Organic Gardening and Farming Magazine." The certification indicated that food bearing the seal was produced without pesticides or artificial fertilizers, grown in soil fertilized with organic matter and natural mineral fertilizers, and was not treated with preservatives, hormones, or antibiotics (Mosier 2017, Nowacek and Nowacek 2008).

Certification programs revolve around a set of standards that establish the practices that allowed under the process in question—in this case, organic food production. The Rodale Press certification program reportedly experienced little conflict in setting the first organic standards—largely because of the authority Rodale and his press held within the organic community (Nowacek and Nowacek 2008). Verifying adherence to the standards, however, proved more difficult. Rodale initially intended to certify with the advantage of product testing, to ensure that certified organic produce carried no pesticides or other prohibited substances. Testing proved to be too high a bar, however, as cross contamination of otherwise organically produced foods would have rendered them uncertifiable. The Rodale Press therefore turned to certifying farms for their adherence to organic practices, such that producers "would be judged by their actions rather than on conditions beyond their control" (Nowacek and Nowacek 2008, 410).

The Rodale Press certification program laid out the basic blueprint for the organic certification schemes that followed, most of which were similarly structured nonprofit associations. After the Rodale Press program was transitioned to the famer operated CCOF in 1974, the Press shifted its attention to facilitating the creation of such associations across the U.S. By the end of the year, an organic certification association was established in each of the U.S. regions (Nowacek and Nowacek 2008), although formal designation sometimes followed years after initiation. It wasn't until 1982, for example, that the certification arm of Oregon Tilth—another contemporary organic certification giant—was founded by the Willamette Valley chapter of the Oregon Tilth organization (Mosier 2017, OTCO 2018).

From the mid-1970s onward, the institutional landscape of organic food governance became increasingly populated and diverse. In the terminology of regulatory scholarship, the nonprofit farmers associations that made up early organic certification programs are best considered "self-regulation" (or two-party) institutions (Levi-Faur 2011), as their standards were collectively established and enforced by members of the organic industry. Around the same time, third-party certification programs emerged. While the first third-party certification programs were arguably initiated by state governments, as discussed below, public sector initiation is not what designates them as "third-party" institutions. Rather, the third-party distinction comes from independence of the organizations that set and enforce standards (the "third-parties") from the certified entities (i.e., organic producers).

As detailed in Samantha Mosier's (2017) account of state-level organic policy diffusion, policy intervention in organic markets began in 1973, when the Oregon Department of Agriculture developed the first governmental organic food standards and certification program in the U.S. State legislation came shortly thereafter, with New York's passage of a 1976 bill directing the state Department of Agriculture to examine the prospect of developing organic rules. California, Connecticut, and Maine followed suit three years later, each establishing their own organic certification programs.

Although federal policy action was still over a decade in coming, national-level attention (and tensions) regarding organic agriculture were evident by 1979, when Secretary of Agriculture Robert Bergland directed the USDA to begin examining organic practices. The Agency published the *Report and Recommendations on Organic Farming* (1980) with the expressed intent of fostering communication between organic farmers and the USDA. This direction was quickly reversed under the Reagan administration just a year later, which attempted to bury the Report and abolished the Organic Resources Coordinator position, recently-established to continue the Agency's research into organic farming methods (Heckman 2006). Around this time the Reagan–appointed Secretary of Agriculture Earl Butz outwardly expressed the resistance to organic practices that the administration's actions had indicated, proclaimed that millions would starve if all farmers adopted organic methods (Lotter 2003).

Federal resistance notwithstanding, the mid 1980s witnessed an expansion of the organic market, more state certification programs, and yet another development in organic governance—the emergence of for-profit third-party certification programs. Several highly visible incidents involving chemical contamination of food brought renewed focus among consumers to agricultural methods and a surge of demand for organic foods. Chief among these was the 1985 nation-wide melon contamination with the pesticide aldicarb—the largest foodborne pesticide outbreak recorded at the time that caused at least six deaths (CDC 1986). The exact impact of the aldicarb incident on the organic market is unknown, but one indicator of its likely influence was a near doubling of CCOF-certified acreage in that same year (Nowacek and Nowacek 2008, 412). Regardless of the cause, the number of farmers seeking certification grew markedly through the 1980s, and private sector certification programs such as Scientific Certification Systems' NutriClean label rushed in to compete with nonprofit certifiers for certification business.

Towards the end of the Reagan administration a growing swell of organic certification and production practitioners were calling for national organic standards. The early self-regulation certification programs established by farmers' associations had largely morphed into third-party arrangements as their memberships grew, their standards-setting and enforcement apparatuses became more formalized and distant from association bodies, and they increasingly found themselves in competition with for-profit counterparts for certification clients (Guthman 2014, Nowacek and Nowacek 2008). Across the country, dozens of nongovernmental certification programs—both nonprofit and for-profit—enforced their own organic standards, ranging in both content and stringency.

Certification professionals became concerned that non-organic food was being sold as organic; concern among some extended beyond sellers independently misrepresenting conventionally raised produce as organic to include lax standards and oversight by (mostly for-profit) certification programs (Mosier 2017). In other words, the integrity of third-party organic certification itself was under threat, as some certification programs were seen as facilitating farms in "making misleading or false claims about the organic nature of their products" (Amaditz 1997). Lax requirements represented one source of inconsistency across different organic certification standards and programs; exceptionally strong standards made up another. Some certification programs competed to set the "gold standard" for organic certification stringency (Marshall and Standifird 2005). Sociologist Brian Obach relays the view of organic certifier personnel reflecting on the resulting dilemma: in the words of certifier Jack Lewin, some certifiers were "playing a very complicated game of 'who's better than who?'" Another commented: "nobody trusted each other. They'd say 'No, ours are better than theirs. We have higher standards'" (as cited in Obach 2015, 60).

Organic standards consistency was no better from a public policy perspective. By 1989, twenty-three states had adopted some sort of organic food policy "ranging from labeling, certification programs, or agreements with [non-governmental] third-party certifiers" (Mosier 2017, 24) leading to a fragmented patchwork of "inconsistent or nonexistent laws . . . threatening the meaning and value of the organic food label" (Baker 2005, 1). In short, the time was ripe for federal-level intervention.

THE ORGANIC FOODS PRODUCTION ACT OF 1990

Three congressional bills aimed at establishing federal-level organic policy were introduced in 1989 but ultimately failed (Lathrop 1991, Mosier 2017). The event credited with galvanizing public, and ultimately federal government, support for national organic standards came later that year with a *60 Minutes* special on alar, a cosmetic additive that was used to give apples a brighter and more uniform color (Baker, 2005). Among other matters, the special highlighted a report by the National Resources Defense Council raising concerns that alar had the potential to cause cancer. The Environmental Protection Agency banned the chemical following subsequent public outcry and consumer interest in verified chemical-free foods spiked. According to one poll conducted that year, 84 percent of consumers stated they would purchase organic foods when presented with an option and 49 percent said they'd be willing to pay more for organic options (Amaditz 1997).

The Organic Foods Production Act of 1990 was introduced by Vermont Senator Patrick Leahy as SB 2108. As reported by Obach (2015, 75), the Act was a revised version of a failed 1989 bill, introduced at the end of the legislative session to solicit comments and feedback. Finding overt resistance from the USDA to assisting with the development of organic policy, Kathleen Merrigan, senior staff member on the Senate Committee on Agriculture, Nutrition, and Forestry, had developed the bill by piecing together material from various state laws and programs, and with input from consumer groups and environmental organizations. After Merrigan worked with organic certifier and farmers association representatives to address their concerns in the failed 1989 bill, the Organic Foods Production Act garnered sufficient political support such that most of its provisions were incorporated in the 1990 Farm Bill. The Bill was signed into law by President George H.W. Bush on November 28, 1990.

A majority of the organic community considered the passage of the Act to be a victory (Obach 2015), even though the content and scope of its objectives had been somewhat altered along the legislative path. This included incorporating elements of a companion bill from House Representatives Peter DeFazio (HR 4156) and DeFazio's later amendment (to HR 3950), as well as incorporations from a bill by Representative Gary Condit (HR 5045). Perhaps most notably, environmental stewardship and sustainable practices provisions contained in Leahy's bill were omitted when it emerged from the Senate-House Conference Committee (Bones 1992), resulting in an Act limited to national standardization and labeling of organically produced foods. The Act's stated purpose was threefold: (i) to establish national standards regulating the marketing of organically produced foods, (ii) to assure consumers that organically produced foods meet a consistent standard, and (iii) to facilitate interstate commerce in organic food products.

Rather than being supplanted by the Organic Foods Production Act, the decentralized organic certification landscape that predated federal action was codified in several important manners. The Act authorized a National Organic Program, a regulatory body that would be charged with overseeing the creation of national organic standards and their enforcement, under the administration of the USDA's Agriculture Marketing Service. The Program was not charged with directly administering organic regulations; instead, loosely following International Organization for Standardization (ISO) principles for third-party accreditation and certification systems, it was to accredit third-party certifiers that would then be responsible for certifying organic operations (such as farms and processing facilities) and inspecting them for regulatory compliance. According to the Act, any governing state official or private group of individuals could be accredited to serve as an organic certifying agent, provided they complete an application for accreditation and demonstrated sufficient expertise in organic practices.

Implementation of the National Organic Program was to alter the role of state governments in organic food governance considerably—but the extent of the change was not clear upon the passage of the Organic Foods Production Act. Consistent with its goal of facilitating interstate commerce of organic foods, the Act clearly prohibited states from discriminating against the importation of organic food from another state, provided it was produced in accordance with federal organic standards (Bones, 1992). As reported by Mosier (2017), states came to have three potential roles in organic certification under the National Organic Program. The first was by operating their own organic programs as "partial preemption agreements" (Mosier 2017, 29), overseeing the administration of the national organic standards. Only one state—California—chose to do so. The second role for state government agencies is as USDA-accredited certifying agents—something a number of state agencies have pursued, as discussed in Chapter 5. Finally, states can choose to participate in one of the two organic certification cost-share programs, which offset organic certification costs for farmers and producers. These cost-share programs are described in greater detail in the next chapter.

The Organic Foods Production Act also called for the Secretary of Agriculture to appoint members of an advisory committee, known as the National Organic Standards Board (NOSB), to assist in the development of national organic standards and the implementation of the National Organic Program. More specific tasks assigned to the Board included developing a National List of allowed and prohibited substances in organic food production and processing, convening technical advisory panels to evaluate substances for inclusion in the National List, and evaluation of botanical pesticides (Bones 1992). The Board was to be made up of fifteen members—representatives from different aspects of organic food production and governance, including organic farmers and growers, organic food handlers and processors, retailers, environmentalists, resource conservationists, certifiers, and consumer interest groups. Decisions of the Board were to require two-thirds vote of all members in attendance at a meeting.

In addition to authorizing the National Organic Program and NOSB, the Organic Foods Production Act outlined the central components of third-party organic certification under federal oversight, many of which were modeled after the procedures established by nongovernmental certification programs that preceded it (Guthman 2014, Obach 2015). The National List was one of these and would prove to be a source of considerable debate and conflict in the later years. The certification process itself revolved around an operation's submission of an organic system plan—an outline for how the operation adhered to the requirements that would be laid out in the to-be-established national organic standards. Recordkeeping requirements for both certified operations and accredited certifiers were also indicated, as well as requirements for the labeling of organic products. An exception from the labeling requirements was made for producers selling less than $5,000 in organic products a year.

As with any legislative act subject to translation into operational policy, the details of organic certification under federal oversight were to be flushed out in the administrative rulemaking process. Nonetheless, the basic structure for regulatory action under the National Organic Program was set, formally adopting the decentralized and organizationally diverse institutional arrangement that had evolved over time. Likely a prerequisite for attracting sufficient support from the organic community (Obach 2007), this design has served as both a strength and a liability for the legitimacy and credibility of organic food governance, as examined throughout this book.

ESTABLISHING NATIONAL ORGANIC STANDARDS

The years immediately following passage of the 1990 Organic Foods Production Act were characterized by little-to-no progress. The U.S. Congress expected National Organic Program implementation to be complete and the Program in operation by October 1, 1993, however, action was stalled by a lack of funds and administrative complications from the Bush-to-Clinton presidential transition (Amaditz 1997, Rawson 1998). No funds were made available from the Department or budget appropriations in fiscal years 1991 and 1992. In 1993, the USDA provided a mere $120,000 under the Federal Advisory Committee Act. Congress finally began appropriating funds for Program activities in 1994, although the support was limited to about $500,000 annually (Rawson 1998).

The NOSB was appointed in 1992 and began slowly but purposefully drafting national organic standards recommendations (Rawson 1998). The Board sought considerable external input, including several meetings a year across the country to gather public comments, and began submitting its recommendations to National Organic Program staff in 1994 (Kuepper 2010). By the end of 1996, the NOSB had generated a wide-ranging "tome" of proposals for the National Organic Program (Amaditz 1997, 545), touching on issues including how the term "organic" should be defined, synthetic inputs that should be allowed in organic food production under the National List, and how organic products should be labeled under a tiered labeling hierarchy.

National Organic Program staff drafted a proposed rule outlining national organic standards based on the NOSB's recommendations, but not in complete conformity with them. The proposed National Organic Program rule appeared on the *Federal Register* on December 16, 1997 (62 FR 65850), and the Program immediately began receiving protests over its contents. Among the most loudly disputed elements were the allowance of the "big three"—irradiation of produce, municipal biosolids (sewage sludge) as fertilizer, and genetically modified organisms—under national organic standards. In addition to the big three, Rawson (1998) identifies six contended issues with the rule:

1. Omission of key concepts such as ecosystem health and biodiversity from the definition of organic;
2. Substitution of NOSB organic standards recommendations with those from the USDA;
3. Overly lax livestock production standards;
4. Loopholes that would allow never-before-used synthetic materials in organic production;
5. Removing certifiers' authority to decertify operations, leaving decertification up to the sole discretion of the USDA; and,
6. Omitting land history from certification requirements, potentially allowing contaminated soils in organic production.

Backlash to the proposed rule was unprecedented, resulting in the largest number of rulemaking comments in the USDA's history (Kuepper 2010, Mosier 2017, "Protests Prompt Delay on Government's Rules for Organic Food" 1998). As the estimated number of certified farms at the time was around 5,000, many assumed that the response largely represented the voice of organic consumers (Kuepper 2010, 10). The Agency received somewhere around 277,000 citizen comments, and many of them argued against the inclusion of one or more of the big three in organic practices (Rawson 1998). As one comment stated:

> A compromised standard, one that yields to pressures from commercial interests and waters down the meaning of "organic" so as to include precisely the elements the organic consumer is trying to avoid, renders certification meaningless and vacates trust in the USDA as a guardian of the people's wellbeing. (As cited in Shulman 2003, 258)

While the response to the proposed rule was notable and had an impact on the USDA's development of organic standards, the number of comments that were received should be considered with an important contextual detail. As indicated by Shulman (2003), the National Organic Program proposed rule was the first fully electronic rulemaking effort in the U.S. While people were able to submit comments by email, fax, or the postal service, electronic comment submission likely encouraged more people than usual to participate, thereby increasing the number of comments when compared to past notice-and-comment methods, to some unknown degree.

The USDA reacted to such criticisms by highlighting that the organic label was never intended to be a food safety or public health claim, but rather was to be implemented for marketing purposes, consistent with the mandates of the 1990 Organic Foods Production Act. Nonetheless, in response to the volume of citizen input, USDA Agricultural Secretary Dan Glickman extended the public comment time period an additional forty-five days, referring to the event as an "exercise in democracy" and stating, "our goal is to develop a final rule that the organic community and all the public can embrace" (as cited in "Protests Prompt Delay on Government's Rules for Organic Food" 1998, 18A).

In May of 1998, the USDA capitulated to protests over the proposed standards, announcing that it would not allow the big three under a Final Rule. Secretary Glickman announced the changes with a written comment which stated: "If organic farmers and consumers reject our national standards, we have failed. Thousands of commenters requested that USDA issue revised proposed standards, and we intend to do so" (as cited in "USDA Abandons Three Contentious Issues in Proposed Organic Standards" 1998, 95). A revised rule was issued in March of 2000 (65 FR 13512), from which the big three were excluded. Overall, the changes were welcomed—particularly from a consumer perspective. Dr. Margaret Mellon, of the Union of Concerned Scientists, noted: "this could turn out to be the most important rule USDA has issued in 20 years . . . the agency has never before been responsive to consumers" (as cited in Burros 2000, 22). The revised rule was released as a final rule in December of 2000 (65 FR 80548), allowing time for organic farmers to comply with the standards. Full implementation of the National Organic Program went into effect in October 2002.

REFLECTIONS ON ORGANIC AGRICULTURE'S INSTITUTIONAL EVOLUTION IN THE U.S.

The preceding evolution of U.S. organic food governance—from the rise of organic farmers' self-regulation, to a patchwork of governmental and nongovernmental certification programs, and finally to USDA regulation—reflects a variety of scholarly notions regarding institutional emergence and evolution. Most relevant to this examination, Bartley (2007) sketches two theoretical perspectives on the emergence of certification systems, which he dubs the "market-based" explanation and the "political construction" approach. According to Bartley, both perspectives are necessary for fully explaining why and how industries choose to self-regulate. The argument is supported by the case of U.S. organic certification, although each of the two theories appear more relevant at different points in time.

The market-based explanation for certification posits that economic actors organize to develop and hold one another accountable to institutions of production to buttress business reputations and preserve privileged market positions (Prakash and Potoski 2007). The explanation recognizes the influence of three actor groups: a social movement, consumers, and industry actors. Social movements draw consumer interest to a concerning dimension of a production activity, such as the labor practices of textile manufacturing or environmental impacts of farming, and consumers respond by seeking production alternatives that address the concern. Recognizing the need for credible information that their products represent such an alternative, industry actors (such as textile manufacturers or farms) construct external accountability systems in the form of certification schemes. Certification labels protect businesses from fraudulent competition—competitors seeking to capitalize on consumer demand for improved practices without substantively altering their processes—often creating a competitive advantage for certified businesses in the process.

Where the market-based explanation of industry self-regulation hinges on businesses' cooperation to generate collective benefits, Bartley's (2007) political construction approach casts certification as arising out of conflict and bargaining. Differing perspectives on how industry is to be regulated give rise to conflict both within a market (i.e., between businesses) and between the market and other actors, such as social movements or other nongovernmental groups. The approach positions governments as potential "institutional entrepreneurs"—sponsors that facilitate or lead the development of certification programs. According to the political construction approach, a certification program ultimately embodies the resolution of differing perspectives regarding how an industry is regulated; the extent to which one group's perspective is institutionalized in the program over another's is a product of the groups' relative political power and bargaining strategies.

The first U.S. organic certification scheme initiated by Rodale in 1971 is a clear example of the market-based explanation for industry self-regulation: as consumer demand for organic products grew throughout the 1960s, organic producers saw the need to protect the organic market from "organic phonies" (Rodale 1971). They found this protection in Rodale Press certification and the subsequent farmer-organized certification schemes that Rodale helped initiate. Although certainly not divorced from political considerations, these early certification efforts occurred outside of governmental purview, reflecting coordination among organic industry actors to exclude conventional farmers from the organic market. Furthermore, shared origins and philosophies among farmer-organized certification schemes meant that the organic standards that they enforced, while not identical, largely aligned (Fetter and Caswell 2002).

As certification programs proliferated throughout the 1970s and '80s, however, and with an increasing diversity of third-party sponsors (from state governments to for-profit firms), disparities between organic certification programs began to concern political officials and the organic community, alike—but for different reasons. As larger agribusinesses took increasing interest in the organic market, political officials worried that organic standards disparities would impede trade and the growth of the organic food sector. Organic farmers worried that the proliferation of certification programs exposed the organic market to cooptation by conventional agriculture interests. Both sets of concerns established favorable conditions and political support for federally established organic standards.

Through Bartley's political construction approach, the resulting passage of the 1990 Organic Foods Production Act and development of national organic standards reflect bargaining and settlement of differences among divergent interests: most notably, those of the organic movement, from which the organic market originated, and corporate agribusinesses, eager to enter the burgeoning market. Conflict existed throughout the process but is most visible in developments surrounding the 1997 National Organic Program proposed rule. A rejection of the "big three" was considered a victory for the organic movement, ensuring that the standards reflected key organic agriculture principles. Political pressures from conventional agriculture interests, however, alongside the USDA's position as an institutional entrepreneur, ensured that organic agriculture stakeholders' vision for national organic standards had a limited influence on the standards codified in National Organic Program regulations (Obach 2015).

Thus, a combination of the market-based and political construction approaches helps explain the emergence and evolution of U.S. organic food governance. Although organic farmers' self-regulation emerged largely in response to market dynamics, understanding the evolution towards government regulation necessitates recognition of the political forces that ultimately shaped the nature and scope of today's USDA organic standards. As importantly, and as documented in the chapters that follow, the ramifications of USDA organic certification's political construction continue to reverberate in contemporary U.S. organic food policy debates, where proponents of traditional organic principles vie with the influence of corporate and conventional agribusinesses over the standards that define "organic" in the U.S.

CONCLUSIONS: THE INSTITUTIONAL LEGACY OF ORGANIC FOOD GOVERNANCE

The history of organic food governance recounted in this chapter sets the stage for this book's largely contemporary analysis of USDA organic certification and it is with this contextual backdrop that the book's findings should be considered. As described above, organic agriculture emerged as a reaction to the technological innovation and "industrialization" that increasingly characterized agricultural practices throughout the twentieth century. In contrast with conventional practices, organic agriculture offered a farming method focused on soil health, minimal reliance on synthetic chemicals and off-farm inputs, and general adherence to "natural" practices. Consumer demand for organic products grew during the 1960s and '70s alongside, and often in connection with, the broader counterculture and environmental movements. Association with parallel social movements arguably had mixed results for organic agriculture proponents: it helped transform organic food from a niche market to a more mainstream industry but also narrowed many consumers' conception of organic methods to those pertaining to environmental sustainability and food quality.

The chapter described how organic certification schemes first emerged as farmer-initiated responses to the need to verify their adherence to organic principles, followed by a proliferation of what are best thought of a third-party certification programs in which independent organizations (often state governments) established and enforced their own organic standards. As a result, by the late 1980s a patchwork of disparate governmental and nongovernmental certification programs was found across the U.S. Congress passed the 1990 Organic Foods Production Act in no small part to harmonize the disparate programs under a uniform set of organic standards, constraining the driving rationale for U.S. organic food regulation to commercial marketing by situating it under the USDA's Agriculture Marketing Service.

This book examines the implications of USDA organic certification's decentralized regulatory design. This design is a direct result of the institutional legacy described in this chapter. Rather than replace the patchwork of third-party organic certification programs of the late 1980s, the Act codified their role as third-party administrators of National Organic Program regulations, creating a regulatory arrangement reliant on a constellation of organizations and individuals, both governmental and nongovernmental, and from within and outside of the Program's formal scope of authority. Furthermore, USDA organic standards were modeled after the certification programs that predated them. For example, beginning with the Rodale Press' *Organic Farming and Gardening* program in 1972, early organic certification schemes certified products based on the practices used to produce them, rather than their end characteristics. Today, USDA organic certification revolves around organic operations' adherence to the practices outlined in National Organic Program regulations, requiring limited product testing only in more recent years.

Finally, as indicated in this chapter's penultimate section, the contemporary political landscape surrounding USDA organic certification is best understood as a by-product of its political construction. The effort to establish organic standards through National Organic Program rulemaking was in many ways a struggle between the objectives and interests of organic agriculture advocates pushing for more restrictive organic standards, and those of commercial and conventional agribusiness seeking more limited regulatory focus and inclusive standards. For many observers, the USDA clearly aligned with the interests of the latter. The struggle to define organic standards did not end with the release of the National Organic Program Final Rule, however, and stakeholders continue to debate the proper scope and elements of organic food policy. The next chapter engages the contemporary debate over the National Organic Program regulations, including how they are developed under NOSB counsel and the implications that stem from some stakeholders' discontent with contemporary standards.

NOTES

1. The opening paragraph in Chapter 3 borrows heavily from David and Rebecca Nowacek's (2008) article "The Organic Foods System: Its Discursive Achievements and Prospects."

2. Ostrom (2005) provides an in-depth examination of the regulatory dimension of institutions, while making a passing mention of institutions' constitutive properties. For more detailed discussions of institutions as constitutive prescriptions, see Searle (1964) and D'Andrade (2006).

3. For an in-depth discussion regarding the foundations and development of organic agriculture as a philosophy and method, see Heckman (2006). Guthman (2004) offers an in-depth examination specific to California. Obach (2015) provides a thorough treatment of the evolution and challenges of the organic movement. This chapter draws heavily from all three sources.

Chapter Four

Systems-Based Regulations and Rulemaking Counsel

USDA National Organic Standards and the NOSB

National Organic Standards Board (NOSB) meetings are usually uneventful affairs. Board members convene in the sterile ambiance of nondescript hotel conference rooms and hold technocratic discussions regarding topics such as revisions to the Policy and Procedures Manual and whether the plant-derived sweetener fructooligosaccharides should be allowed under the organic standards as a flavor enhancer. The April 2014 NOSB meeting, however, was not typical. In what reporter Nathanael Johnson (2014) refers to as the "showdown at the organic standards board," deliberations were brought to a halt when protesters entered the meeting, took positions at the front of the room, and began deliberately chanting in a monotone unison "don't change sunset." The protest ended when police handcuffed one of the protesters—Organic Consumers Association Political Director Alexis Baden-Mayer. Awkwardly grasping her elbows and ankles, police carried the still-chanting Baden-Mayer from the conference room.

At issue was a USDA revision to NOSB procedures for vetting materials approved for use in organic food production under the National List of Allowed and Prohibited Substances. Prior to the change, allowed synthetic materials were removed from the List by default after five years unless re-approved by a two-thirds NOSB vote. After the revision, synthetic substances remained on the List unless the Board voted to remove them. Although the revision may seem like a minor reorganization of bureaucratic routines, for advocates such as those from the Organic Consumers Association it was an affront to the principles that traditionally guided organic agriculture.

Although the 2014 NOSB meeting "showdown" is admittedly among the more dramatic demonstrations against the USDA organic standards, it is nonetheless indicative of discontent expressed by some organic policy stakeholders. The National Organic Program Final Rule, released in 2000, established U.S. organic policy's constitutive and regulatory dimensions by operationalizing the mandates of the 1990 Organic Foods Production Act. From a policy perspective, and as intended by the advocates that pushed for federal organic policy, the Final Rule addressed key regulatory ambiguities by providing a formal definition of organic agriculture and establishing the standards against which organic practices are evaluated. According to the National Organic Program Final Rule, organic production is defined as:

> . . . a production system that is managed in accordance with the Act and regulations in this part to respond to site-specific conditions by integrating cultural, biological, and mechanical practices that foster cycling of resources, promote ecological balance, and conserve biodiversity. (7 C.F.R. pt. 205.2)

Through this definition, National Organic Program regulations set the federally recognized scope and objectives of organic agriculture. The parameters do not, however, resolve conflicts between the assumptions, perceptions, and philosophies held by organic movement proponents and those of the broader agricultural sector. As early as Kathleen Merrigan's 1989 draft bill, organic activists voiced concerns that the agribusiness-friendly USDA would undermine the true purpose and spirit of organic agriculture (Obach 2015) and the 1997 Proposed Rule controversy directed such skepticisms at the USDA's organic standards (Amaditz 1997). By 2002, the standards had come to embody this concern in the minds of more fervent organic agriculture proponents (Guthman 2014, Obach 2015). Finally, full implementation of the National Organic Program placed the standards at the center of struggles over who organic food policy is meant to serve and which sectors of the agricultural industry should have the greatest influence over organic food governance.

This chapter examines the organic standards established in National Organic Program regulations. While most of this book focuses on regulatory *administration*, how the National Organic Program regulations are monitored and enforced is inevitably shaped by the nature of the standards they encompass. Perhaps more importantly, the extent to which organic agriculture stakeholders view the standards-setting process as just and adequately protecting their interests heavily influences the relative legitimacy with which the standards—and the National Organic Program more generally—are perceived. Decreased perceived legitimacy, in turn, holds the potential to undermine the long-term durability of organic food policy under the USDA.

The chapter begins with an overview and description of the USDA organic standards, including select criticisms lodged against standard's limited scope. It then takes an in-depth look at the key institutional mechanism by which the National Organic Program regulations are meant to shape regulatee behavior. For example, May (2007) differentiates between prescriptive, systems-based, and performance-based regulations. Dating back to Rodale's original 1972 certification program, organic operations have been certified on by their processes, rather than the characteristics of the products they generate (Deaton and Hoehn 2005). Organic certification under the USDA can therefore be considered systems-based regulation, where operations are evaluated for compliance with process-oriented specifications (i.e., an organic system plan), rather than production outcomes, such as the presence of pesticide residue or genetically modified organisms (May 2007).[1]

Regulatory theory suggests that the inherent flexibility of systems-based approaches can leave them vulnerable to overly creative regulatee interpretation of regulatory standards, causing such programs to become more prescriptive over time. The chapter uses the evolution of the National Organic Program regulations' organic livestock standards to illustrate the challenge of USDA organic standards as systems-based regulation. The evolution indicates that systems-based regulations *may* become more prescriptive in response to concerns of overly loose standards interpretations, but that the tendency towards more prescriptive principles can be impeded where sufficient commercial or political interests intervene.

The chapter's third section turns to how National Organic Program regulations are developed. USDA organic standards are informed by the NOSB, a non-discretionary advisory committee authorized under the provisions of the Federal Advisory Committee Act of 1972. Rulemaking with advisory committee counsel offers notable benefits, for example, the ability to leverage stakeholder expertise towards more informed rulemaking and increased credibility in the eyes of stakeholders (Cook and Rinfret 2013). Perceived legitimacy can be undermined, however, if advisory committee composition or decision processes are seen to favor the interests of some stakeholders over others (Coglianese 2002). As discussed in this chapter, critics charge that the NOSB has evolved to represent the interests of corporate agribusinesses over smaller and more "genuine" organic operations—claims that suggest diminished Board legitimacy in some corners of the organic community.

The chapter's fourth section considers the implications of USDA organic standards' decreased legitimacy in the eyes of some stakeholders. The discussion centers on the emergence of supplementary certification programs in response to perceived National Organic Program shortcomings, in particular, and what such programs might signal in regard to USDA organic certification's long-run viability. A concluding section recaps the chapter's central lessons.

THE USDA NATIONAL ORGANIC STANDARDS

The National Organic Program regulations translate 1990 Organic Foods Production Act provisions into organic standards against which operations' practices are evaluated. The regulations that are directly applicable to organic food production and handling can be considered in four parts: organic crop production standards, organic livestock and poultry standards, organic product handling standards, and the National List of Allowed and Prohibited Substances (referred to as the "National List" for short). The central contours of each are described in brief below. Because the USDA considers the National Organic Program's primary purpose to be marketing, as evidenced by the Program's housing under the Agriculture Marketing Service, the regulation's labeling provisions are also described. The section concludes with a discussion of the of USDA organic standards allowances, limitations, and the organic agriculture dimensions that the standards do not address.

Organic Crop Standards

The National Organic Program regulation's crop standards most directly reflect aspects of organic agriculture's early focus on soil referenced in the previous chapter. The regulations direct farmers to manage soil fertility and crop nutrients through methods such as tillage (preparing soil through mechanical agitation), crop rotations, and cover crops. Notably, the regulations allow these methods to be supplemented with natural fertilizers and approved synthetic materials. Famers are required to address pests, weeds, and diseases through physical, mechanical, and biological methods. Where these practices are found insufficient, biological and botanical substances such as herbicides and pesticides may be used, as well as approved synthetic substances. The regulations require farmers to use organic seeds when available and require land to have gone at least three years since the application of a prohibited substance for an operation to harvest organic crops from it. The regulations specify a separate set of standards for the harvesting of wild crops and products, such as mushrooms, herbs, and maple syrup.

Organic Livestock and Poultry Standards

The National Organic Program regulations for livestock and poultry apply to animals that are raised for meat, milk, eggs, and other animal products. Among the requirements, feed must be 100 percent organic, although vitamin and mineral supplements are allowed, and animal health is to be ensured through preventative management practices. Livestock producers are prohibited from withholding treatment from sick animals but may not sell products as organic from animals treated with a prohibited substance, including those from treatment medications. Animals raised for slaughter must be raised under organic management methods from the last third of gestation and no later than the second day of life, in the case of poultry; for milk products to be labeled organic, the animal must have been managed under organic standards for twelve months or more. The regulations also address requirements for animals' access to the outdoors, which are discussed in greater detail later in this chapter.

Organic Handling Standards

National Organic Program regulation handling requirements apply to operations that prepare, transport, and process organic products. The regulations direct handlers to establish procedures that prevent the comingling of organic and non-organic products and protect against the contact of organic products with prohibited substances. They also set requirements for handling facilities' pest management practices. Under the required pest management practices, a handler is allowed to use a synthetic substance (such as a pesticide) that is not allowed by the National List of Allowed and Prohibited Substances only *after* they have attempted to address the problem with National List-consistent methods.

The National List of Allowed and Prohibited Substances

The National List of Allowed and Prohibited Substances identifies the synthetic substances which may be used in organic food production or processing (i.e., "allowed substances"), as well as the non-synthetic substances that are prohibited (i.e., "prohibited substances"). The List also stipulates the purposes and conditions under which synthetic substances are allowed. As is evident, the term "synthetic" is central to the National List. According to the National Organic Program regulations "synthetic" is defined as:

> A substance that is formulated or manufactured by a chemical process or by a process that chemically changes a substance extracted from naturally occurring plant, animal, or mineral sources, except that such term shall not apply to substances created by naturally occurring biological processes.

As a general rule, synthetic substances are prohibited unless explicitly allowed by the National List and non-synthetic substances are allowed unless prohibited by the National List. The National Organic Program website's introduction to the National List provides the following example: "a vaccine used to prevent pinkeye in livestock is an allowed synthetic substance and arsenic is an example of a prohibited natural substance." In 2018, the National List contained approximately 47 synthetic substances approved across organic crop and livestock production and handling uses. To put the National List in perspective, organic advocates often contrast the List against the substances that are used in conventional agriculture. The Organic Trade Association's website attests that while the EPA registers over 900 synthetic pesticide products for use in conventional farming, the National List approves only 25 for organic agriculture.

Importantly, the National List identifies only *general* substances, rather than the name of manufactured commercial formulas or products, such as a brand name fertilizer or pesticide, that might contain an allowed or prohibited substance. As a consequence, responsibility for reviewing commercial formulas and products for their compliance with USDA organic standards and the National List falls to individual accredited certifiers, often in consultation with an organic materials review organization, such as OMRI. The materials review process and how it should be regulated have proved consistent challenges for the National Organic Program, as discussed in greater detail later in this book.

Product Labeling Requirements

Under 1990 Organic Foods Production Act mandates, food products marketed and sold as "organic" in the U.S. must have been produced, handled, and processed in accordance with USDA organic standards by operations certified USDA organic. An exception is made for operations that gross less than $5,000 annually in organic product sales; these operations are required to adhere to the organic standards but are not required to be certified. Although exempt operations are allowed to use the term organic, they are prohibited from using the USDA organic seal or representing their products as certified organic. Retail establishments (such as grocery stores) that handle, but do not process, organic foods are also exempt from the certification requirement.

For certified operations, the National Organic Program regulations outline detailed requirements for how the term organic and the USDA organic seal may be used, as well as where they can appear on a product. They also require retail products to disclose the name of manufacturers' accredited certifier with a "Certified organic by . . ." statement (which certifiers refer to as the "COB" statement). There is a four-tier labeling scheme for multi-ingredient products made with organic ingredients:

- Products that are made entirely out of organic ingredients can be labeled as "100 percent organic." They may also carry the USDA organic seal. Water and salt are excluded from the organic ingredient requirement, as the Program already considers these "natural." Most certified unprocessed and raw products are considered 100 percent organic.

- Products that contain a minimum of 95 percent organic ingredients (excluding water and salt) can use the term organic on their principal display panel. They may also carry the USDA organic seal. The product's information panel must identify organic ingredients.
- Products that contain at least 70 percent organic ingredients can use the phrase "made with organic . . ." followed by up to three ingredients or ingredient categories. These products may *not* use the USDA organic seal. The product's information panel must identify organic ingredients.
- Products that contain less than 70 percent organic ingredients can list the ingredients as such in the products' information panel. They may not use the USDA organic seal or the term "organic" in the primary display panel.

Allowances, Limitations, and Omitted Standards

A variety debates have emerged and subsided over the years regarding the proper scope and content of USDA organic standards. Many of these revolve around the extent to which specific agricultural practices conform or depart from organic principles. For example, some argue against the allowance of hydroponics—soilless plant cultivation—given the centrality of soil health to the development of organic methods. Others revolve around the mechanics of implementing a given standard, such as how aquaculture can be certified organic absent a way of verifying that the food consumed by wild fish is organic. Although such disputes are too numerous to allow for a comprehensive accounting here, there are several debates that reflect broader disagreements regarding the purpose and scope of national organic standards.

A first of these is the allowance of synthetic substances. Consumers are often surprised to find that the National Organic Program regulations allow for the use of synthetic inputs in organic methods. Contemporary organic practitioners, in contrast, seem to have accepted limited allowance as a general rule, although what specific substances are allowed under the standards draws considerable debate. Organic advocates voice a range of other objections, however, regarding the limited scope of the USDA organic standards and requirements or principles that they omit. For many critics, the standards effectively replace holistic organic agriculture principles with a narrow set of prescribed requirements. The sentiment was expressed by one farmer during the standard's initial development: "I look at [the National Organic Program rule] as something that puts a cap on the standards that we are now living by . . . it caps the standards at the USDA level[s], which are very low" (as cited in Vos 2000, 249).

A second debate centers on worker welfare standards. More strict adherents to traditional organic principles criticize the USDA organic standards for ignoring issues related to worker wellbeing—a dimension that organic movement advocates consider integral to organic agriculture. For example, International Federation of Organic Agriculture Movements (IFOAM) standards include social justice and social rights considerations under the general principle of fairness. As explained by IFOAM (2014, 63): "The fairness principle of organic agriculture emphasizes that those involved in organic agriculture should conduct human relationships in a manner that ensures fairness at all levels and to all parties involved." Requirements in support of the principle include recognition of indigenous land rights, guaranteed worker collective bargaining rights, and protections against retaliation for employees that miss work due to illness.

A third and more commonly voiced critique dates back to the passage of the Organic Foods Production Act. At issue is whether the USDA organic standards facilitate the cooptation of the organic market by the broader agriculture and food production industries; "conventionalizing" organic agriculture (Buck, Getz, and Guthman 1997). For some, the simple presence of corporate agribusiness in the organic market is an affront to organic agriculture values, while others criticize lax sustainability requirements that allow for off-farm inputs such as commercial fertilizers (Guthman 2004b). Proponents of more stringent environmental protection standards, for example, advocate requirements such as on-farm compost making, mulching, and the application of green manure (plowing growing plants back into the soil). The USDA organic standards' limited requirements regarding animal welfare have also drawn considerable attention. The topic is discussed in greater detail in the following section as it pertains to outdoor access for ruminant livestock and poultry.

NATIONAL ORGANIC STANDARDS AS SYSTEMS-BASED REGULATION

As described in this chapter's introduction, USDA national organic standards are best characterized as systems-based regulations. Rather than mandate exact procedures by which organic operations implement organic standards (with the exception of the National List), producers and handlers develop their own organic system plans that spell out how the operations will adhere to the National Organic Program regulations. The plan is reviewed by a certifier for organic standards conformance and a representative of the certifier inspects the operation for with compliance with the plan. As CCOF (2018b) explains to potential certification applicants: "Your [organic system plan] acts as an agreement between you and CCOF. It defines how you remain in compliance with the organic standards, and explains what you do, how you do it, and what you use while doing it."

Systems-based regulations empower regulated entities to tailor how they conform to regulatory standards, allowing leeway to account for the characteristics of their operations and the contexts they operate in. The approach is found across regulated sectors that are populated by diverse products, methods, and operational characteristics, such as industrial safety regulation, nuclear energy operations, and food safety governance (Coglianese and Lazer 2003). A systems-based approach works well when no single technology or process defines the practice or outcomes of interest, or where "the production systems of firms are too complicated to be able to effectively prescribe regulatory fixes" (May and Wood 2003, 10). In the realm of organic agriculture, systems-based regulation affords agricultural producers and food processors operational leeway to craft processes that are responsive to the regional, economic, and environmental conditions that they face, and within the capacities and constraints of their operations.

Of course, the benefits of systems-based regulation come with vulnerabilities. Among these is the potential for regulatee-devised systems, while conforming to regulatory standards, to fail in bringing about the anticipated or desired policy outcomes. For example, certified organic methods may prohibit the use of most synthetic chemicals, but they do not guarantee that organic products are free of chemical residues. In some cases, program outcomes can be supported by augmenting systems-based regulation with performance-based design elements, such as supplementary product monitoring. The 1990 Organic Foods Production Act outlined such a hybrid design, mandating at least some product testing for prohibited substances. When finalized, however, National Organic Program regulations allowed—but did not require—product testing (OIG 2010). It wasn't until around 2013 that the Program issued guidance requiring certifiers to test 5 percent of the products they certify for prohibited substances.[2]

A second concern with systems-based regulation is variation in the stringency with which regulatees translate regulatory standards into operational practices, as the flexibility inherent in systems-based standards leaves them more vulnerable to overly lenient interpretation by bad actors (Black 2008, May 2007). Excessive variation in standards interpretation undermines program fidelity and can threaten program rationale if such variation deviates from policy intents. Furthermore, overly creative standards interpretations may undermine perceived program legitimacy if consumers or other stakeholders regard the practices allowed under program oversight to run contrary the program's principles, goals, or underlying philosophy.

Regulatory theory suggests that programs are inclined to make systems-based regulations more prescriptive over time: as some regulatees inevitably exercise overly lenient standards interpretations, programs respond by "ratcheting up" standards and increasing the prescriptive detail with which standards are specified (Bardach and Kagan 1982, Judge-Lord, McDermott, and Cashore 2018). In the context of organic certification, the tension between general standards and prescriptive detail is perhaps most visible in the evolution of organic livestock requirements. The case supports the proposition that systems-based designs face pressures to become more prescriptive over time. It also indicates that the tightening of systems-based standards is not inevitable—at least in the medium term—and may be resisted to protect politically and economically powerful stakeholders' interests.

Principles versus Prescription in Organic Livestock and Poultry Standards

The brief history of organic livestock requirements under the National Organic Program is one in which the regulations first stipulated general principles but the actions of some certified operations motivated the Program to develop more detailed prescriptions over time. The standard in question outlines requirements for organic livestock welfare, which reads:

> The producer of an organic livestock operation must establish and maintain livestock living conditions which accommodate the health and natural behavior of animals, including (1) Access to the outdoors, shade, shelter, exercise areas, fresh air, and direct sunlight suitable to the species, its stage of production, the climate, and the environment; (2) Access to pasture for ruminants[.] (7 CFR 205.239(a)(1-2))

The first operation officially accused of overly lenient organic livestock standards interpretation was the Massachusetts egg producer Country Hen, which claimed that the screened chicken-sized porches installed on its poultry facility met the regulations' requirements for outdoor access. Baystate Organic Certifiers (also known as Massachusetts Independent Certification)—the organic certifier that Country Hen was seeking organic certification through—disagreed, and in 2002 denied the operation's application (Jaffee and Howard 2010). Country Hen appealed the decision with the USDA and despite protests and court petitions from Baystate Organic, the USDA overturned the denial and compelled the certifier to issue the certification. While largely ignored by the media, the case sparked off a debate within the organic industry regarding the appropriateness of process–based livestock welfare standards that allowed for a diversity of interpretations, thereby facilitating the growth of the organic sector, and more prescriptive requirements, which would maintain the intent and spirit of organic agriculture advocates.

A second case of lenient standards interpretation came to light three years later—this time catching the attention of activists and the media, alike. A January 2005 *Chicago Tribune* article showcased Aurora Organic Dairy's 5,300 cow dairy operation to illustrate a rift in the organic industry over the interpretation of organic livestock requirements (Martin 2005). Organic agriculture advocates decried Aurora's use of large dirt-floor pens and processed organic feed, arguing that the practices fell short of the regulations' access to pasture requirements. The Colorado operator countered that the cows had the required outdoor access, but that the climate of an arid Western state precluded sufficient pasture for all its animals to graze.

Perhaps because of the national attention garnered by the *Chicago Tribune* article, and subsequent media coverage, the USDA took action. The NOSB began considering new access to pasture requirements language that same year, and in 2006 the USDA published an advanced notice of proposed rulemaking asking stakeholders to weigh in on questions concerning pasture access, including whether pasturing is essential to organic milk production in the eyes of consumers, and what scientific evidence had to say about ruminant animal nutrition and pasturing. A proposed rule followed in 2008, and in 2010 the USDA issued regulations establishing the new parameters for pasture grazing of ruminant livestock, under the label "the Pasture Rule." The Pasture Rule specified prescriptions constituting "access to pasture" under the National Organic Program regulations, including:

- The definition of "dry matter intake," a term for feed that ruminant animals eat by grazing on pasture;
- The definition and minimum length of a grazing season, during which animals must be grazed on pasture;
- The organic system plan requirements for a pasture management plan, outlining the system by which an operation would meet the Pasture Rule requirements, and;
- Recordkeeping requirements to document that the operation had adhered to the Pasture Rule.

While resolution to the organic pasture controversy was relatively quick, USDA action regarding outdoor access for poultry was a prolonged process—likely in-part because the incident went largely unnoticed by the media and consumers. The NOSB recommended outdoor access requirements revisions in 2002, and again in 2009. Shortly thereafter, a 2010 Office of the Inspector General report called on the USDA to clarify the standards—citing inconsistencies in the way both organic operations and organic certifiers were interpreting regulations pertaining to the treatment of organic poultry. The National Organic Program responded with a 2010 draft guidance to the regulations' outdoor access requirements, but the move was immediately met with skepticism by those who claimed that the guidance did little to strengthen or clarify the ambiguous standards (Kane 2010).

It wasn't until 2015 that the USDA released a proposed Organic Livestock and Poultry Practices Rule, requiring each hen have a square foot of space when indoors and precluding screened-in porches as outdoor access. The move was met with support from many in the organic community, including animal welfare groups, the Organic Trade Association and consumer interest organizations, and organic certifiers seeking authoritative USDA guidance on how to administer National Organic Program regulations (Curry 2017). A final Rule was published in January 2017 and slated to go into effect in March of that year. As with the proposed rule, the final Organic Livestock and Poultry Practices Rule engendered considerable support for balancing the "complexities of commercial scale farming with the expectations of organic consumers," as evidenced by an Organic Trade Association letter signed by 334 organic livestock farmers submitted to the federal registrar (OTA 2017b).

Instead of implementing the regulations, however, Secretary of Agriculture Sonny Perdue surprised the organic community by issuing a second proposed rule—this time calling for public comment on four possible actions for the final Organic Livestock and Poultry Practices Rule: enact it, suspend it, delay it, or withdraw it (Curry 2017). In a December 2017 Federal Register Notice the USDA withdrew the rule under the rationale that the Agency lacked the authority to issue rules beyond those pertaining to livestock health, and that the continued growth of the organic market was evidence that the current standards were effective *without* the rule change. Over the protests of supporters, the rule was withdrawn in March 2018.

Drawing Lessons from the Evolution of Organic Livestock Standards

The most obvious explanation for why the 2017 Organic Livestock and Poultry Practices Rule was withdrawn is that the Obama-era regulation, issued immediately prior to President Trump's inauguration, fell victim to the Trump administration's anti-regulatory mission. Such an explanation, however, fails to account for the years in which the Obama administration delayed organic poultry standards revisions. It also underplays the outsized influence that a minority of organic egg producers may have come to hold over USDA organic standards development as their share of the organic market has grown. As pointed out by food and agricultural journalist Lynne Curry (2017):

> . . . as the organic market has bloomed, a few massive and influential shell egg companies—including Herbruck's Poultry Ranch in Michigan, Rose Acre Farms in Indiana, and Hidden Villa Ranch in California—that represent just five percent of all U.S. egg producers, have dominated organic egg sales. And they do not want to give up their rapidly growing market share or their cost of production advantages from raising millions of birds in multistory aviaries.

Regardless of the precise cause of the Organic Livestock and Poultry Practices Rule withdrawal, the evolution of organic livestock requirements illustrates the tension that the National Organic Program faces in balancing systems-based regulation through general standards and providing regulatory detail that encourages consistent standards interpretation and practices. More flexible standards, such as those that are currently make up poultry outdoor access requirements, may best serve the Program's goal of encouraging a robust organic food market—at least in the short term. The benefits of flexible standards may not hold in the long run, however, if they contribute to dissatisfaction with the National Organic Program among organic practitioners or undermine consumer confidence in the organic label. Indeed, the relative leniency of the Program's livestock requirements is cited as a central rationale for the rise of supplementary organic certification programs, as discussed at the end of this chapter.

On the other hand, the prescriptive detail that was realized in the case of the Pasture Rule and cheered by much of the organic community may carry unintended consequences. Chief among these is the additional cost to producers of the Pasture Rule's recordkeeping requirements—documentation requirements of the sort that usually accompany more prescriptive regulations. Such recordkeeping costs and associated administrative obligations can deter otherwise qualifying operations from pursuing certification, thereby decreasing overall program participation. The challenge of balancing regulatory stringency and administrative burden is discussed in Chapter 5.

Importantly, both the 2010 Pasture Rule and the 2017 Organic Livestock and Poultry Practices Rule were informed and supported by the NOSB. Yet, as recounted in this section, the USDA's withdrawal of the Organic Livestock and Poultry Practices Rule rejected a unanimous recommendation from the Board. To those skeptical of organic policy under the USDA, the move added to evidence that the NOSB's role in organic regulation was being undermined by the agency it is meant to advise. The remainder of this chapter focuses on the NOSB's function in the organic food regulatory arrangement and the implications of such criticisms for the future of USDA organic certification.

NOSB COUNSEL IN ORGANIC STANDARDS RULEMAKING

This section shifts the discussion from USDA organic standards' content to how the standards are developed and, in particular, the role of the NOSB in advising National Organic Program rulemaking. The extent to which, and how, advisory committee counsel shapes regulatory standards is dependent on several factors. An advisory committee's influence is largely determined by the weight afforded to committee determinations; in other words, the extent to which program decisions should follow or may deviate from committee recommendations.

The *content* of committee recommendations is shaped by the committee's composition, or "who has a seat at the table." Literature examining advisory committee influence in other policy making venues demonstrates that that the extent to which committee representation is concentrated to particular stakeholder groups is often a direct determinant of whether the benefits of committee input are narrowly captured by special interests or are more broadly accessible (Mitchell 1997, Henry and Harms 1987). Simply put, the more a stakeholder group dominates an advisory committee, the more likely committee decisions are to further that stakeholder group's interests and objectives.

The content of advisory committee recommendations is further influenced by the decision rules a committee uses to develop its recommendations. Particularly influential is a committee's "default position" in key decision situations or topics. Default positions specify the assumed position of a committee on a given issue (absent express indication otherwise), and thereby establish where the burden of proof for justifying deviations from a default position lies (Wright 1977). For example, because the default position of the NOSB is that synthetic substances are to be prohibited from national organic standards, the burden of proof is on industrial agriculture stakeholders to justify why exceptions should be made to the rule.

All three factors—advisory committee authority, composition, and decision rules—have proved sources of conflict throughout NOSB's history. Perhaps the greatest single threat to the NOSB's rulemaking role was witnessed early in the implementation of the National Organic Program. Although this early acute threat to NOSB authority was never realized, anecdotal evidence suggests that the Board's influence may be gradually diminishing over time. The trend—even if only a perceived one—arguably constitutes a considerable threat to the NOSB's legitimacy among organic agriculture advocates, as explored below.

Rulemaking Influence and Stakeholder Interests at the NOSB

The NOSB's statutory mission is "to assist in the development of standards for substances to be used in organic production and to advise the [Secretary of Agriculture] on any other aspects of the implementation of this title" (OFPA, Sec. 2119 (a)). To fulfill this role, the NOSB is charged with seeking stakeholder input and public comments, convening technical advisory panels, and working collaboratively with the National Organic Program (NOSB 2016). A key Board function—and one that affords it a somewhat unique statutory authority—is the recommendation of materials as approved or prohibited in the production of organic foods listed in the National List of Allowed and Prohibited Substances.

The earliest challenge to the NOSB's rulemaking influence came with the release of the 1997 National Organic Program Proposed Rule. Although citizen backlash to the Proposed Rule was directed at the inclusion of the "big three" in national organic standards (as described in Chapter 3), long-time organic advocates also condemned the Rule's transfer of National List recommendations authority from the NOSB to National Organic Program staff. The NOSB's National List advisory role was ultimately maintained in the subsequent Final Rule and today the Board submits National List recommendations directly to the Secretary of Agriculture without Program intervention (NOSB 2016). More recent events, however, suggest that the NOSB's rulemaking influence may be threatened in more subtle manners. For example, the NOSB's authority to set its meeting agendas was stripped under the Obama administration (Cornucopia Institute 2018) and subsequent Trump-appointed Secretary of Agriculture Sonny Perdue decided against several NOSB National List determinations, such as a recommendation to remove the emulsifier carrageenan as an allowed input for organic products (Charles 2014) and the controversial decision to withdraw NOSB-supported 2017 Organic Livestock and Poultry Practices Rule recounted earlier in this chapter.

Despite concerns of eroding NOSB influence in organic standards rulemaking, perhaps that most fervently argued critique of the NOSB is that its processes and recommendations have become coopted by large-scale industrial agriculture and conventional agribusinesses. The Board's official membership composition is fifteen volunteer stakeholders representing seven stakeholder groups or professional backgrounds. Presented in order of representative weight, these include:

1. Four representatives that own or operate an organic farming operation
2. Three representatives with expertise in the fields of environmental protection and resource conservation

3. Three representatives who represent public interest or consumer interest group
4. Two representatives that own or operate an organic handling operation
5. One representative that owns or operates a retail establishment with significant trade in organic products
6. One representative with expertise in the fields of toxicology, ecology, or biochemistry
7. One representative from a USDA-accredited organic certifying agent

Despite the diverse *official* composition of the NOSB, many organic agriculture advocates charge that the individuals appointed to the Board increasingly fail to meet the criteria for their selected positions. The Cornucopia Institute, an organic policy advocacy nonprofit and self-proclaimed industry watchdog, is among the most vocal of such critics. The Institute argues that beginning with the George W. Bush administration, the USDA began filling key positions with corporate employees and industry lobbyists (Cornucopia Institute 2018). A few of the appointments that the Institute puts forth as inappropriate include: an employee of Driscoll (the largest berry supplier in the U.S.) with no farming experience, but who was appointed to an organic farmer Board position; a market development specialist from PurePak, Inc. with no background in environmental science, but who was appointed to an environmental protection/resource conservation position, and; a General Mills employee who was appointed to a scientist position following backlash at her placement in a consumer interest slot (Cornucopia Institute 2013).

Through an analysis of National List recommendations compiled in a NOSB member voting record Scorecard, the Institute contends that the Board's balance has been undermined, leading to a gradual loosening of national organic standards. For example, the Scorecard found that three NOSB members voted in favor of more restrictive organic standards 90 percent of the time in 2017, while another two were what the Institute refers to as "swing voters," voting between 50 and 70 percent for more restrictive standards. The remainder voted in the direction of more restrictive standards 50 percent of the time, or less. While the Scorecard has yet to be subject to rigorous external assessment, the Cornucopia's overall argument of NOSB cooptation by conventional agribusinesses engenders limited support from scholarly research (Dimitri and Bronsing 2015, Jaffee and Howard 2010).

Finally, NOSB decision rule changes have also fallen under criticism from organic agriculture advocates. The most notable of these is the USDA's sunset provision revision referenced in this chapter's opening paragraphs. Before 2013, a synthetic material that was approved under the National List of Allowed and Prohibited Substances fell off the list by default after five years, unless the Board re-approved the material through a majority vote of two-thirds. After the revision, synthetic substances remained on the List unless the Board voted to remove them. While some in the organic community recognized that the original sunset provisions created a considerable time burden for the National Organic Program's small staff (Behar 2014), others contended that it constituted a reversal of the long-recognized principle that, in the words of former NOSB chairman James Riddle, "the use of synthetic substances in organic production and processing is an exception, not an entitlement" (as cited in Cornucopia Institute 2013). The revision became the subject of a lawsuit brought by the Center for Food Safety and thirteen consumer interest groups (Temkar 2015), in addition to the Organic Consumers Association political director's arrest at the spring 2014 NOSB meeting, when protesters brought the meeting to an abrupt halt (Johnson 2014).

How Rule Development Impacts Program Administration

As described in this section, the NOSB's role in USDA organic certification is important for both operational and symbolic reasons. Operationally, NOSB recommendations are intended to represent a compromise between the differing perspectives that vie for institutionalization in USDA organic standards. The content of those recommendations, combined with whether the USDA decides to accept and act on them, effectively define organic food as it appears on grocery store shelves. Symbolically, the NOSB has become a representation among the more fervent organic policy advocates of the outsized influence that they perceive "Big Ag" to hold over that definition. Whether that influence is over- or underestimated, it shapes the politics surrounding U.S. organic food regulation.

The central focus of this book is the administration, rather than the development, of USDA organic standards. Nonetheless, the way National Organic Program regulations are determined shapes the regulatory context in which they are administered. The most obvious way that organic standards development shapes their administration is in the regulatory requirements that are established. As indicated above, however, where regulatory standards are informed by expert counsel, the composition of that counsel and the extent to which a regulatory authority takes heed of advisory recommendations are likely to be observed and critiqued by policy advocates and other interested stakeholders. In this manner, the extent to which organic standards rulemaking is seen as credible impacts the perceived legitimacy of the Program, as a whole. The narrative in this section suggests that some organic agriculture stakeholders perceive NOSB-advisement process to be corrupted in one way or another. The following section therefore examines the implications that stem from decreased NOSB legitimacy, and that of the National Organic Program more generally, in the eyes of key organic agriculture stakeholders.

THE EMERGENCE OF SUPPLEMENTAL CERTIFICATION PROGRAMS

It's important to note that discontent with the NOSB, and National Organic Program more generally, is not shared universally among the organic agriculture and certification communities. For example, in a 2014 letter to then-Secretary of Agriculture Thomas Vilsack, the ACA responded to the aforementioned NOSB meeting protest with a vote of confidence for the Program and the NOSB. Representing the ACA's 2014 membership of forty-nine domestic USDA-accredited certifiers, Board of Directors Chair Scott Rice proclaimed: "We believe that the USDA National Organic Standards are stronger than they've ever been. . . .We support the [National Organic Program's] work and have faith in their leadership to the highest degree in the history of the [Program]" (2014, 1).[3]

Such support notwithstanding, it is clear that some within the organic community believe that the NOSB's processes and decisions have failed to adequately navigate divergent stakeholder interests and this discontent holds potential ramifications for the viability of organic certification under the National Organic Program. The most evident consequence of such dissatisfaction is the emergence of supplementary certifications offering a layer of stringency beyond the standards specified by USDA organic standards (Howard and Allen 2006). For example, in 2018 the Rodale Institute (organizational decendent of the originator of the first organic certification program in the U.S.) announced Regenerative Organic Certification, a program that "builds upon the standards set forth by USDA Organic . . . particularly in the areas of animal welfare and farmer and worker fairness" (Rodale Institute n.d.). The same year witnessed the launch of the Real Organic Project, a coalition of small-scale producers working "to create an add-on label to USDA certified organic to provide more transparency on organic farming practices" (Real Organic Real Organic Project n.d.).

Organic community members have expressed concerns that additional labels may contribute to consumer confusion over the meaning of organic certification, or worse, undermine consumer confidence in the USDA organic label altogether. Mark Kastel, co-founder of the Cornucopia Institute and one of the more vocal National Organic Program critics, expressed unease over the potential for unintended consequences from supplementary labels: "There's a real risk that the new seals will turn products that just have the federal seal into second-class citizens, unable to command the premium prices needed for even the most basic organic production" (as cited in Strom 2018). The Organic Trade Association expressed similar reservations in a letter to the Rodale Institute commenting on the Regenerative Organic Certification program:

> The good intention of the regenerative organic certification scheme, in fact, does present a serious risk to the success of the USDA Organic label. . . . As the awareness of this standard spreads, so may the misconception that USDA organic standards do not include requirements for soil health, biodiversity and animal welfare. Although not intended, this could present an unfortunate disservice to the livelihood of the organic sector and organic farmers across America. (OTA 2017a, 3)

It has yet to be seen whether such "add-on" certification programs indeed undermine the meaning and value of USDA organic certification, as suggested in the OTA's letter, or serve to support the National Organic Program, as is the stated intent of the Rodale Institute. Alternatively, it is possible that they will follow the path of programs advertised as alternatives to USDA organic certification, such as the farmer sponsored Certified Naturally Grown: attracting only limited attention from organic operations and consumers, alike. Regardless, supplementary organic certification programs are concrete indications that a sizeable contingent of the organic agriculture community is discontent with the scope and stringency of national organic standards (Howard and Allen 2006, Ikerd 2018).

CONCLUSIONS: SYSTEMS-BASED REGULATIONS, RULEMAKING COUNSEL, AND THE POLICY IMPLICATIONS OF DECREASED LEGITIMACY

Given the central role that organic standards occupy in the politics surrounding the National Organic Program, this chapter focused on the content and development of the USDA's national organic standards. The standard's scope and contours are reflected in their crop, livestock, handling, and labeling requirements. The standards allow for a limited amount of synthetic inputs (such as chemicals) when no viable organic alternative is available, under the National List of Allowed and Prohibited Substances. They also omit dimensions of agricultural production that some consider to be central to organic agriculture, such as worker welfare. Not all stakeholders are content with the extent to which the regulations incorporate the values and principles of organic agriculture, criticizing them for mainstreaming watered-down organic standards and an inferior "organic lite" market (Guthman 2004b).

The chapter traced the evolution of organic livestock standards to illustrate the tension between general principles and prescription that is inherent in systems-based regulation. Regulatory theory suggests that systems-based regulations are inclined to become more prescriptive over time as overly loose standards interpretations are discovered, however, that the tendency is subject to resistance from influential opposition. In the case of organic standards, the National Organic Program strengthened access to pasture requirements for ruminant animals under a 2010 Pasture Rule but withdrew an analogous strengthening of outdoor access requirements for poultry in 2017. For critics, withdrawal of the Organic Livestock and Poultry Practices Rule was an example of conventional agribusiness influence in, and dilution of, USDA organic policy.

The latter half of this chapter examined the role of the NOSB in National Organic Program rulemaking, with particular attention to claims that NOSB influence, stakeholder composition, and decision processes have been coopted by the conventional agriculture and food production sector. Although the discussion revolved around the claims of the National Organic Program's most fervent critics, they find some support from scholarly sources (e.g., Jaffee and Howard 2010). The claims also seem to have material consequences, as discontent with the USDA organic standards has proved sufficient to give rise to "supplemental" certification programs offering more stringent organic standards interpretations and filling in requirements that the USDA organic standards lack.

Although this chapter illustrated core issues regarding USDA organic standards and their development, it also identified a need for further research regarding how National Organic Program regulations are determined and to what ends. As noted earlier, scholarly research has yet to systematically assess advocates' claims of NOSB cooptation by conventional agribusiness. Furthermore, the process by which NOSB recommendations are incorporated or ignored by the USDA is opaque and difficult to interrogate. As stated by Vos (2000, 254): "The governmental/regulatory process in this case has a 'black-box' quality to outsiders and remains mysterious and confusing." Future research regarding how and when NOSB recommendations are accepted or rejected by the USDA offers not only a better understanding what shapes USDA organic standards but can also provide empirical insights into the promise and limitations of rulemaking advisory board counsel.

Such limitations notwithstanding, the chapter's analysis highlights key insights into the regulatory implications of stakeholder perceptions of the USDA organic standards and the role of the NOSB. Most notably, the criticisms documented in this chapter may signal more than political discontent—they are indicative of decreased perceived legitimacy within organic stakeholder communities, and potentially, consumer markets. Furthermore, the emergence of supplementary certification programs offers concrete evidence of perceived legitimacy declines.

When considered in light of the dimensions outlined in this book's framework for examining decentralized regulatory administration (Chapter 2), this decreased perceived legitimacy indicates a potential threat to the durability of USDA organic policy. Following May and Jochim (2013), policy durability is defined as the sustainability of the political commitments represented by a public policy. The preceding critiques of the NOSB and USDA organic standards are illustrative examples of how policies that fail to live up to those commitments in the eyes of key stakeholders undermine the policy's legitimacy, thereby turning supporters into opponents (May and Jochim 2013, 433). If sufficient policy support remains among key organic agriculture and certification stakeholders, such as that expressed by the ACA letter earlier in this chapter, the threat that decreased legitimacy poses to policy durability may be small.

However, when a program repeatedly delivers undesirable outcomes to already disillusioned stakeholders, the resulting legitimacy declines can engender negative feedback in which the cadre of detractors continues to grow. The evidence presented in this chapter offers some indication that the emerging supplemental label programs may create such negative feedback—most notably in the OTA's warning of the potential impacts of the Rodale Institute's Regenerative Organic Certification. If at least some observers of supplementary organic certification labels take their existence and adoption by producers to be indicative of USDA organic standards inadequacies (either real or perceived), stakeholder disillusionment with USDA organic policy is likely to grow. Ultimately, and as indicated by the OTA's caution, whether such programs represent a threat to the durability of organic food policy under the USDA is likely contingent on their influence on organic food consumers and the resulting impact on the consumer market for organic food, as a whole.

The National Organic Program has thus far remained silent on the topic of supplemental certification programs, but it is clearly aware of the criticisms described in this chapter and the hazards of decreased legitimacy. One manner that the Program seeks to address these concerns is through administrative initiatives—concerted efforts to focus the Programs regulatory activities and improve consumer confidence in what it calls "organic integrity." It pursues these initiatives alongside, and sometimes as part of, its other regulatory responsibilities; most notably, oversight of accredited certifying agents. The following chapter examines the National Organic Program as the USDA organic certification regulatory authority, focusing on the Program's initiatives and accreditation oversight of organic certifiers, and the resulting implications for USDA organic certification regulatory fidelity and program feedback.

NOTES

1. Elsewhere in the literature, systems-based regulation is also referred to as process-based (Coglianese, Nash, and Olmstead 2003) and management-based (Coglianese and Lazer 2003).

2. It's worth noting that the Program declined to mandate how certifiers should interpret the requirement, resulting in evident between-certifier product-testing disparities (Whoriskey 2017a).

3. It should also be noted that the ACA publicly supported the 2017 Organic Livestock and Poultry Practices Rule and pushed the USDA to support and implement the Rule in several letters.

Chapter Five

The Regulator

The National Organic Program

In 2010, on the heels of a critical Office of the Inspector General audit, newly appointed USDA Deputy Administrator Kathleen Merrigan announced the dawning of an "Age of Enforcement" at the National Organic Program. "In the past USDA has not played a strong enough role in enforcement and this administration intends to change that," she declared, "this is the age of enforcement. We will protect farmers who play by the rules and consumers who pay premiums for organic products" (as cited in Harsch 2010). The move was prompted by more than a critical audit—a number of highly publicized news investigations had recently raised serious concerns over the effectiveness of organic regulation under the USDA, alarming organic policy activists and the broader industry, alike.

Almost a decade later, it would be generous to say that the Age of Enforcement's success at quelling the concerns is unclear. News articles continue to question the credibility of the USDA organic label. While early critiques were often ignorant of how organic food is regulated, resorting to broad claims of weak regulatory initiative, contemporary criticisms dig deeper into the vulnerabilities of organic certification's design. Investigative journal Richard Read's writing is a case in point: referring to USDA organic certification as a "conflicted system," he introduces one article with the following observation: "The U.S. Department of Agriculture allows producers to hand-pick—and pay—the certifiers responsible for verifying that food meets organic standards" (Read 2017). Although he does not say as much outright, the implication is that certifiers paid by regulatee-clients are unlikely to enforce the regulations with sufficient rigor.

The implication has not gone unnoticed in regulatory scholarship. Using the language of "regulatory intermediaries" introduced in Chapter 2, Abbott,

Levi-Faur, and Snidal (2017b, 30) note "if the [regulatory] targets pays for the intermediary's services . . . then the intermediary may become overly responsive to the target's needs, especially if targets can engage in 'intermediary shopping.'" Preventing certifier shopping is just one tasks that that the National Organic Program is charged with. The Program's position at the top of a chain of regulatory action further saddles the Program with managing institutional tensions—challenges that stem directly from USDA organic certification's design, reflected in "the nature of the [Program's] rules and standards and the means for gauging adherence to them" (May 2007, 9). With these tensions come parallel, and sometimes competing, mandates. Perhaps most importantly, the National Organic Program is simultaneously charged with maintaining the integrity of organic regulation through stringent standards and enforcement while also promoting organic label adoption and the growth of the organic sector.

This chapter is concerned with the National Organic Program's role in U.S. organic certification, how the Program navigates institutional tensions while executing its oversight function, and the resulting implications for organic certification fidelity, integrity, and program feedback. As a regulatory arrangement, organic certification defies simple classification under the typologies usually applied by regulatory scholars. Rather, its design is a combination of several institutional features. As discussed in Chapter 4, two of these features are rulemaking with advisory committee counsel and systems-based regulation. This chapter focuses on two additional features: USDA organic certification's quasi-voluntary nature and the competitive third-party administration of organic regulations. As is described throughout the chapter, the tensions that are introduced by each of these features create administrative challenges with which the National Organic Program must contend.

The chapter begins with an overview of the National Organic Program's structure, functions, and select challenges created by its quasi-voluntary nature and competitive third-party design. Drawing on a combination of secondary evidence and published research, I then document the Program's administrative evolution, from early Program deficiencies, to the Age of Enforcement, and the contemporary "Sound and Sensible" initiative. The evolution portrays resource constraints the Program has faced and the concerted efforts that it has undertaken to buttress organic industry stakeholders' confidence in USDA organic certification. It also illustrates the Program's efforts to reduce barriers to organic certification while ensuring robust regulatory oversight.

In the third section, I examine National Organic Program oversight of organic certification agents through accreditation requirements. I describe the accreditation process and assembles USDA records to depict the Program's accreditation actions over time. I also identify a key gap in accreditation oversight in the Program's failure to track the enforcement actions of accredited certifiers. The chapter concludes with an assessment of the Program's administrative initiatives and accreditation activity, as they pertain to organic certification regulatory fidelity, integrity, and program feedback. The ending discussion identifies opportunities for research pursuing a more complete understanding of National Organic Program operations and effectiveness.

THE NATIONAL ORGANIC PROGRAM: STRUCTURE, MANDATES, AND CHALLENGES

As discussed in the preceding account of U.S. organic certification's evolution, the National Organic Program was implemented as a regulatory arm of the USDA's Agriculture Marketing Service. By most any measure it is a small program that operates with a limited budget; Deputy Administrator Miles McEvoy made this point in a 2017 interview following his retirement: "The [National Organic Program] is small with a $9 million budget for a $50 billion market" (McEvoy 2017). Despite its size, the Program juggles an array of responsibilities. In addition to regulating organic certifiers, its responsibilities include coordinating with and supporting the NOSB, developing the regulations and related guidance documents that specify organic standards and the National List of Allowed and Prohibited Substances, enforcing Program regulations through violation complaints investigations and enforcement actions, and overseeing Organic Certification Cost Share programs administration. The Program also facilitates international organic commerce through equivalency agreements and other organic import and export policies.

The National Organic Program's small staff, numbering forty-five in 2015, is organized in four divisions. The Office of the Deputy Administrator sets general Program policies and oversees core programmatic functions such as administration, budgeting, and personnel. The Standards Division is the Program's authoritative voice on organic standards interpretation, responsible for rulemaking, standards guidance development and associated communications, and coordination with the NOSB. The Accreditation and International Activities Division manages certifier accreditation activities, California State Organic Program oversight, and negotiates international organic trade policies. The Compliance and Enforcement Division processes regulatory compliance complaints, conducts investigations, and takes regulatory noncompliance enforcement actions.

While the National Organic Program has many responsibilities, the two that arguably constitute its core mandates are front and center in its 2015–2018

Strategic Plan (AMS 2015b). The first goal outlined in the Plan is to "protect organic integrity" through consistent regulatory enforcement and effective accreditation oversight. The second is to facilitate organic market access, in large part by supporting candidate and currently certified organic operations. The tension in simultaneously achieving the two goals is identified in the Program's third goal of implementing clear standards, which involves "develop[ing] sound and sensible policies that support certifier and operation compliance, while also reducing recordkeeping burdens" (AMS 2015b, 5). As I've pointed out with co-authors Tyler Scott and Nadia Mahallati (2017), the tension is not unique to the National Organic Program, but rather one it shares with all regulatory programs that are voluntary in nature. The challenge this presents and how the Program has tried to address it is the focus of the following section.

The second challenge examined in this chapter is central in the National Organic Program's effort to "protect organic integrity." The Program is charged with ensuring regulatory fidelity and integrity in the administration of USDA organic standards though third-party certifying agents. The responsibility is compounded by the competitive design of USDA organic certification: operations seeking organic certification choose their certifier and pay them a fee for certification services, creating a competitive environment in which certifiers compete for regulatee-clients. Competitive third-party designs are vulnerable to several threats to regulatory fidelity and integrity—threats which the National Organic Program attempts to address through accreditation requirements and regulatory conflict of interest provisions. The contours of the Program's accreditation oversight are discussed in the latter half of this chapter, along with the available evidence of the Program's accreditation activities.

ORGANIC CERTIFICATION AS QUASI-VOLUNTARY REGULATION

As an institutional feature, "quasi-voluntary regulation" references the extent to which compliance with a regulatory program's rules is compulsory. For example, compliance with traditional command-and-control regulations is required, whereas in the case of voluntary programs firms *opt into* standards oversight (Potoski and Prakash 2009).[1] The National Organic Program is best thought of as a quasi-voluntary program, because producers and processors can opt out of its requirements by using alternative phrases, such as "natural" or "sustainable," but must be certified under the Program and adhere to Program regulations to market or sell their products as organic.[2] Regardless of the *quasi*-voluntary nature of organic certification, many of the considerations and dynamics of voluntary programs also apply to the National Organic Program. Central among these is the tension that voluntary programs face in establishing meaningfully stringent and credible program standards, on one hand, while encouraging program participation, on the other.

In business-to-consumer markets, certification is a way for businesses to distinguish their products from those their competitors. In the words of consumer affairs scholarship, certification labels are quality cues, communicating credence attributes (such as sustainability) that are otherwise difficult to gauge (Grunert and Aachmann 2016). Certification thereby enables a firm to access and charge a premium in markets where verified credence attributes are highly valued (Carter and Cachelin 2018). While evidence regarding the economic return on organic certification is mixed, product differentiation and higher prices are among the top motivations for operations to pursue certification (Oberholtzer, Dimitri, and Greene 2005).

Stringent standards and strong enforcement create the most credible "signal" for consumers, thereby offering the greatest benefit for certified businesses. Indeed, the desire for credible organic standards was a central driver for the first organic certification programs (Obach 2015). Stringent standards and strong enforcement also offer the greatest public policy payoff, as they are most likely to result in meaningful production improvements—such as a reduction in the use of pesticides—that benefit society overall.[3] Stringent standards and strong enforcement come at a cost, however, as the high entry barrier that they create may impede prospective program participants. Insufficient participation, in turn, can undermine the benefits of program membership if the program is not widely enough adopted to be recognizable, and threaten program viability if it fails to attract sufficient membership (Prakash and Potoski 2007). Certification programs are therefore faced with an inherent institutional tension: the barrier to entry created by voluntary standards serves as both an incentive and a deterrent to potential program participants.

The National Organic Program has sought to address this challenge in recent years through an administrative effort dubbed the Sound and Sensible initiative. The initiative is best understood in the context of the Program's administrative evolution; the remainder of this section describes this evolution. The Program's early years were characterized by resource constraints and operational deficiencies, documented in two OIG Audit Reports (2005, 2010). 2010, in turn, marked the beginning of the proclaimed Age of Enforcement, in which the Program sought to leverage bolstered resources to improve its credibility through more vigorous regulatory enforcement. More recently, the Program has sought to maintain stringent regulatory enforcement while at the same time encouraging USDA organic certification uptake through "sound and sensible" organic regulation.

Early Program Deficiencies

The first OIG Audit Report to document operational deficiencies at the National Organic Program was published in 2005. The audit, while officially aimed at evaluating the Agriculture Marketing Service's control over the Program, provided an early assessment of Program performance, as it focused largely on the National Organic Program's operating policies, procedures, and guidelines from fiscal years 2003 and 2004. Based on fieldwork at Agriculture Market Service headquarters, two State Departments of Agriculture, accredited certifiers CCOF and the Northeast Organic Farming Association of New York, and nine certified organic operations, the audit findings highlighted two central areas of concern: insufficient guidelines for Program coordination with the NOSB and inadequate internal operating procedures at the Program.

The Report identified three problems that resulted from insufficient guidelines for coordination with the NOSB. The first regarded the extent to which the National Organic Program was required to consult with the NOSB, as the OIG Report found that the Program initiated regulatory revisions related to pesticide use and livestock medications and feed without NOSB involvement. The omission prompted the Secretary of Agriculture to rescind the revisions and directed the NOSB be consulted on new revisions. The second regarded procedures for processing NOSB National List recommendations, as the Report found that the Program had failed to act on twenty-six recommendations as of the time of the audit. The third was a lack of protocols for resolving conflicts between Program personnel and the NOSB.

Several internal National Organic Program procedures were deemed inadequate, reflecting deficiencies in the Program's oversight of accredited certifiers and enforcement of organic regulations. At the time of the audit, accreditation applications reviews and audits were handled by the Agriculture Marketing Service's Audit, Review, and Compliance division and then passed to the National Organic Program for final review and determination. The OIG audit found that Program staff had been failing to review accreditation applications and inspection reports, instead simply forwarded Agriculture Marketing Service recommendations to the Secretary of Agriculture. In addition to inadequate accreditation procedures, the Program lacked standardized methods of providing certifiers with Program-relevant information. According to the OIG Report, certification personnel expressed concerns that this likely resulted in certification inconsistencies between accredited certifiers (2005, 12). Finally, the audit found eight complaints unresolved by the National Organic Program, despite the fact that the Program had almost three years to address them.

A second OIG audit was carried out from late 2008 into 2009 to follow up on the Agriculture Marketing Service's implementation of corrective actions in response to the 2005 Audit Report. The findings were released in a 2010 Report. To conduct the audit, the OIG review included site visits to Agriculture Marketing Service headquarters, the California State Organic Program, four accredited certifiers, and twenty certified organic operations.[4] Audit findings indicated that the Agriculture Marketing Service had implemented eight of the ten corrective actions issued following the prior audit. The two corrective actions identified as lacking were implementing procedures for disseminating Program-relevant information (such as regulatory provision clarifications) to accredited certifiers and establishing protocols for processing and resolving noncompliance complaints.

The OIG's audit identified a range of National Organic Program deficiencies in addition to the unfulfilled corrective actions. The example, the Program had failed to incorporate Organic Foods Production Act provisions that required periodic residue testing for prohibited substances. As a result, none of the four certifiers the OIG visited during the audit had conducted residue testing at any of the 5,000 certified operations they for which they were responsible (OIG 2010, 2). The Program had also failed to assemble a peer review panel to annually evaluate its accreditation procedures, as required by Program regulations. The OIG's audit found a range of issues at the California State Organic Program that required National Organic Program attention; these issues are discussed in greater detail in Chapter 8.

Finally, the OIG audit identified a number of operational deficiencies that threatened USDA organic certification regulatory fidelity. For example, among the Program oversight inadequacies identified in the OIG Report were differences in certifiers' criteria for minor and major noncompliance issues and inconsistencies in certifiers' USDA standards interpretations, such as poultry outdoor access requirements and procedures to prevent comingling of organic and conventional products at split operations. The Report credited such inconsistencies to insufficient accreditation review guidelines, communication breakdowns between National Organic Program staff and upper management, and inadequate Program guidance to certifiers. The OIG issued fourteen recommendations to National Organic Program officials to address the deficiencies raised in the Report.

The Age of Enforcement

As reflected in the OIG findings, the National Organic Program's early years were characterized by a lack of funding and insufficient resources (Harsch 2010). Things took a turn in 2009—the same year in which the second OIG audit was conducted—when author of the Organic Foods Production Act Kathleen Merrigan was appointed USDA Deputy Administrator by Secretary of Agriculture Tom Vilsack. Recognizing the threat that a lack of enforcement posed for consumer confidence in the organic label, Merrigan immediately took several actions that were welcomed by organic food proponents (e.g., Caughlan 2010), including announcing a 75 percent National Organic Program funding increase and an expansion of the Program's severely limited staff, the 2009 follow-up OIG audit discussed above, and an independent audit from the Department of Commerce's National Institute of Standards and Technology.

Along with Merrigan's appointment, many applauded the hiring of Miles McEvoy as the Deputy Administrator of the National Organic Program. McEvoy was a highly regarded in the organic community for his "solid credentials" in organic agriculture (IOIA 2009).[5] Beginning his career as an organic inspector, McEvoy spent the twenty years prior to his appointment at the Program as the head of the Washington State Department of Agriculture's (WSDA) Organic Food Program. During that time, McEvoy had made notable contributions to organic certification, generally, by overseeing the development of the WSDA Brand Names Materials List, helping establish the National Association of State Organic Programs, and assisting several states (including Montana and Oregon) to establish their own organic certification programs (IOIA 2009).[6]

In 2010, McEvoy announced a refocusing at the National Organic Program on regulatory stringency, under the Age of Enforcement (McEvoy 2012). With this revised trajectory, the Program initiated investigation and enforcement proceedings of fraudulent organic certificates, applying civil penalties for serious violations, and working with the Department of Justice to address fraud. In the words of McEvoy: "Our work on some significant fraud cases ended up with people doing jail time as a result" (as quoted in McEvoy 2017). The Program also instituted efforts to tighten the monitoring and enforcement practices of accredited certifying agents (Warner 2010a) and clarify organic standards "gray areas," such as the livestock access to pasture requirements discussed in the preceding section.

The Age of Enforcement was a welcome development to many concerned with a perceived lack of Program stringency prior to Merrigan's and McEvoy's appointments (Warner 2010a). As the Program began to focus more concertedly on regulatory enforcement, however, another concern began to draw the attention of organic industry proponents and policy makers: the associated costs that were passed on to prospective and continuing certified operations. Concerns over onerous certification paperwork, recordkeeping, and certification fees had been around since the National Organic Program's implementation (Guthman 2004a), especially as they pertained to smaller operations. Evidence began to build, however, that a focus on strong enforcement was compounding the administrative burden born by those seeking organic certification. As noted at the International Federation of Organic Agriculture Movements (IFOAM) 18th World Congress:

> Farmers have reported spending more time completing forms and maintaining records. A certain amount of records are essential to ensure organic farmers are meeting the organic standards, such as planting non-genetically modified seeds or raising dairy cattle on organic pasture. But, too much focus on paperwork can detract from farming activities that support organic principles, such as conservation and cycling of resources. (Yang 2014)

Evidence suggests that the administrative burden of National Organic Program requirements had caught the eye of at least some policy makers, as well. For example, Sam Farr, U.S. Congressional Representative from the agriculture-heavy state of California commented: "[T]he concern here is how do the smaller growers, who may not have the resources to pay the cost and do all the background information that's necessary for certification—the regulatory process is growing exponentially in terms of cost," (as quoted in Hattem 2013). Finally, indication that the concern was on the minds of USDA officials is found in an Agency review of the Program, highlighting the comments of an accredited certifier:

> [C]omments received from clients regarding the regulations were mostly concerned with the amount of paperwork required for recordkeeping, which some considered to be excessive and burdensome. This certifying agent stated there is a need to streamline paperwork and recordkeeping requirements for all organic operations. (NOP Regulations; Section 610 Review 2015, 25899)

"Sound and Sensible" Organic Regulation

The most visible indication that the National Organic Program recognized the tension created between stringent organic standards and encouraging Program participation is found in the Program's 2014 Sound and Sensible initiative. The initiative represents both a guiding philosophy for the Program and the accredited certifiers it authorizes, and a collection of projects and products aimed at reducing the learning and compliance costs associated with being certified organic. The overarching goals of the initiative are to identify and remove organic certification barriers, streamline certification process, focus enforcement activities on more serious regulatory violations, and "[work] with organic producers and handlers to correct small issues before they become larger issues" (NOP Regulations; Section 610 Review 2015, 25899). These goals are supported by five Sound and Sensible principles:

1. to promote efficient processes through the elimination of bureaucratic requirements that do not contribute to organic integrity;
2. to streamline recordkeeping requirements to ensure that records support organic integrity and are not a barrier for farms and businesses to maintain organic compliance;
3. to encourage common sense organic system plans that clearly capture organic practices;
4. to take only fair and focused enforcement actions; and,
5. to focus on factors that impact organic integrity, as opposed to administrative details.

As part of the initiative, the Program claims fourteen year-long projects aimed at making organic certification more "accessible, attainable, and affordable while maintaining high standards, ensuring compliance, and protecting organic integrity" (USDA 2015c). The results of these projects include seventy-five facts sheets, sixteen training workshops and curricula, and fifteen online videos that outline the national organic standards, explain regulatory requirements related to organic system plan development, certification processes, recordkeeping, and inspections, as well as the "value proposition" of transitioning to organic practices (USDA 2015c). For example, the NOP co-produced a series of "how to" guides with Baystate Organic Certifiers that include primers on transitioning from conventional to organic practices, retail and wholesale labeling under USDA organic certification, and what operations qualify as exempt from organic certification, among other topics (Carter, Scott, and Mahallati 2017).

Around the time that the National Organic Program implemented the Sound and Sensible initiative, it also revised its Penalty Matrix. The Matrix is intended to serve as a guide for accredited certifier personnel faced with issuing sanctions—directing certifiers to the appropriate sanctions based on the relative gravity of the noncompliance issue in question. For example, the Matrix dictates that recordkeeping inconsistencies fall under the category of "minor noncompliances" and call a notification of the noncompliance to the operation and a correction, rather than a more serious enforcement action that might put an operation's certification in peril (AMS 2015a).

Finally, it is worth noting that two cost-share programs—while not part of the Sound and Sensible initiative nor administered by the National Organic Program directly—are offered to help address the financial costs created by certification fees. The first is a National Organic Certification Cost Share Program, available to operations in all fifty states. The second is an Agricultural Management Assistance Organic Cost Share Program, available to livestock and crop producers in sixteen states.[7] The Programs enable operations to recoup up to 75 percent of their certification costs, totaling up to $750 for each certification scope held (crops, livestock, handling, and/or wild crops). The extent to which the Programs make a meaningful difference in the financial burden of organic certification is difficult to know, but according to the USDA's 2014 survey of certified organic producers, organic certification fees make up less than 1 percent of production expenses overall ($19 million out of $4 billion; NASS 2014).

The Role of "Sound and Sensible" beyond Alleviating Burden

It's too early to assess whether the Sound and Sensible initiative has translated to a meaningful reduction in the administrative burden faced by prospective and ongoing certified organic operations. Regardless of whether the National Organic Program successfully devised a way to navigate the tension of balancing stringent enforcement and program participation in its Sound and Sensible approach, both the initiative and the preceding Age of Enforcement reflect more than Program efforts to address the challenge. The efforts also reflect attempts to shape how certifiers perceive and understand their regulatory role—what May and Burby (1998, 162) label regulatory agencies' "enforcement philosophies"—constituting the extent to which an agency views itself as "proactive or reactive, as an educator or policeman, or as providing persuasion or punishment."

Influencing certifiers' enforcement philosophies affords the National Organic Program an indirect avenue for shaping the strategies that agencies apply when executing regulatory functions. For example, certifiers motivated out of a formalistic philosophy are likely to emphasize deterrence strategies by conducting frequent inspections and readily issuing harsh penalties. Others, in contrast, may chose operate from a more facilitative philosophy, focusing on identifying education and tools that assist in regulatees' efforts to comply with organic standards. Of course, certifiers may find a responsive approach most effective—adjusting the strategies and tactics they employ according to the attitudes and actions of the operations that they are charged with regulating (Ayres and Braithwaite 1992). Indeed, the National Organic Program's intent with the Penalty Matrix revisions seems aimed at ensuring a measure of responsiveness, albeit very structured one, in certifiers' sanctioning behaviors on the basis of the seriousness of regulatory noncompliances that they encounter.

NATIONAL ORGANIC PROGRAM ACCREDITATION OVERSIGHT

A defining element of regulatory design is which entities are authorized to monitor and enforce compliance with regulatory directives. For example, under traditional regulatory programs regulatory authorities both set and enforce standards. In self-regulation contexts, standards are set by an industry and monitored and enforced by and among industry members (Levi-Faur 2011). Following the less formal arrangements that predated it, USDA organic certification exhibits a third-party design in which the National Organic Program accredits independent certifiers to certify operations as organic and monitor them for compliance with national organic standards.

As illustrated in the 2010 OIG Audit Report, a key National Organic Program concern is the extent to which Program regulations are delivered consistently and in accordance with Program goals—referred to in this book as regulatory fidelity. Organic certification's competitive third-party design creates challenges for the Program in ensuring regulatory fidelity. Delegation of its monitoring and enforcement responsibilities to a cohort of diverse certifying agents introduces the possibility that some may lack the organizational expertise and resources to faithfully execute regulatory duties. Where third-party certifiers exhibit sufficient capacity, differences in organizational cultures, objectives, and priorities may lead to considerable variation in how they administer the regulations. As the regulatory authority charged with regulatory oversight, the National Organic Program bears the responsibility of vetting certifiers for adequate capacity and ensuring that certifiers fulfill their regulatory role in a manner that conforms to the Program's regulations and vision.

A perhaps more concerning implication that stems from USDA organic certification's third-party design is the possibility that perverse incentives established by the design promote regulatory capture, or otherwise undermine the integrity of program administration. As highlighted by Abbott, Levi-Faur, and Snidal (2017b) third-party designs in which regulatees pay third-parties for monitoring and enforcement "services" create a leverage point through which regulatees can influence, or attempt to control, the decisions of third-part certifiers. Coglianese and Lazer (2003, 718) specify a less dramatic take on the implication: "third-party certifiers probably face incentives to satisfy their clients through at least marginally more lax enforcement."

The Program's central oversight mechanisms are accreditation procedures, through which each certifying agent is vetted for its ability to adequately administer USDA organic standards. As of July 2018, the National Organic Program accredited a total of eighty certifying agents to administer organic standards, forty-seven of which are based in the U.S., with another thirty-three based internationally. Twenty-one additional certifiers are indirectly authorized to administer standards through certification equivalency agreements the USDA arranges with foreign governments. For example, the USDA has facilitated export agreements that allow USDA certified products to be sold as organic without additional certification requirements in Canada, the European Union, Japan, the Republic of Korea, Switzerland, and Taiwan (USDA 2016a). Only the eighty USDA accredited certifiers are subject to National Organic Program oversight; certifiers authorized under trade agreements are regulated by their countries' respective organic programs.

The Accreditation Process

The accreditation requirements outlined in the National Organic Program regulations cover a range of organizational attributes and processes, including a certifier's administrative policies and procedures (e.g., quality assurance manuals, program manuals, standard operating procedures), personnel expertise and qualifications, service fee schedules, and conflict of interest procedures and disclosure reports, among others. The National Organic Program collects accreditation fees, which can easily exceed the initial $500 application fee, as the Program charges by the hour for staff time and requires reimbursement for audit-related travel expenses. According to the Program, as of 2010 the average cost of a desk audit was $4,428 and the average cost of an on-site inspection of a foreign certifier was $24,082 (USDA n.d.).

In many ways, certifier accreditation resembles that of certification for organic operations. Organic certification begins with submission of a certification application and organic system plan, followed by an on-site inspection. Certifier accreditation begins with a prospective certifier applying to the National Organic Program's Accreditation and International Activities Division, which is in charge of reviewing new and renewal accreditation applications and administering subsequent accreditation procedures. According to the Division, application document review can take up to three months and is followed by a "pre-decisional" audit to determine whether the application is capable of complying with the Organic Foods Production Act and USDA organic standards (USDA 2015a). The pre-decisional audit, which is conducted within six months of the application document review, is composed of both off-site document inspections and on-site witness inspections, as well as interviews with certification personnel.

Accreditation oversight revolves around several audit types, including and beyond the pre-decisional audit. A certifier may be granted accreditation following favorable findings of a pre-decisional audit, at which point the certifier is authorized to certify operations and administer national organic standards. After accreditation is granted, an "initial" audit is conducted to verify implementation of any corrective actions that were called for in the pre-decisional audit and determine if the certifier is competently complying with accreditation requirements. Accreditation renewal audits are then administered in five-year cycles, interspersed with mid-term "desk" audits at the two-and-a-half-year mark between renewal audits.

National Organic Program Accreditation Actions

While the National Organic Program publishes some audit findings and the current accreditation documentation for each certifier on the Program's website, as of the time of this writing no database exists by which audit findings can be readily aggregated and analyzed. Absent such a database, an Accreditation and International Activities Division analysis of the thirty-nine accreditation audits conducted in 2015 offers a window into Program oversight actions. The Division's analysis indicates an average certifier compliance of 96 percent, reflecting the average percent of regulatory provisions with which certifiers complied, as recorded on audit checklists (NOP Form 2005).

The most frequently cited provisions with which certifiers were found out of compliance were National Organic Program general requirements for accreditation. Thirty-three of the thirty-nine certifiers were found to be out of compliance with the general requirements, and the Accreditation and International Activities Division highlighted certifiers' administrative capacities and insufficient or missing annual performance evaluations as key problem areas across the cited audits. The second most frequently cited noncompliance type was certifiers' administration of on-site inspections of organic operations, found to be an issue in twenty-seven of the thirty-nine audits. Twenty-five of the thirty-nine audits found noncompliances in certifiers' procedures for issuing proposed certification suspensions or revocations, and twenty-one audits turned up noncompliances related to certifiers' annual reports and/or recordkeeping.

Accreditation oversight can be further observed in the accreditation determinations administered by the National Organic Program. According to a USDA-published list (USDA 2015b), between 2002 and 2015 the Program revoked two certifiers' accreditations and suspended another two. Forty-three certifiers had surrendered their accreditations for reasons ranging from a lack of financial resources for accreditation fees to consent orders from the National Organic Program's Compliance and Enforcement Division. Twenty-three of these accreditation surrenders—a majority of the thirty international accreditation surrenders—were the result of international certification equivalency agreements with the European Union and Canada. The status and USDA-reported reason for the associated accreditation action for all domestic certifiers on the list are summarized in Table 5.1.

Table 5.1. Surrendered and revoked domestic certifier accreditations 2002–2015

Certifier name	*State*	*Accreditation status*	*Reason for accreditation status*	*Year*
Organic Growers of Michigan	MI	Surrendered	Membership voted to cease certification activities	2006
American Food Safety Institute, International	WI	Revoked	n/a	2006
Integrity Certified International Inc.	IA	Surrendered	n/a	2006
Northeast Organic Farming Association of New Jersey	NJ	Surrendered	n/a	2007
California Crop Improvement Association	CA	Revoked	Failure to submit timely corrective actions	2008
Guaranteed Organic Certification Agency	CA	Surrendered	Surrendered pursuant to settlement agreement	2010
North Carolina Crop Improvement Association	NC	Surrendered	Lack of funding	2010
Certified Organic Inc.	IA	Surrendered	Surrendered pursuant to settlement agreement	2011
Hawaii Organic Farmers Association	HI	Surrendered	No official reason provided; informally due to financial reasons	2011
Mississippi Department of Agriculture and Commerce	MS	Surrendered	Inability to provide proper administrative capacity per USDA organic regulations	2011
Global Organic Certification Services	IA	Surrendered	Withdrew re-accreditation request due to lack of financial resources	2012
Louisiana Department of Agriculture and Forestry	LA	Surrendered	Lack of sufficient resources to comply with USDA organic regulations	2012
Organic National and International Certifiers	IL	Surrendered	n/a	2014

NOTE: n/a = No reason provided on USDA (2015b) list

As displayed in the table, the National Organic Program revoked the accreditation of two domestic certifiers from 2002–2015. One of the revocations is reported as due to the certifier's failure to submit corrective actions to regulatory noncompliances; no explanation is provided for the other revocation. Eleven domestic certifier accreditations were surrendered over the seven-year period. Of the eight accreditation surrenders for which the Program cites a reason, three were due to an inability to meet the financial burden of accreditation fees, two were the result of settlement agreements, two were due to insufficient administrative capacity and/or resources to fulfill certification duties, and one was a decision of the certifier's voting membership to stop certification activities.

Gaps in Accreditation Oversight

As an oversight mechanism, National Organic Program accreditation audit effectiveness is contingent on successful identification of the operational processes that, if properly conducted, result in appropriate and consistent certification agent behavior. In other words, accreditation guidelines must identify and assess the right certification behaviors with an adequate depth and specificity to hold certifiers accountable in any meaningful manner. Indeed, a central finding of the OIG's second audit was that inconsistencies between certifiers "occurred because the review guide that the [Agriculture Marketing Service] used to evaluate certifying agents' compliance with [National Organic Program] regulations was not sufficiently focused to identify the types of problems we noted" (2010, 3). A focus on processes alone, however, leaves a regulatory authority blind to the manners in which intermediaries wield the regulatory authority that has been granted to them.

The National Organic Program's accreditation processes appear to exhibit precisely this blind spot. While the National Organic Program compiles and publishes the certification status of all certified organic operations in its Organic Integrity Database, it makes no effort systematically assemble or assess all of the enforcement actions that organic certifiers take on its behalf. How organic certifiers oversee certified operations is described in greater detail in Chapter 6; in general terms, certifiers have a graduated system of sanctions that they can issue in response to regulatory noncompliances. For serious violations, certifiers can issue a proposed suspension or revocation of an operation's organic certification. Although it is not obvious that the National Organic Program factors certifiers' suspension and revocation decisions into accreditation decisions, suspension and revocation rates can be compiled and compared by sorting Organic Integrity records by certifier. As my analysis in Chapter 6 shows, doing so reveals considerable variation in certifiers' propensity to suspend or revoke organic certifications.

For less serious "minor" violations, certifiers issue "notices of noncompliance," which outline regulatory violations and corrective actions needed to address them. Although certifiers are required to notify the National Organic Program of the notices they issue, the Program seems to make no effort to make use of these records, beyond saving them. Indeed, a Freedom of Information Act request revealed that the Program was unaware of even the overall number of noncompliance records that had been issued in a given year. As discussed in the final section of this chapter, and further illustrated in the Chapter 6 discussion of accredited certifiers, by not assembling or analyzing notice of noncompliance data, the National Organic Program overlooks a key opportunity to understand the extent to which, under what conditions, and to what purposes accredited certifiers are exercising the regulatory authority that the National Organic Program delegates to them.

Addressing Conflicts of Interest

In addition to general accreditation requirements, such as the administrative procedures and personnel qualifications discussed above, the National Organic Program regulations include provisions expressly aimed at combating the potentially detrimental incentives created by USDA organic certification's competitive third-party design. The conflict of interest provisions target several conflict of interest sources, from monetary inducements, such as gifts, to relation-based conflicts of interest, such as those that might develop between an inspector and a farmer during the process of an on-site inspection. The requirements specified by the provisions include:

- A certifier cannot certify an operation if the certifier, certification personnel, or family members of either party, have a commercial interest in the operation
- A certifier must exclude any personnel, including contractors, from being involved in an operation's certification if they or their family members have had a commercial interest in the operation in the year prior to certification application
- A certifier and certification personnel cannot accept any gifts beyond prescribed fees from applicants and certified operations[8]
- A certifier and certification personnel cannot provide advice or consultation to applicants or certified operations "for overcoming identified barriers to certification"

- A final certification approval/denial decision cannot be made by the individual that performed an initial document review or inspection
- All certification personnel must complete annual conflict of interest disclosures

Underlying many of the provisions is an intent to preserve USDA organic certification's "third-party" design. As detailed earlier in this book, the first organic certification systems were effectively self-regulation: farmers inspected one another's operations, verifying standards that the farmers themselves often developed collectively. Third-party certification, in contrast, is built on the idea that regulation is more credible and less vulnerable to corruption when the individual elements of the regulatory arrangement are independent. The is perhaps best explained by Roger Blobaum, director of the Americans for Safe Food Project and an advocate involved in the push for federal-level organic food policy during the 1980s (as cited in Obach 2015, 190):

> [The National Organic Program has] a separation-of-functions principle. The inspectors cannot be involved in the decision making. The decision makers can't be involved in the inspection, and neither of them can be involved in running the organization or hiring and firing. . . . There's this functional requirement that is what makes it truly an arm's-length, third-party system.

No publicly available data exists to offer a credible assessment of the National Organic Program's ability to combat either perceived conflicts of interest or outright corruption through the application of these provisions. Anecdotal evidence suggests that, at least historically, the provisions have failed to prevent *all* of such instances. This is most apparent in accounts of "certifier shopping," in which operations "shop" from among USDA accredited certifiers, looking for a certifier with less stringent standards interpretations (ACA 2010). As described in 2011 by Ed Maltby, executive director of the Northeast Organic Dairy Producers Association:

> What has become increasingly apparent is that different certifiers will allow different products for different applications, and that has caused some certifier shopping. There also seems to be a lack of consistency of what kinds of records are needed, and how to review those records. (As cited in Sircely 2011, 17)

Although illustrative of the type of behavior the National Organic Program is meant to address, such anecdotal evidence provides no indication of the *prevalence* of certifier shopping, or similar types of inappropriate regulatory practices. Certifier shopping and related threats to the USDA organic certification integrity are clearly of concern to the organic agriculture community (e.g., ACA 2010). It's also clear that the potential for conflicts of interest—whether real or perceived—is on the National Organic Program's radar. As stated by a program representative in a research interview:

> The dilemma of organic regulation is that the regulatory organizations are in competition with one another, which at times may lead to an inconsistent application of standards and regulations. The [National Organic Program] is addressing this challenge by keeping an eye on the fees charged by certifiers through audits, to ensure they are not cutting deals with operations, and looking for conflicts of interest. (Research interview, Fall 2012).

While the majority of organic stakeholders seem to support the intent behind the National Organic Program's conflict of interest provisions, many contest individual provisions as ineffective and event detrimental. One often-voiced objection is that they impede organic operations' advocacy on organic policy matters. For example, exclusion of certified organic producers and processors from involvement in the organizations that certify them is argued by some to undermine the collective policy influence of organic operators:

> Many view USDA's regulation that prohibits organic farmers from sitting on their own organic certification boards as having "decapitated" organic farmers and stifled their meaningful participation in the organic regulatory process. This has led to the loss of an organized organic farmers' voice, despite the fact that it was the organic farmers themselves who launched and developed many of the organic certification programs that currently exist. (Hoodes et al. 2010, 29)

Others point out that the provision barring certifiers from consulting leaves an information "void" by impeding inspectors and other certification personnel from offering advice on how to adhere to USDA organic standards or correct noncompliance issues (Thilmany 2006). These critics point out that inspectors could be key information sources for regulatees, particularly when it comes to interpreting and adhering to technical or legally worded directives. The claim finds support in the academic literature, which shows that inspectors are instrumental resources for regulatees across many regulatory contexts (e.g., Scholz 1991), as discussed in the following conclusion. While it may create a challenge for operations in understanding and complying with USDA organic standards, the non-consultation provision likely benefits one group, as in lieu of providing their own guidance or advice certifiers refer their certification clients to organic agriculture consultation services firms (e.g., Oregon Tilth n.d.).

CONCLUSIONS: THE NATIONAL ORGANIC PROGRAM AS REGULATOR

As the organic certification regulatory authority, the National Organic Program is charged with a range of responsibilities, in spite of the limited resources and personnel it is afforded to fulfill them. Among these responsibilities, the Program coordinates with and supports the NOSB, develops USDA organic standards and related guidance documents, carries out regulatory violation complaints investigations and subsequent enforcement actions, and oversees administration of Organic Certification Cost Share programs. Furthermore, the quasi-voluntary Program attempts to encourage organic certification uptake by reducing the burdens associated with organic regulation, while simultaneously ensuring the rigorous regulatory monitoring and enforcement of third-party certifiers through accreditation requirements.

The evidence presented in this chapter illustrates some of the inherent challenges the National Organic Program faces in implementing a quasi-voluntary program through third-party administrators. The Program shoulders a dual mandate of encouraging a robust organic market while also ensuring regulatory fidelity and integrity. The administrative evolution from the Age of Enforcement to the Sound and Sensible initiative suggests that the Program has been aware of and responsive to both mandates: it's likely that after striving to overcome the operational and regulatory deficiencies of its early years through an emphasis on robust regulatory action, the Program found that some flexibility in regulatory administration was needed to sustain growth in organic certification uptake and a robust organics sector.

As referenced earlier, it's too early to assess whether the Sound and Sensible initiative has succeeded in reducing the administrative burden faced by prospective and ongoing certified organic operations. Preliminary evidence is promising; in a 2017 press release, the National Organic Program announced that 2016 witnessed the highest rate of certification uptake since 2008, reflecting a 13 percent increase in the number of domestic certified organic operations (USDA 2017). Regulatory scholarship offers a cautionary warning, however, to affording too much attention or emphasis on metrics such as certification numbers. Most notably, Carrigan (2017) points out that regulatory agencies saddled with dual mandates exhibit lower performance, on average, when compared to their single-mandate counterparts. Furthermore, to the extent that an emphasis on non-regulatory functions (i.e., encouraging growth in the number of certified operations) over regulatory ones (i.e., ensuring compliance with standards) requires a shift in attention and resources, efforts such as the Sound and Sensible initiative run the risk of undermining the stringency of organic standards enforcement.

As an accreditor, the National Organic Program has an undeniable track record of exercising its oversight authority—even during its leanest years. For example, it is worth noting that the Program's first serious oversight action occurred in 2006 with the revocation of American Food Safety Institute's accreditation—three years before Merrigan's Age of Enforcement and during a period in which the Program was widely considered to be grossly underfunded and understaffed. Furthermore, although only two domestic accreditations were revoked by the Program between 2002 and 2015, several of the accreditation surrenders that occurred during this time appear to be the result of accreditation oversight and enforcement, including Guaranteed Organic Certification Agency's and Certified Organic's accreditation surrenders resulting from settlement agreements, Mississippi Department of Agriculture and Commerce's accreditation surrender for lack of sufficient administrative capacity, and Louisiana Department of Agriculture and Forestry's accreditation surrender for lack of resources to comply with Program regulations.

This chapter thus demonstrates that the National Organic Program has been active in its accreditation oversight role. Ultimately, a lack of sufficient data means that this chapter's analysis falls short of capturing *the extent to which* National Organic Program accreditation oversight ensures fidelity and integrity in the administration of USDA organic standards. Program accreditation arguably provides for a more rigorous certification environment when compared to similar programs that lack the same oversight—from the organic certification alternative Certified Naturally Grown to privately sponsored sustainability certifications—if for no other reason than the systematic audit requirements that provide an objective evaluation of regulatory compliance based on documented characteristics of effective oversight, such as oversight independence, compliance measurement, and verification (Power 1997). It is for such reasons that USDA organic certification is regarded by many as the "gold standard" of natural or sustainable certification programs.

At the same time, the anecdotal accounts to certifier shopping referenced in this chapter show that accreditation oversight, while superior to no formal oversight at all, likely fails to *completely* counteract the incentives that a competitive third-party certification arrangement creates. More importantly, in this chapter I've identified a key oversight mechanism that the National Organic Program seems to ignore: the potential to measure and assess certifiers' enforcement activity through the noncompliance records that the Program already collects. Although it is beyond my ability to determine with the evidence provided here, it may very well be that the budgetary and personnel limitations make such records compilation efforts impossible. Regardless, the fact that the Program fails to track certifiers' administration of regulatory sanctions highlights a weakness in accreditation oversight and a missed opportunity to better understand how the USDA's delegated regulatory authority is applied by organic certifiers, how this application might differ between certifiers, and to what ends.

My discussion in this chapter also speaks to some of the likely unintended consequences of National Organic Program's conflict of interest provisions. While designed to prevent improper regulatory behaviors—either real or perceived—the provisions seem to exacerbate the burdens facing potential and continuing certified operations by limiting the information and assistance that certifiers and inspectors offer. Indeed, a non-consultation conflict of interest provision may have contributed to the reasons the Program felt compelled to develop the Sound and Sensible initiative. As important, conflict of interest provisions may impair program feedback. The National Organic Program relies heavily on certifiers for information regarding challenges both in, and caused by, the administration of USDA organic standards. Barring organic farmers and processors from the decision-making bodies of certification organizations likely dilutes their ability to relay relevant experiences and information to the Program, or at minimum creates an additional layer through which such program feedback is conveyed.

Finally, the chapter raises a number of promising avenues for future research in the realm of organic certification and beyond. Perhaps chief among these is a more detailed analysis of the National Organic Program accreditation process, starting with the specific organizational and operational indicators that accreditation requirements capture and omit, and an assessment of the extent to which the indicators are valid measures of consistent and appropriate regulatory behavior. Such research will no doubt involve considerable data compilation efforts. For example, a robust analysis of National Organic Program accreditation effectiveness will necessitate the compilation of accreditation audit findings, determinations, and corrective actions over time.

Although limited in scope and detail, by providing the most in-depth analysis of the National Organic Program-as-accreditor to date, this chapter begins to address a gap in regulatory scholarship examining decentralized regulatory administration: the question how third-party regulators are themselves regulated. A strong, yet largely untested, presumption in the literature is that accreditation is one avenue for ensuring effective third-party regulation (Abbott, Levi-Faur, and Snidal 2017b). This chapter urges scholars to look beyond simply whether accreditation offers regulatory oversight to instead question the extent to which accreditation ensures *both* regulatory fidelity and integrity, and perhaps most importantly—*how*. The following chapter continues to pursue these questions by shifting attention from the National Organic Program to the third-party administrators of USDA organic certification—accredited certifying agents.

NOTES

1. Much of the policy literature (e.g., Prakash and Potoski 2007) deals more specifically with voluntary environmental programs (VEPs), however, many of the theoretical and empirical dynamics derived in this literature arguably also apply to socially oriented voluntary programs, such as those that specify working conditions and fair wages.

2. Following the National Organic Program regulations, operations that sell less than $5,000 of organic produce annually are exempt from Program requirements.

3. In economic or policy analysis terms, stringent standards and strong enforcement should lead to the greatest generation of positive externatilities (Prakash and Potoski 2007).

4. Certifiers that were included for site visits during the 2008–2009 OIG audit included the Organic Crop Improvement Association, Pennsylvania Certified Organic, Quality Assurance International, and Quality Certification Services.

5. McEvoy stepped down as head of the National Organic Program in 2017. While he still enjoyed considerable support within the organic agriculture community, he also developed vocal detractors during his eight-year tenure, including calls for him to resign from organizations such as the Cornucopia Institute (Dixon and Kastel 2017).

6. The National Association of State Organic Programs was an organization established by state organic programs to address the challenges specific to governmental certifiers. It was later absorbed into the ACA.

7. The National Organic Certification Cost Share Program is also available to operations in the District of Columbia, the American Samoa, the Commonwealth of the Northern Mariana Islands, the Commonwealth of Puerto Rico, Guam, and the United States Virgin Islands. The sixteen states in which the Agricultural Management Assistance Organic Cost Share Program is available are Connecticut, Delaware, Hawaii, Maine, Maryland, Massachusetts, Nevada, New Hampshire, New Jersey, New York, Pennsylvania, Rhode Island, Utah, Vermont, West Virginia, and Wyoming.

8. An exception to this provision is made for nonprofit certifiers, which may accept voluntary labor from certification clients.

Chapter Six

The Third-Party Administrators

Accredited Certifying Agents

Although the National Organic Program is the regulatory authority of USDA organic certification, organic certifiers are the linchpin around which the integrity of organic certification system revolves. The case of Aurora Organic Dairy featured in the book's opening paragraphs, for example, showed how inadequate monitoring practices at the Colorado Department of Agriculture allowed the mega-dairy to skirt organic livestock access to pasture requirements (the 2010 Pasture Rule). When investigative journalists visited the High Plains complex in the summer of 2016, rather than observing thousands of grazing cattle, they were met with mostly empty fields. The Colorado Department of Agriculture would have presumably seen the same had they inspected the operation during the grazing season. The Department instead scheduled its annual inspection in November—outside of the grazing season—thereby making it impossible for its inspectors to verify the complex's Pasture Rule compliance.

Of course, certifiers need not represent a vulnerability to organic standards integrity. As recounted in Chapter 4, for instance, when Massachusetts egg producer Country Hen argued that its chicken-sized screened porches met the USDA's poultry outdoor access requirements, certifier Baystate Organic denied it organic certification. It was only when the USDA overturned the denial—over Baystate Organic's protests and petitions—that Country Hen was granted organic certification. Baystate's position, while undermined by the subsequent USDA reversal, remains supported by a wide swath of the organic agriculture community and the ongoing legal effort to strengthen organic poultry outdoor access requirements.

Thus, certifiers occupy a critical position within the USDA organic certification regulatory arrangement. Certifiers (and the personnel they hire) represent the only interaction that most organic farmers and processors have with USDA organic standards and their enforcement. Certifiers review organic system plans, employ or contract with inspectors to perform on-site inspections, and are responsible for determining whether an operation complies with the requirements laid out in the National Organic Program regulations. In the process, certifiers interpret sometimes vague regulatory provisions, issue notices of noncompliance to operations that fail to comply with those regulations, and may suspend operations that fail to correct noncompliances.

Organic certifiers exhibit considerable organizational diversity: they come from across the for-profit, nonprofit, and public sectors, vary widely in size and experience, and their service areas range from regional to international in scope. Such diversity raises questions such as how differences in organizational characteristics translate to divergences in regulatory practices, and the extent to which regulatory practice disparities undermine the fidelity of USDA organic standards administration. Of central concern is whether the intermediaries charged with regulatory monitoring and enforcement have the requisite expertise to detect noncompliances and effectively sanction, when necessary (Abbott, Levi-Faur, and Snidal 2017b).

Furthermore, USDA organic certification's institutional design situates organic certifiers to face competing incentives. On one hand, they operate with the Program's delegated regulatory authority and bear the responsibility of ensuring Program integrity. In this role, they face the formal institutional pressures of accreditation oversight and less-formal pressures from organic agriculture stakeholders to exercise consistency and stringency in organic standards administration. On the other hand, certifiers provide, and are paid for, certification services. In this role, they face pressures to exercise discretion, flexibility, and otherwise meet the customer service expectations of certification clients. The accounts of certifier shopping presented in the preceding chapter suggest that the customer service expectations of certification clients may shape some certifiers' certification decisions, at least some of the time, but fall short of an assessment regarding whether competition between organic certifiers impacts National Organic Program integrity in the aggregate.

This chapter takes a deeper look at the characteristics and role of organic certifiers as the third-party administrators of USDA organic standards, with an emphasis on those headquartered in the U.S. In the first section I provide a more detailed description of the diversity that is observed across the domestic certifier cohort. I then compile Organic Integrity certification status data to depict and compare the enforcement actions taken by certifiers under USDA-delegated authority. In the third section I offer a more nuanced discussion of certifiers' administration of USDA organic standards with a synthesis of research findings related to certifiers' regulatory behaviors and services, as perceived by certified organic producers. I close the chapter with an assessment of the available evidence as it pertains to lessons for USDA organic certification regulatory fidelity and integrity.

THE DOMESTIC ORGANIC CERTIFIER COHORT

As of 2018, the National Organic Program accredited of 80 certifying agents to administer USDA organic standards. Forty-seven of these are based in the U.S., while 33 are headquartered internationally. Of the 47 domestic organic certifiers, 14 are for-profit businesses, another 14 are IRS-recognized nonprofit organizations, and the remaining 19 are public entities. Public sector certifiers can be further broken down into three types: 15 are housed under state department programs, 3 fall under California county governments, and 1 operates out of Clemson University's Department of Plant Industry. Details, such as names and the state in which each domestic certifier is headquartered, are depicted in Table 6.1.

As seen in the table, USDA accreditation records indicate that a majority of domestic certifiers predated the National Organic Program's implementation, as 36 of the 47 held accreditation in 2002. Ten certifiers became accredited from 2003 to 2010. The most recent organic certifier to gain accreditation was Basin and Range Organics, a nonprofit startup based in Nevada, which was accredited in 2015.

According to the National Organic Program's Organic Integrity Database, the number of certification clients served by certifier varies widely across the domestic organic certifier cohort. CCOF—a California-based certifier that is the present-day outgrowth of Rodale's initial certification program (as recounted in Chapter 3) holds largest organic certification client base, at 3,568 operations. Monterey County Certified Organics certifies the fewest operations, with a client base of 14. Certifiers' organic certification client bases tend towards the lower end of this spectrum, generally speaking, as the median number of clients per certifier is 218, and only 10 certifiers serve 1,000 clients or more.

Organic certifiers' service areas also vary widely. For example, governmental certifiers' services are geographically restricted to areas within, or immediately adjacent to, their state or county jurisdictions. An exception can be seen in the case of the WSDA, which certifies operations in 14 states, from Alaska to Missouri. The service areas of 7 certifiers are limited to a single state (6 of these certifiers are from the public sector), while Quality Assurance International is the sole certifier to operate in all 50 states. CCOF and Oregon Tilth tie for second in state coverage, as each operates in 49 states. The me-

Table 6.1. The 2018 domestic organic certifier cohort: certifiers and certifier characteristics

Certifier	*Accreditation year*	*Client number*	*Headquarters state*	*Number of states certifying in*	*Certifies internationally*
For-Profit Sector Certifiers					
Quality Assurance International (QAI)	2002	1641	CA	50	Yes
Global Organic Alliance, Inc. (GOA)	2002	1073	OH	38	Yes
Organic Certifiers, Inc. (OC)	2002	990	CA	33	Yes
International Certification Services, Inc. (ICS)	2002	901	ND	43	Yes
Nature's International Certification Services (NICS)	2007	874	WI	24	No
Organic Crop Improvement Association (OCIA)	2002	817	NE	39	Yes
ECOCERT ICO (ECO)	2002	636	IN	43	Yes
OneCert, Inc. (ONE)	2003	500	NE	39	Yes
Primus Labs (PRIM)	2006	307	CA	16	Yes
Americert International (AI)	2009	160	FL	15	Yes
Agricultural Services Certified Organic (ASCO)	2006	157	CA	13	No
A Bee Organic (ABO)	2010	136	CO	23	Yes
Natural Food Certifiers (NFC)	2002	113	NY	17	Yes
SCS Global Services (SCSG)	2002	85	CA	19	Yes
Nonprofit Sector Certifiers					
CCOF Certification Services, LLC (CCOF)	2002	3568	CA	49	Yes
Midwest Organic Services Association, Inc. (MOSA)	2002	2012	WI	28	No
Oregon Tilth Certified Organic (OTCO)	2002	1895	OR	49	Yes
Pennsylvania Certified Organic (PCO)	2002	1546	PA	24	No
Ohio Ecological Food and Farm Association (OEFFA)	2002	1278	OH	16	No
Quality Certification Services (QCS)	2002	1196	FL	46	Yes
Northeast Organic Farming Association of New York (NOFA)	2002	1000	NY	9	No
Vermont Organic Farmers, LLC (VOF)	2002	692	VT	5	No
MOFGA Certification Services, LLC (MOFGA)	2002	519	MA	1	Yes

Minnesota Crop Improvement Association (MCIA)	2002	500	MN	13	No
Baystate Organic Certifiers (BOC)	2002	467	MA	22	No
Stellar Certification Services (SCS)	2002	202	OR	33	Yes
Georgia Crop Improvement Association, Inc. (GCIA)	2002	112	GA	7	No
Basin and Range Organics (BRO)	2015	47	NV	4	No
Public Sector Certifiers					
Washington State Department of Agriculture (WSDA)	2002	1181	WA	14	Yes
Iowa Department of Agriculture and Land Stewardship (IDALS)	2002	360	IA	9	No
Idaho State Department of Agriculture (ISDA)	2002	264	ID	8	No
Montana Department of Agriculture (MTDA)	2002	218	MT	6	No
Texas Department of Agriculture (TDA)	2002	207	TX	4	No
Kentucky Department of Agriculture (KDA)	2006	205	KY	4	No
Colorado Department of Agriculture (CDA)	2002	189	CO	2	No
Oklahoma Department of Agriculture, Food and Forestry (ODAFF)	2002	166	OK	6	No
Oregon Department of Agriculture (ODA)	2009	131	OR	2	No
New Hampshire Department of Agriculture, Markets and Food (NHDAMF)	2002	118	NH	3	No
New Mexico Department of Agriculture (NMDA)	2002	113	NM	3	No
Maryland Department of Agriculture (MDDA)	2002	105	MD	1	No
New Jersey Department of Agriculture (NJDA)	2007	102	NJ	2	No
Clemson University (CLEM)	2002	67	SC	7	No
Yolo County Department of Agriculture (YCDA)	2006	58	CA	1	No
Utah Department of Agriculture and Food (UDAF)	2002	56	UT	1	No
Marin Organic Certified Agriculture (MOCA)	2002	51	CA	1	No
Rhode Island Department of Environmental Management (RIDEM)	2002	17	RI	1	No
Monterey County Certified Organics (MCCO)	2002	14	CA	1	No

NOTE: Table figures reflect USDA Organic Integrity data as of July 2018; certifiers listed by client number within their respective groupings by sector (for-profit, non-profit, public) dian number of states domestic certifiers operate in is 13. Finally, 18 domestic certifiers also provide services outside of the U.S., in countries ranging from Canada to India.

DEPICTING ORGANIC STANDARDS ADMINISTRATION THROUGH CERTIFICATION STATUSES

Just as Chapter 5 used National Organic Program accreditation decisions to provide a window into the Program's oversight activities, one way of understanding organic certifiers' regulatory behaviors is through their certification determinations: the certifications they grant and the apparent predisposition they exhibit towards enforcing USDA organic standards through certification suspension or revocation. To understand certification determinations, it is first helpful to have a grasp of certifiers' responsibility in certification process. This section first provides an overview of how certifiers monitor and enforce USDA organic standards compliance. It then discusses the available data on certifiers' certification determinations.

Organic Certifiers' Role in Enforcing USDA Organic Standards

Organic certification revolves around an organic system plan that details how an operation will adhere to USDA organic standards. To become certified organic, an operation submits an organic system plan to an accredited certifier. Once the certifier has reviewed and approved the plan, an employee or contract inspector is sent to the operation to inspect it for plan adherence. Certification must be renewed once a year, which entails submission of changes to the organic system plan and an on-site inspection. Unannounced inspections may be carried out between yearly scheduled inspections and may include product testing for prohibited substances, at the discretion of the certifier.

To guide certifier enforcement of the organic standards, USDA guidance distinguishes between "minor" and "major" noncompliances, with the primary difference being that major noncompliances represent systematic failures that impede an operation from being able to comply with the organic regulations (AMS 2015a). The USDA requires that any certifier actions taken in response to noncompliances be supported by a preponderance of evidence, defined as indication that signals more than a 50 percent likelihood that a noncompliance occurred, such as firsthand or secondhand witness testimony, documentation or photographs, and test results. Following USDA guidelines, certifier responses to noncompliances can take one of four forms:

(i) A simple mandate that an operation correct a noncompliance, issued without formal documentation or notification to the National Organic Program when the certifier deems the noncompliance to be minor issue not justifying a corrective action plan.
(ii) A Notice of Noncompliance, in which the National Organic Program is notified of the noncompliance and the operation is required to develop a corrective action plan to ensure and verify compliance.
(iii) A notice of proposed suspension (or denial of certification, in the case of new applicants), issued when an operation fails to correct a noncompliance. A notice of proposed suspension may be issued alongside a Notice of Noncompliance, instead of after it, in the cases of major noncompliances.
(iv) A notice of proposed revocation (or denial of certification, in the case of new applicants), issued when a certifier finds evidence of deliberate violation of the USDA organic regulation, falsification or concealment of records, inspection refusal, or continued noncompliance following a notice of proposed inspection.

Certification Statuses across Domestic Certifiers

Certifiers are required to notify the National Organic Program when they take three of the four possible enforcement actions: Notifications of Noncompliance, certification suspensions, and certification revocations. As discussed in the preceding National Organic Program chapter (Chapter 5), although the Program retains Notice of Noncompliance records, it makes no effort to compile or aggregate the information in any usable format, meaning that the extent to which certifiers issue Notices of Noncompliance, either individually or collectively, is unknown—presumably including by the National Organic Program and USDA. As a result, USDA-compiled data regarding the certification determinations of accredited certifiers is limited to the status of each operation's certification.

These limitations notwithstanding, organic certification statuses provide a window into the enforcement actions taken by organic certifiers. Perhaps more importantly, compiling certification status data by certifier allows for a valuable, if bounded, comparison of organic certifiers' enforcement behaviors. Figure 6.1 provides a visual representation of a descriptive analysis of 2018 Organic Integrity certification status data (USDA 2018). The figure depicts surrendered, suspended, and revoked certifications as a percentage of all certifications the USDA reports for each organic certifier. Active certifications have been omitted from the figure but can be inferred as the remaining percentage needed, by certifier, to make up 100 percent. Surrendered certifications—certifications that were not renewed when an operations' recertification time came around—are included because they *may* be indicative of a certifier's enforcement action. For example, an operator might choose to let her certification lapse if she found it impossible to correct an ongoing noncompliance issue. Alternatively, a certification might be surrendered because the operation closed, the operator found the cost of organic production to exceed its benefits, or for any number of other reasons. The difficulty of interpreting surrendered certifications is returned to towards the end of the section.

Certification status figures vary considerably across the domestic certifier cohort. Surrendered, suspended, and revoked certifications collectively make up anywhere from 1 percent of a certifier's issued certifications to almost 48 percent, in the case of Clemson University's Department of Plant Sciences. Five of the forty-seven domestic certifiers exhibit no certification suspensions, and the suspension rates for the remaining certifiers range from under 1 percent (Pennsylvania Certified Organic and the Montana State Department of Agriculture) to over 26 percent (Clemson University). According to the USDA data, clients of eight of the certifiers have had their certifications revoked. Among these, the Montana Department of Agriculture exhibits the highest rate of revocation, at just under 1 percent of all issued certifications. The other certifiers for which clients with revoked certifications are listed include Organic Certifiers, the Iowa Department of Agriculture and Land Stewardship, Global Organic Alliance, Oregon Tilth, CCOF, Natures International Certifiers, and Stellar Certification Services.

The comparison of organic certification statuses by certifier suggests considerable variation in regulatory enforcement actions across domestic certifiers and a possible source of concern for USDA organic standards administration fidelity. That said, the conclusions that can be drawn from the analysis are limited by three important considerations. First, without relevant Notice of Noncompliance data, distinguishing between surrenders, suspensions, and revocations is problematic. For example, it may be the case that some certifiers are more willing to issue surrenders and/or revocations, while others let suspended certifications ride until an operation's recertification comes around—at which point still-noncompliant operations' certifications are considered surrendered. Similarly, if a certifier takes a long time to follow up on Notices of Noncompliance, certifications may be surrendered before a notice of proposed suspension can be issued.

Second, it's impossible to know from these data the extent to which differences in status percentages are caused by certifiers' propensity to take enforcement actions, or whether they reflect differences in client bodies. For example, it is plausible that Montana Department of Agriculture's relatively high revocation rate is due to an under-resourced or less-competent clientele

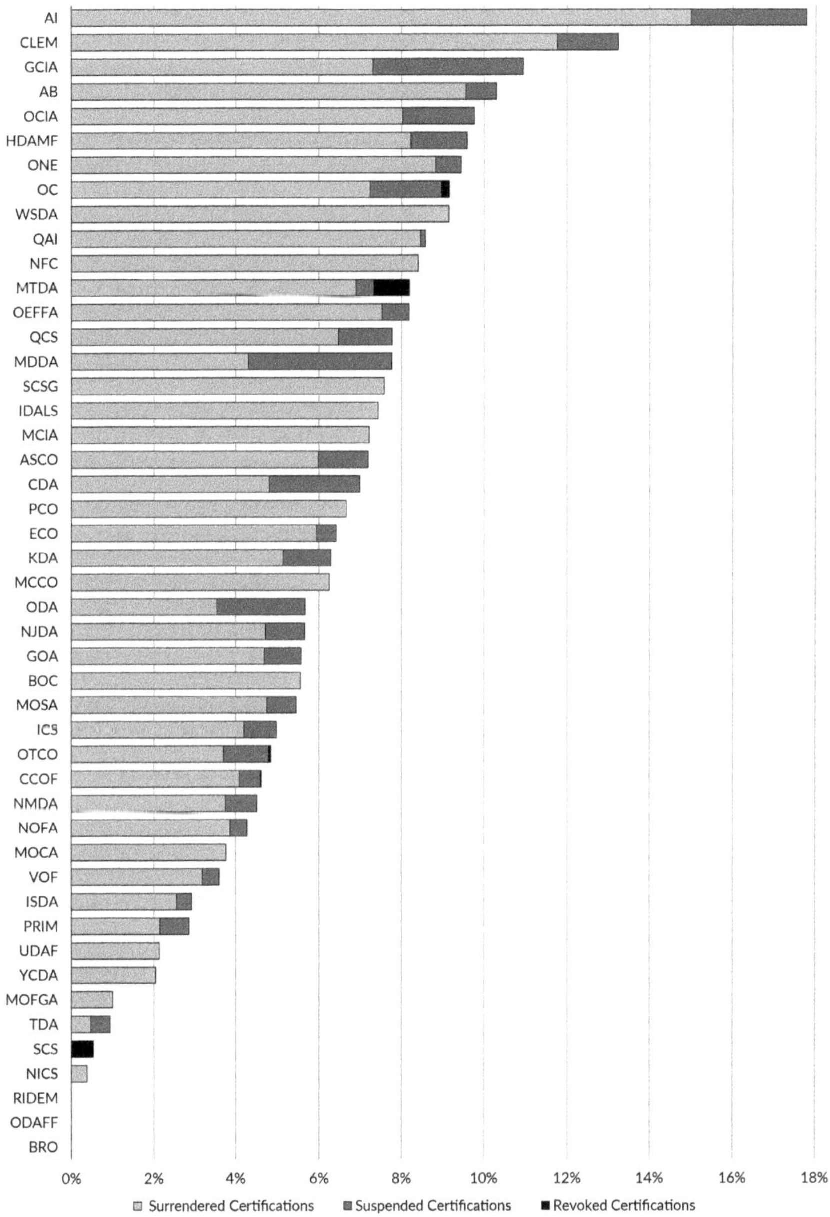

Figure 6.1. Surrendered, suspended, and revoked organic certifications as a percent of all certifications by certifier

SOURCE: Author

NOTE: Figure generated with data from the USDA's Organic Integrity Database (USDA 2018)

that struggles to maintain regulatory compliance. It is also possible, although arguably less so, that none of the Washington State Department of Agriculture's clients are culpable of major noncompliance violations that warrant certification suspension or revocation. Furthermore, the final outcome of enforcement actions taken by certifiers, such as a proposed suspension or revocation, are subject to USDA approval. Thus, it is impossible from these data to know if certifiers have proposed enforcement actions that were later reversed by the USDA.

Finally, certification statuses, while relatively easy to compile and compare, are limited to certification determinations and say little about differences in *how* organic certifiers administer USDA organic standards. The regulatory literature depicts considerable variation in regulatory agents' strategies for encouraging compliance with regulatory standards, from the extent to which they apply regulatory standards "to the letter" to the relative willingness with which they provide regulatees with information and assistance. In the next section, I discuss the findings of several studies in which I examined differences in certifiers' organic standards administration, including and beyond such aspects of certifiers' regulatory behavior. The findings not only provide a better understanding of standards administration differences—they also help identify likely organizational causes of some differences.

BEYOND CERTIFICATION STATUSES: EXPLAINING DIFFERENCES IN USDA ORGANIC STANDARDS ADMINISTRATION

A more nuanced understanding of how the administration of USDA organic standards varies across certifiers can be found in a couple of publications through which I examined certifiers' standards administration through the perceptions of certified organic producers. The first examines differences in how organic certifiers fulfill their monitoring and enforcement function, which I refer to as certifiers' "regulatory approaches" (Carter 2016). The second focuses on the service-provision aspect of organic certification by studying differences in certifiers' service emphases and service quality (Carter 2017d). Data for both studies come from the Organic Regulation Research Project nation-wide survey of certified organic producers described in this book's introductory chapter. It's worth noting that because the email addresses of several certifiers' clients were not listed in the USDA database that the Project relied on for contact information, the analysis is limited to forty-one domestic certifiers. Despite omitting seven certifiers, the survey data capture the diversity of the domestic organic certifier cohort, including varying sectoral affiliations, geographic locations, and sizes—as illustrated in the analyses that follow.

It's further worth noting that relying on regulatee survey data deviates from much of the existing regulatory literature, representing both a research limitation and strength. Cross-sectional survey data do not provide, for example, the rich descriptive data captured by in-depth case studies. Additionally, surveying regulated entities limits collected data to actions observed, remembered, and reported by regulatees. These limitations notwithstanding, the national survey offers a valuable window into the actions of the organic certifiers. Most notably, and as referenced above, it allows me to look beyond the limited perspective of certification statuses to investigate how monitoring and enforcement behaviors and services vary across certifiers. Furthermore, a considerable strength of the approach over studies that rely on self-reported regulator data (e.g., May and Burby 1998, May and Winter 2000) is that regulatees arguably face fewer pressures to report "favorable" regulatory actions in a manner that biases study findings.

In addition to providing a more nuanced understanding of certifiers' administration of the USDA organic standards, the studies allowed me to examine a question central to this book's analysis: Do organic certifiers alter the manner in which they administer the USDA organic standards to compete for regulatee-clients? There are two ways that I investigate the impact of competition. One is looking for differences between certifiers on the basis of sector, as governmental, nonprofit, and for-profit. Because for-profit certifiers, and to a lesser degree, nonprofit certifiers, are more reliant on client fees for revenue, my presumption is that sectoral differences in the administration of organic standards may expose certifiers' responses to variable exposure to competitive pressure. The second manner in which I examine the impact of competition is through the concentration of the certification markets in which organic operations are embedded. Each of these approaches is discussed in greater detail, below.

While the primary data for each of the studies came from the producer survey, I drew on USDA data to fill in some missing measures. In particular, I used Organic Integrity (USDA 2018) records to construct a client base measure for each of the certifiers, which I used as a rough proxy for organization sizes in all three analyses. I also used the Organic Integrity data to construct the certification market concentration measures referenced immediately above. Finally, as explained below, I drew on website coding for some of the data used to examine certifier services. The rationale, focus, and central theoretical concepts of each of the studies are presented in this section, followed by an explanation of how I constructed certification market concentration measures from Organic Integrity data. Following the overviews, I present a synthesis of the study findings as they relate to explaining differences in certifiers' organic standards administration. Complete information regarding the relevant theories, data, and analytical methods can be found in the original article publications.

Regulatory Approaches as a Dimension of Organic Standards Administration

Understanding organic certifiers' monitoring and enforcement behaviors beyond the certification statuses determinations discussed earlier requires a manner in which to conceptualize and compare certifiers' aggregate certification actions—what I refer to as certifiers' regulatory approaches (Carter 2016). Conceptualizing regulatory enforcement is complicated by the myriad of ways scholars approach the task and variety of terms that they use. Many scholars take a continuum approach, characterizing regulators' activities as situated somewhere between deterrence, representing an emphasis on enforcement and sanctioning, and accommodation, representing a more flexible and responsive approach (Ayres and Braithwaite 1992, Bardach and Kagan 1982, Potoski and Prakash 2009). Others take a multi-dimensional approach, such as May and Burby's (1998) facilitative and systematic dimensions, or May and Winter's (2001a) formalism and facilitation.

Given the diversity of constructs offered by regulatory scholarship, my research strikes a middle-ground by conceptualizing certifiers' regulatory approaches as being situated along a deterrence-accommodation continuum but comprised of different attitudinal and behavioral dimensions. These dimensions include (i) the strictness with which a regulator interprets regulatory provisions, (ii) their propensity to administer sanctions for noncompliance, (iii) the flexibility the exhibit in allowing regulatees to correct noncompliance before issuing sanctions, and (iv) their willingness to provide technical assistance. Strictness in regulatory interpretation is intended to reflect May and Winter's (2000) formalism, or "rule-bound stances." Propensity to administer sanctions and flexibility relate to coercion or deterrence. Willingness to provide assistance indicates an organization's inclination to aid regulatees to come into compliance (Scholz 1991), akin to what Winter and May (2001a) dub "facilitation."

Measurement of certifiers' regulatory approach dimensions involved asking certified organic producer survey respondents to indicate their level of agreement with several prompts on to a five-point scale ranging from *strongly disagree* to *strongly agree.* The prompts were:

- Strictness in regulatory interpretation: "My certifier strictly interprets the [National Organic Program] regulations."

- Propensity to administer sanctions: "My certifier always administers notices of noncompliance for serious issues."
- Flexibility: "Before administering a formal notice of noncompliance, my certifier always allows me to correct the noncompliance issue."
- Willingness to provide assistance: "My certifier frequently offers information and/or assistance that help me comply with [National Organic Program] regulations."

As foreshadowed in the early paragraphs of this section, my examination of regulatory approaches hinged on the theoretical impact of competitive certification environments on regulatory behavior. I posited that in competitive markets certifiers would be more inclined to exhibit accommodative regulatory approaches—for example, by being less strict in their regulatory interpretations and more willing to offer help—to attract and retain certification clients. Furthermore, private certifiers likely face the greatest exposure to competitive pressures, largely because they are reliant on fees-for-service for organizational revenue (Bozeman 2004), and I therefore expected private-sector organic certifiers to exhibit the most accommodative regulatory approaches. Public sector organizations are typically more constrained in their service areas, are held accountable to more than the "bottom line," and can draw on budget appropriations for revenue (Boyne 2002, Bozeman 2004, Meier and O'Toole Jr. 2011). As a result, I suggested public certifiers would exhibit more deterrent regulatory approaches. Finally, I anticipated nonprofit certifiers to be situated between their private and public counterparts on the deterrence-accommodation spectrum, due in part to reliance on fees for service that is tempered by more diverse revenue portfolios, often including member fees, grant funding, and donations (Chang and Tuckman 1994).

Services as a Dimension of Organic Standards Administration

In a departure from most regulatory scholarship, I consider certifiers' customer-service orientations to reflect an important element of USDA organic standards administration (Carter 2017d). In a competitive certification environment, certification services may offer a valuable competitive edge—particularly if a certifier is regarded as offering desirable service types or superior quality services. Assuming certifiers' behaviors are shaped by their enforcement philosophies (as first discussed in Chapter 5), for example, whether a certifier views itself as "proactive or reactive, as an educator or policeman, or as providing persuasion or punishment" (May and Burby 1998, 162), a certifier's relative emphasis on service provision constitutes an influential element of the certifier's regulatory administration.

The first manner in which I examined organic certifiers' services was by identifying the services offered on domestic certifier websites and coding each website for whether it exhibited three service categories: educational services, advocacy services, and additional certification or labeling services beyond USDA organic.[1] The definition of each category is provided below. The second manner in which I examined certifiers' consumer service orientations was through perceived service quality data collected in the producer survey: survey respondents were asked to indicate the quality of the of their certifiers' aforementioned service categories on a five-point scale, ranging from *poor* to *excellent.*

- Educational services: Education related to organic practices including workshops, webinars, and training opportunities
- Advocacy services: Political representation of organic producer interests, such as in Washington, DC and at NOSB meetings
- Additional certification services: Certification and labeling services in addition to USDA organic certification such as "Certified Gluten-Free" and "Food Alliance Certified"

I theorized that organic certifiers' service emphases would be most heavily influenced by their sector. Due to the constraints of legislation, associated statutes, and organizational mandates (Andrews, Boyne, and Walker 2006), public certifiers are least likely to provide or emphasize services beyond their regulatory responsibilities. I posited that nonprofit organic certifiers, influenced by their historical role in the evolution of the organic industry and its governance (Guthman 2014, Nowacek and Nowacek 2008), would emphasize education and policy advocacy. Finally, organizational strategy literature suggests that private-sector organizations seek the most efficient means of tailoring services for competitive advantage. Because the replication of existing services attracts new clients while requiring minimal input costs, involving ". . . a mere duplication of a well-conceived system . . ." as opposed to ". . . a minor or major redesign of the system with a fair chance of unwelcomed negative consequences" (Carman and Langeard 1980), I predicted that private-sector organic producers are more likely to focus on providing certification services including, and beyond, USDA organic certification.

Examining the Impact of Competitive Certification Markets on Organic Standards Administration

As discussed throughout this book, overlapping certifier service areas, combined with operations' ability to choose their organic certifier, creates an environment in which certifiers compete for organic regulatee-clients. Several certifier representatives acknowledged the competitive pressures that they experienced during the course of research interviews. For example, the manager of one state government certifier recounted visiting the operations of organic farmers to try and convince them to be certified under the State Department, rather than a nonprofit or private-sector certifier (Research interview, Winter 2012/2013). Similarly, a representative of a different certifier described organic certification as a "mini business under the umbrella" of the State Department of Agriculture in question (Research interview, Winter 2012/2013). The interviewee went on to remark that her organization's response to competition was to ensure that operating costs were kept to a minimum, thereby allowing the organization to offer the lowest fees-for-service possible.

My examination of whether competition shapes certifiers' administration of USDA organic standards takes advantage of the fact that the competitiveness of certification environments is not uniform across the U.S.; rather, they vary geographically. One way of conceptualizing the competitiveness of regional certification environments is in market concentration, roughly understood as the number of certifiers in a given market relative to the number of certified operations. When market concentration is used as an indicator of competition, the more concentrated a market, the less competitive it is assumed to be (Hannan 1997). Market concentration arguably works as a good proxy for competitiveness in the case of organic certification because, perhaps as result of certifiers' regional clustering in the early years of organic certification, overlap in certifiers' service areas does not correspond tightly with organic operations' geographic distribution. In other words, some parts of the country have many organic operations and few organic certifiers, while other parts of the country fall under many certifiers' service areas but exhibit relatively few operations.

To measure certification market concentrations, I used data from the National Organic Program's Organic Integrity Database to generate a Herfindahl-Hirschman Index (HHI) value for each state (with states representing geographical certification "markets"). Following previous constructions of HHI measures (e.g., Hannan 1997), I first calculated a market share value for each certifier operating in a given state by dividing the number of clients for each certifier in the state by the total number of certified operations in the state. I then squared each certifier market share value, and the results summed for all certifiers in a state, producing a state HHI value with potential to range from 0 (not concentrated/more competitive) to 1 (highly concentrated/less competitive).

State market concentration values can be interpreted relative to Department of Justice guidelines, which defines HHI scores between 0 and 0.15 as not concentrated, 0.15–0.25 as moderately concentrated, and 0.25–1.0 as highly concentrated. To correspond with the date range of this chapter's

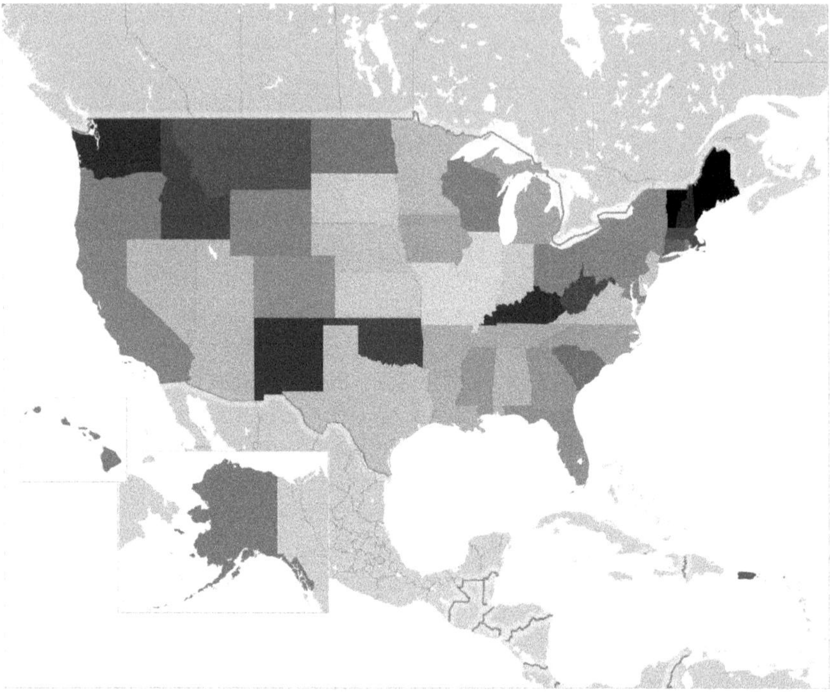

Figure 6.2. State certification market concentration as represented by 2014 HHI values
SOURCE: Author
NOTE: Lighter shades represent less concentrated state certification markets and darker shades represent more concentrated markets

survey date-based analyses (below), HHI measures represent data from the year 2014, although it should be noted that the relative differences in state market concentrations have changed little in the subsequent years. In 2014, the average state organic certification was fairly concentrated, reflected in a mean HHI value of 0.44. The lowest HHI value was 0.14 (Delaware) and the highest was 0.90 (Vermont). The map in Figure 6.2 depicts how state certification market concentrations vary across the U.S., where lighter shades reflect lower HHI values (less concentrated markets) and darker shades reflect higher HHI values (more concentrated markets).

Findings: Explaining Differences among Certifiers' Organic Standards Administration

Before turning to the analysis findings, it is instructive to compare my descriptive regulatory approach findings with the certification status data presented earlier in this chapter. While comparing the percentage of surrendered, suspended, and revoked certifications suggests considerable variation in enforcement actions across certifiers, survey data seems to indicate greater between-certifier consistency. The descriptive findings are depicted in Figure 6.3, where each marker represents a certifier represented in the survey data and the markers are positioned by where the certifier-specific survey respondent mean falls relative to each regulatory approach dimension. For example, the first panel of the figure maps each certifier by their mean "strictness of regulatory interpretation" value. The left end of the spectrum represents the minimum number of -2 equating to "strongly disagree" on the survey and is interpreted as reflecting low strictness of regulatory interpretation on the part of a certifier. The right end of the spectrum, in contrast, represents the maximum number of 2 equating to "strongly agree," and is interpreted as reflecting high strictness of regulatory interpretation.

As can be seen in the figure, the dimension in which certifiers exhibited the least amount of variation was strictness of regulatory interpretation, analogous to May and Winter's (2000) regulatory formalism construct, as most producers reported that their certifiers strictly interpreted the National Organic Program regulations.[2] The dimension in which certifiers exhibited the greatest variation was in their willingness to provide information and assistance to regulatees—similar to Winter and May's (2001a) "facilitation" construct. All in all, the descriptive findings suggest that certifiers are collectively seen as strictly

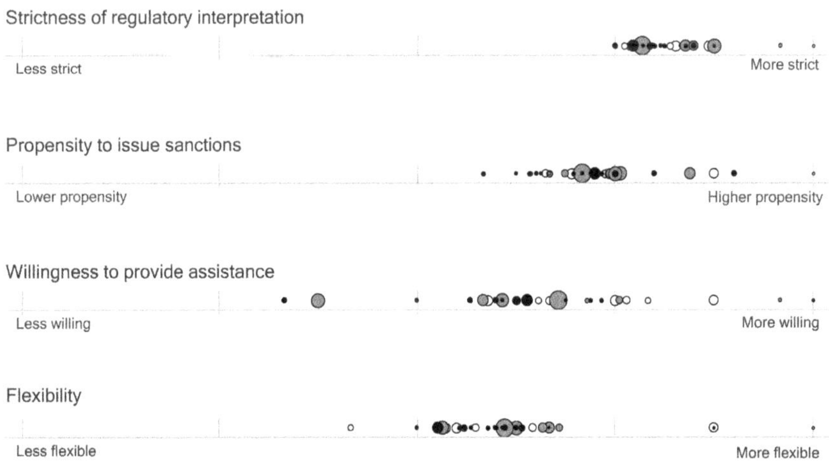

Figure 6.3. Survey findings depicting organic certifiers' regulatory approaches
SOURCE: Author
NOTE: Circle marker location represents mean survey value by certifier; Circle size reflects each certifier's total client number: the larger the marker, the bigger the certifier's client base; Circle color reflects certifier sector, where black = public, grey = nonprofit, and white = private

interpreting USDA organic standards and willing to sanction but are at the same time inclined to offer regulatees assistance and display *some* flexibility when issuing sanctions.

Analysis findings from the two studies are summarized in Table 6.2. The studies applied multiple regression procedures to examine the relationship between certifier characteristics, such as sector and number of certification clients, and the dependent variables of interest: regulatory approach behaviors and service qualities. The competitiveness of the certification markets in which producers were located, measured by state certification market HHI values, was also included as an independent variable in each of the analyses. Model specifications varied somewhat between the studies, but each controlled for theoretically influential confounding factors, such as respondents' operational characteristics (e.g., size, certification tenure, certification scope) and respondent perceptions and experiences, such as the relative difficulty that they reported in complying with the National Organic Program regulations.

As can be seen in the table, my analysis seeking to explain differences in certifiers' regulatory approach dimensions turned up largely null results. Public certifiers were associated with a lower willingness to provide information and other assistance, when compared with their nonprofit and private-sector counterparts. Certifier size, measured by the number of certification clients each certifier has, seemed to have an influence, as larger certifiers were found to exhibit a greater propensity to issue sanctions and less likely to allow producers to correct noncompliances before sanctioning them. Importantly, no support was found for the notion that the competitiveness of certification environments influences certifiers' regulatory approaches, as no relationship was detected between market concentration—the proxy indicator of market competitiveness—and any of the regulatory approach dimensions.

The element of USDA standards administration that was best explained by organic certifiers' characteristics was service differences. First, my coding of the services offered on domestic certifiers' websites indicated a clear pattern. Public sector certifiers were notably constrained in the services they listed outside of USDA organic, mentioning only verification of origin labeling, such as Rhode Island State Department of Agriculture's "RI Certified. Get Fresh. Buy Local" label. Private-sector certifiers were most likely to offer services related to other certification programs, with programs ranging from gluten-free certification to Fair Trade found on eight of seventeen private-sector certifier websites. Nonprofit certifiers, in turn, were very likely to offer educational services (found on eight of eleven nonprofit certifier websites) and had the only websites which mentioned advocacy-related services (on five websites).

Table 6.2. Research findings examining differences in producer-perceived certifier regulatory approaches and services

	Sector	*Number of certification clients*	*Certification market concentration*
Regulatory approach			
Strictness of regulatory interpretation	N.S.	N.S.	N.S.
Propensity to administer sanctions	N.S.	Larger certifiers are more likely to administer sanctions for serious issues	N.S.
Flexibility	N.S.	Larger certifiers are less likely to allow for noncompliance corrections prior to sanctioning	N.S.
Willingness to provide assistance	Public certifiers are less likely to offer information and assistance	N.S.	N.S.
Services			
Educational services	Nonprofit certifiers are more likely to offer, and exhibit higher quality of, educational services	N.S.	N.S.
Advocacy services	Nonprofit certifiers offer, and exhibit higher quality of, advocacy services	N.S.	N.S.
Additional labeling services	Private-sector certifiers offer and exhibit the highest quality of other certification services. Nonprofit certifiers exhibit higher quality of other certification services than public certifiers.	N.S.	N.S.

SOURCE: Summary of research findings from (Carter 2016, 2017d)
NOTE: N.S. = relationship is not statistically significant at the $p < 0.05$ level

Analysis of service quality data from the certified producer survey tells a similar story, assuming the quality of certifiers' educational, advocacy, and additional certification services are reflective of certifiers' customer service focuses. Private-sector certifiers exhibited higher additional certification service qualities than both nonprofit and public certifiers. Nonprofit certifiers exhibited the highest quality educational and policy advocacy services. Collectively, the findings of the organic certifier services study suggest that certifier service provision is shaped by certifiers' sectoral affiliations. Public certifiers limit their services to administration of USDA organic standards, while private-sector and nonprofit certifiers "bundle" peripheral services in distinctive ways, with private-sector certifiers pursuing increased revenues through diversification of certification programs and nonprofits focusing on mission-aligned educational and advocacy services.

The results of the two studies offer key insights into the administration of USDA organic standards through third-party certifiers. Only limited differences in certifiers' regulatory behaviors can be explained by their organizational characteristics: larger certifiers may be more stringent in aspects of their regulatory enforcement and public certifiers appear less generous in assisting regulatees. In contrast, certifiers' sectoral designations as public, nonprofit, and for-profit seems to explain the different patterns observed in certifiers' service emphases. As I concluded in the original publication, the latter findings align with organizational theory regarding organizational responses to competitive environments (e.g., Andrews, Boyne, and Walker 2006). They also have practical implications for USDA organic standards administration:

> [S]tudy findings support predictions that organizational responses to competition are not uniform and vary according to organizational characteristics. . . . As a result, and as illustrated by study results, including third-party administrators from the nonprofit and private sectors in the administration of regulatory standards leads to peripheral services that are "bundled" with regulatory activities and systematic differences in service quality. (Carter 2017d, 814)

When considered collectively, however, the findings of the two studies offer a more profound conclusion with direct relevance to USDA organic certification regulatory integrity. In light of evidence that suggests certifiers' respond to a competitive environment through the services they offer and emphasize, combined with a lack of evidence that their regulatory approaches correlate with theoretically relevant indicators of exposure to competitive pressures, it may be that certifiers find it less risky, more efficient, or simply more effective to compete through the service bundles they offer rather than through their monitoring and enforcement behaviors. The explanation is substantiated by an organic certification consultant that I interviewed in the course of this research, who when reflecting on organic certification before-and-after National Organic Program implementation commented: "It used to be that certifiers would compete on standards, but they cannot do that anymore . . . so now that leaves customer service and types of certification . . . kind of a range of services" (Research interview, Fall 2012).

CONCLUSIONS: ORGANIC CERTIFIERS AS THIRD-PARTY ADMINISTRATORS

This chapter examined accredited certifying agents as the third-party administrators of USDA organic standards to depict the organizational diversity of U.S.-based certifiers, investigate differences in certifiers' administration of USDA organic standards, and assess the extent to which certifiers support or undermine the regulatory fidelity and integrity of USDA organic certification. The findings show that the domestic cohort of 47 organic certifiers is diverse, comprised of 14 for-profit businesses, 14 nonprofits, and 19 public organizations, with governmental certifiers taking the form of state department of agriculture programs, county government programs, and a university department. Certifier client numbers vary considerably, from 12 to over 3,500, as do their geographic scopes of service—ranging from the boundaries of a county to national and international in scope. The competition of the certification markets in which certifiers offer their services also differ, as reflected in state certification market HHI concentration measures from not concentrated (HHI of 0.14 out of 1.0) to extremely concentrated (0.90).

The two data sources that I leveraged in this chapter's analyses offered somewhat contradictory findings when it comes to disparities in certifiers' administration of the USDA organic standards. My descriptive analysis of USDA data regarding organic certification statuses as active, surrendered, suspended, or revoked showed considerable variation among certifiers' propensity to take enforcement actions. Organic certification suspension rates by certifier ranged from 0 to 26 percent, and only eight certifiers exhibited detectible revocation rates, with the highest totaling under 1 percent. Considering in light of the regulatory administration dimensions identified in Chapter 2, these figures raise concerns regarding the fidelity with which certifiers administer organic regulations. At a minimum, they suggest discrepancies in certifiers' enforcement behaviors.

Data from the Organic Regulation Research Project's nation-wide survey of certified organic producers depicted greater consistency between certifiers on the basis of producer-perceived certifier regulatory approach behaviors, such as how strictly certifiers interpret National Organic Program regulations and their relative propensity to administer noncompliance penalties. Synthesizing the findings of my published research (Carter 2016, 2017d), I sought to explain differences in certifiers' administration of the USDA organic standards on the basis of their organizational characteristics and certification markets in which they operate. The most apparent explanation of differences between certifiers was found in the relationship between certifiers' sectors and their service emphases. Governmental certifiers tend to limit the services they offer to those related to USDA organic certification. Nonprofits, in contrast, tend to emphasize advocacy and educational services alongside their certification services. Private-sector certifiers tend to offer additional certification services, such as non-GMO labeling and gluten-free verification. Notably, when measured by the relative concentration of state certification markets, the competitiveness of the markets in which certifiers operate seems unrelated to the regulatory approaches they adopt when administering the USDA organic standards and the quality of the services they offer.

This chapter's analyses speak directly to two of the chief regulatory design implications discussed throughout this book: the regulatory fidelity and integrity with which USDA organic standards are administered. The preceding chapter showed that the National Organic Program is capable of exercising its regulatory oversight, for example, by revoking certifiers' accreditations for failing to comply with USDA accreditation requirements. Beyond anecdotes of certifier shopping, however, the chapter was unable to address whether accreditation effectively translates to consistency and stringency in organic certifiers' behaviors. This chapter indicates that variation exists in certifiers' regulatory decision making, raising some regulatory fidelity concerns, but there is no evidence in the findings to indicate that certifiers respond to competitive certification environments in a manner that threatens the integrity of the USDA organic label.

Evidence of regulatory fidelity concerns is found in the variation exhibited in certifiers' certification determinations. The chapter's analysis of certification status data, as discussed above, suggests that many certifiers may have difficult identifying, or are reluctant to take enforcement actions in the face of, major noncompliance issues: eighteen of the forty-seven domestic certifiers recorded no certification suspensions, and a vast majority had not issued revocations at a rate high enough to be picked up in the analysis. On the other hand, a majority of certifiers appear willing to suspend operations, and select few *do* revoke clients' certifications, up to a rate of almost 1 percent.

These data contrast somewhat with the findings of producer survey-based studies, as the latter indicate relative consistency in certifiers' regulatory actions. Potential contributors to the differences may be found in data limitations, including the challenges of using certification status data as a measure of enforcement actions (as discussed above), potential survey sample biases, or faults with survey operationalization and measurement. A perhaps more compelling explanation for at least some of the apparent discrepancy is my inability to incorporate certifiers' issuances of less serious, although not inconsequential, noncompliance sanctions in my analysis of USDA records data. As recounted in the preceding chapter, the National Organic Program seems to make no effort to analyze or even compile Notice of Noncompliance records. It is possible that accounting for these missing data may bridge the gap between the two sets of findings—particularly if certifiers exhibit more consistency in their propensity to administer Notices than in their propensity to suspend or revoke certifications.

The implications for regulatory integrity that stem from USDA organic certification's competitive third-party design constitute a recurring theme throughout this book. The aforementioned limitations notwithstanding, this chapter's analyses provide the most direct test for whether competitive pressures undermine the integrity of USDA organic certification by incentivizing certifiers to exercise lax regulatory oversight to attract and retain clients. On the basis of the analyses presented here, there seems to be little evidence to substantiate the concern. Incorporating the service-provision aspect of organic certification offers an additional piece to the puzzle: certifiers are not restricted to altering their regulatory behaviors to compete for regulatee-clients. In a context where baseline expectations for regulatory action are established by accreditation standards, certifiers might find altering their services to be the most effective—and least risky—way of appealing to client desires.

Of course, organic certifiers are not the sole monitoring and enforcement intermediaries that shape USDA organic standards administration. Nor is the National Organic Program the sole actor that seeks to maintain regulatory fidelity and integrity in USDA organic certification. The chapters that follow examine two additional regulatory intermediary categories that play important roles within the design of USDA organic certification. The following chapter examines organic inspectors—the "regulatory frontline" of USDA organic food regulation—to investigate the manner in which organic inspectors balance the multiple, and often competing, roles that these street-level regulatory actors fulfill. The discussion then turns to the professional associations, the IOIA and ACA, that serve as coordinating intermediaries both within certifier and inspector communities and between these cohorts and external organizations—most notably, the National Organic Program.

NOTES

1. Service categories for the examination of organic certifier services were identified through interviews with organic certification practitioners and industry members (see Carter 2017d).

2. The standard deviation for the "strictness of regulatory interpretation" variable was 0.75 (where the mean = 1.20, min = –2, and max = 2). The standard deviation for the "willingness to issue sanctions" variable was 1.04 (mean = 0.63, min = –2, and max = 2). Details regarding these findings and more can be found in the original publication.

Chapter Seven

The Inspection Intermediaries

Organic Inspectors

Organic inspectors are one of the most overlooked aspects of USDA organic certification. When they are mentioned, inspectors are typically treated as extensions of the accredited certifying agents they work for, yet, the function they perform is both distinct and crucial. Whether it be for new applicant inspection, certification renewal, or an unannounced "spot" inspection, when organic inspectors are dispatched to farms and facilities, they are likely the only certifier representative to set foot at an operation. Furthermore, organic inspectors are the only face-to-face contact that many organic farmers and food handlers have with National Organic Program authority. How organic inspectors carry out their monitoring and enforcement functions is therefore central to the fidelity and integrity of USDA organic certification.

Although the work of inspectors may be undervalued in the context of organic certification, regulatory scholars readily recognize the importance of inspectors in regulation, more broadly. In the words of Peter May and Robert Wood (2003):

> Within broad parameters established by agency guidelines and routines, inspectors typically have a good deal of autonomy and discretion in how they go about enforcing regulations. They have discretion over the thoroughness with which they conduct inspections and over the manner in which they interact with regulatees. In other words, inspectors are classic examples of street-level bureaucrats.

Following street-level bureaucracy theory (Lipsky 1980), much of the research on regulatory inspectors examines how inspectors exercise discretion; for example, how inspectors may "be alternately informative, cajoling, educating, or punitive as needed to produce the desired levels of cooperation and compliance" (May and Wood 2003, 118). The findings of this research suggests that just as organic certifiers vary in the regulatory approaches that they apply, organic inspectors also likely differ—to some extent—in their monitoring and enforcement styles (May and Winter 1999, 2000). For example, some seek a more "responsive" style by considering how contexts and motivations differ across regulatees. Others seek more uniform and rigid stances (Ayres and Braithwaite 1992).

A range of influences shape how inspectors fulfill their monitoring duties, from the design of regulatory provisions (May 1993), to political signals written into regulatory directives (May and Winter 2007), and the personal values held by inspectors (Hedge, Menzel, and Williams 1988). Research further highlights the social contexts in which inspections take place. Inspection styles are not simply the product of the signals embedded in regulatory provisions or inspectors' personal values—they also reflect inspectors' accumulated interactions and experiences with regulatees (Fineman 1998, Nielsen 2007). Where regulatees are also paying service recipients, such as is the case for producers and processors seeking USDA organic certification, inspectors may face pressures to emphasize customer service over policy goals (Fountain 2001), possibly threatening regulatory program integrity.

This chapter examines how organic inspectors understand and approach their role, and the resulting implications for USDA organic certification. The chapter begins with an overview of the Organic Regulation Research Project's organic inspector study by which the research team and I collected organic inspector data. It then draws on these data to describe what we know about the organic inspector cohort and inspectors' relationships with the organic certifiers they work for. The third section draws on my published research (Carter 2017c) to assess how organic inspectors understand their regulatory roles and how these role perceptions likely shape the administration of USDA organic standards.

THE ORGANIC INSPECTOR STUDY

Our investigation of individuals that inspect farms and other facilities for USDA organic standards compliance comprised a discrete study under the broader Organic Regulation Research Project. We collected quantitative data through a survey of inspectors and qualitative through in-depth interviews. The following description reviews key survey elements, provides an overview of the interviews, and compares the survey and interview samples. More details are provided in the Methodological Appendix.

As stated above, no publicly available list identifies the individuals that conduct inspections for USDA organic, much less provides a description of their employment details. We used organizational affiliations and snowball sampling techniques (Atkinson and Flint 2001) to generate a list of potential organic inspectors (see the Methodological Appendix). The names and contact information of 260 individuals thought to be inspectors of organic standards were collected and 92 serviceable surveys were returned (35 percent of the initial 260 requests sent). The data collected, as discussed later in this chapter, included questions pertaining to inspectors' interactions with their employing certifiers, the roles that inspectors perceive themselves to fulfill in organic certification, inspectors' attitudes towards the use of discretion, and demographic and employment information.

Qualitative data were collected through semi-structured interviews conducted via telephone with a subsample of ten inspectors. Our interview sample frame was purposeful and designed with the goal of achieving appropriate representation of population sub-groups (referred to as a parallel sampling frame by Onwuegbuzie and Leech 2007), including inspectors that worked as both part/full-time employees and on a contract basis, and inspectors that worked for governmental and nongovernmental (nonprofit or for-profit) certifiers. In the end, we received a higher interview request response rate from government-affiliated inspectors; in our final interview sample five participants were part-time or full-time employees of government certifiers, two were contract inspectors that worked for both government and private certifiers, and three were inspectors that contracted exclusively with private certifiers. Interview question topics mirrored those of the survey.

Comparing survey and interview participant characteristics indicates that the interview sample reflects the survey sample fairly well, with the exceptions of overrepresentation among governmental employee inspectors and those identifying as male. Five of the 10 interviewees had been conducting organic inspections for over ten years, while 44 of the 92 survey respondents had more than ten years of experience. One was a new organic inspector as of the preceding year and the 4 remaining inspectors had conducted organic inspections for between four and six years. By comparison, 10 survey respondents had two years or less of experience, leaving the remaining 38 survey respondents with three to ten years of experience. Four interviewees were women and 6 were men; 51 survey respondents identified as women and 41 identified as male. The interviewees were not asked for their exact age, however, two were likely over 65 years old, six were "middle aged," and the remaining two inspectors were under 30 years old. Eleven of the 92 survey respondents were 35 years old or younger, another 37 fell between the ages of 36 and 55, 32 were between 56 and 65, and 12 were over 65 years old.

ORGANIC INSPECTORS' FUNCTION, EMPLOYMENT CHARACTERISTICS, AND RELATIONSHIP WITH CERTIFIERS

Before considering organic inspectors' backgrounds, employment characteristics, and relationship with certifiers, it is helpful to understand what organic inspectors do. A considerable amount of an inspectors' time is spent traveling to operations in remote rural areas (Crandell 2003). While inspectors may perform inspections close to their place of residence, they are often dispatched to more distant parts of their home state or region. Our interviews with organic certifiers and inspectors indicated that this is particularly the case when an operation requires specific areas of expertise that are not readily exhibited by the average inspector.

As recounted in Chapters 4 and 6, USDA organic certification revolves around the organic system plan that an operation submits as part of a certification application to an accredited certifying agent. National Organic Program regulation conflict of interest provisions (discussed in Chapter 5), stipulate that the person that makes certification decisions cannot be the same individual that inspects an applicant's operation. Therefore, after certification personnel approve a plan as compliant with the standards specified in regulations, the certifier dispatches an inspector to the operation. The inspector is responsible for determining whether the operation's practices and processes are congruent with the organic system plan, recording any deviations from the plan, and reporting the findings to their employing certifier. As stated succinctly in Erin Crandell's (2003) interview with organic process inspector Nancy Ludwig:

> [The inspection] includes inspecting buildings and equipment, contamination risks, pest management, and sales and production records. . . . Although samples may be collected and analyzed during an inspection, Nancy emphasized that it is the process itself, and not the products resulting from it, that is the focus of the inspection.

The National Organic Program Handbook specifies two inspection objectives in addition to verifying that the operation's organic system plan is representative of the operation's actual practices: to assess the operation's compliance with Program regulations and ensure that no prohibited substances have entered organic processes or have been applied to organically labeled products (NOP Form 1100). The latter objective requires inspection of physical facilities and processes, such as sufficient "buffer zones" from neighboring farms to guard against herbicide or pesticide drift, and examination of the records documenting the operation's practices, such as audit invoices, records of material applications, organic product sales, and harvest and yield data (McEvoy 2014).

The final step of an organic inspection is an "exit interview" with an authorized representative of the operation. The purpose of the exit interview is to review any potential noncompliances observed and documented during the inspection. The inspector might also use the exit interview as an opportunity to request any necessary information missing from the operation's organic system plan and make updates to the plan as part of the inspection report that they forward to the certifier.

Organic Inspectors' Backgrounds and Employment Characteristics

Organic inspectors come to their job through a variety of avenues and may play any number of roles in the organic industry. In terms of organic inspectors' backgrounds, our survey findings indicated that 40 of 92 survey respondents (43%) had held been employed by organic certifiers in positions other than as inspectors. Forty-two (46%) had owned or operated an organic operation. About 1 in 4 (26%) identified themselves as "organic policy advocates" and almost three quarters of survey respondents (72%) characterized themselves as organic food consumers.

Although some organic inspectors have a degree in plant sciences or a related field, no formal educational requirement is specified for the job. National Organic Program regulations require that certifier personnel, including inspectors, have sufficient expertise in organic production and handling to carry out their assigned duties. The regulations stop short, however, of specifying what types of education, experience, or training constitute "sufficient expertise." In practice, organic inspectors attain training in two ways. First, inspectors that are hired as part-time or full-time personnel from an accredited certifier may receive in-house training. Second, many inspectors (both employee and contract) pursue training through the IOIA. According to Margaret Scoles, IOIA executive director: "[the IOIA is] the industry standard. There is no rule that requires that anyone take our training, but almost all inspector trainees have taken a basic course with us" (Scoles 2013). IOIA training may involve coursework and apprenticeship, with apprenticeship lasting up to two years (Crandell 2003).

Because of the lack of available data regarding organic inspectors, one objective of our survey was to paint a better picture of their employment affiliations and statuses. The findings are presented in Figure 7.1. The majority of survey respondents (72; 80%) reported working mostly for nongovernmental (i.e., nonprofit and for-profit) certifiers and the majority of these (56) did so on a contract basis. Twelve survey respondents (13%) worked mostly for governmental certifiers, 9 of whom were either full- or part-time

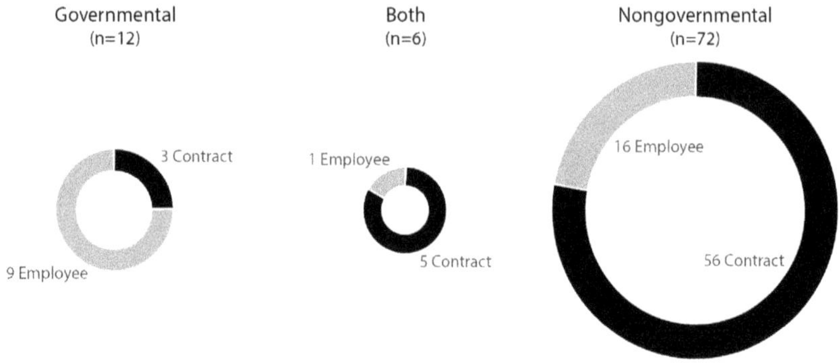

Figure 7.1. Inspector survey respondents by governmental affiliation and employment status

SOURCE: Author

NOTE: Chart sizes are representative of relative number of survey respondents by affiliation category; Shading reflects respondents' employment statuses, where darker shading represents contracted inspectors and lighter shading represents full or part-time employees

employees. Another 6 respondents reported working for governmental and nongovernmental certifiers more or less evenly.

Not depicted in the figure, the survey also queried inspectors about the number of certifiers they had worked for in the preceding year. Thirty-six survey respondents (39%) reported performing organic operations for a single certifier. Twenty-nine (31%) had worked for two or three certifiers and another 23 (25%) had worked for four or five. Four respondents had worked for six or more certifiers in the prior year. Finally, 36 survey respondents (39%) reported performing inspections for programs or food labels other than USDA organic, such as gluten free, GLOBAL G.A.P., or fair trade.

The Certifier-Inspector Relationship

Given the range of certifiers that an inspector might work for in a given year and the fact that many of them do so on a contract basis, it is worth considering how organic certifiers oversee the work of the inspectors they employ. If considered through a principal-agent framework (Scholz 1991), it's apparent that there is an information asymmetry between a certifier (the principal) and the inspectors they employ (the agents); certifiers likely find it difficult to observe the extent to which inspectors exercise discretion in their monitoring and reporting duties, for example, by overlooking minor noncompliance issues or treating some organic operations less stringently than others. In response to the asymmetry, certifiers may try to restrict inspector discretion through means such as narrowly-defined goals and checklist-style work routines. Regulatory scholarship suggests, however, that such efforts to tightly control inspectors' behaviors can decrease inspection effectiveness if they mechanize the process to the point inspectors fail to, or are constrained in their ability to, observe and record noncompliance issues that span or fall outside the bounds of pre-determined conditions or processes (Pires 2011).

The manner in which we examined the relationship between organic certifiers and inspectors was through a survey battery which asked inspectors to indicate their level of agreement with six prompts. Relative agreement was measured on a scale from 1 to 5, in which 1 represented "strongly disagree" and 5 represented "strongly agree." Given the variation in certifiers types, sizes, and resources (as discussed in the previous chapter), the prompts were constructed to assess certifiers' general approaches to overseeing organic inspectors' practices. They were also worded to account for the fact that many inspectors work for more than one certifier. The prompts were:

- The certifier(s) closely tracks my inspection practices.
- The certifier(s) knows very little about my inspection practices.
- I am frequently in contact with certification personnel during the course of inspections.
- Certification personnel frequently accompany me on inspections.
- The certifier(s) enforces ethical standards on my inspection practices.
- There are few repercussions from the certifier(s) if my inspections deviate from the National Organic Program regulations.

The findings are depicted in Figure 7.2. According to the findings, most certifiers exercise at least some oversight over their inspector personnel, as a majority of surveyed inspectors (71%) agreed that their employing certifiers closely track their inspection practices. Confirming the finding, roughly the same number of inspectors (74%) disagreed that certifiers knows little about their inspection practices. The findings suggest, however, that certifiers track inspectors' decisions and behaviors through secondary measures such as inspection reports, as only eleven percent of inspectors report that certifier personnel accompany them during inspections and less than half (44%) report being in frequent contact with certifiers during inspections. The most robust finding of the question battery regards certifiers' ethical-behavior expectations, as 77 percent of inspectors indicated that their employing certifiers enforce ethical standards, and 75 percent deny that there are few repercussions for deviating from the National Organic Program regulations.

All-in-all, the findings suggest that most certifiers emphasize adherence to the National Organic Program regulations, as well as general ethical standards, and track the decisions and behaviors of their inspector personnel—most

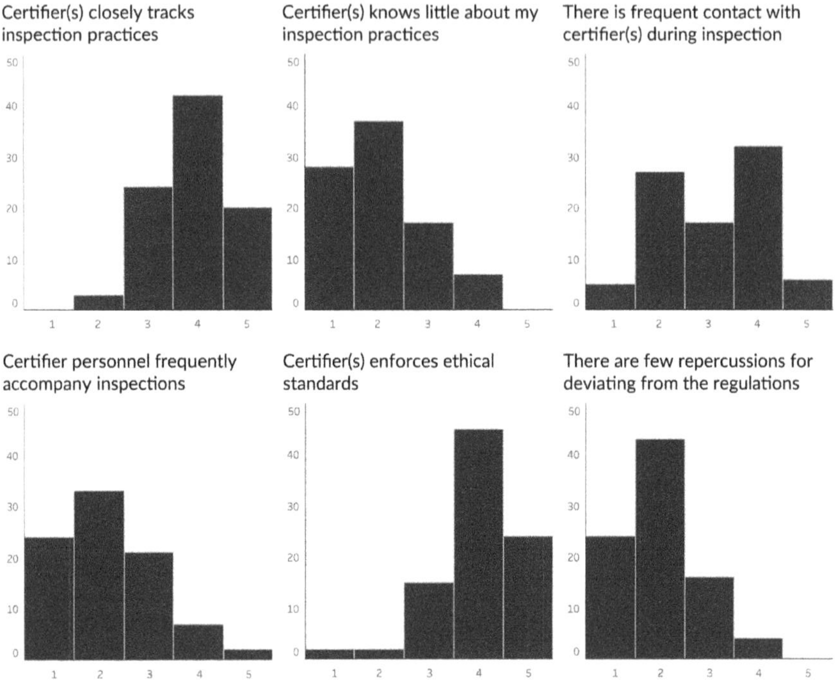

Figure 7.2. Inspector survey findings pertaining to statements reflective of the relationships and interactions between organic inspectors and employing certifiers

SOURCE: Author

NOTE: Vertical axes indicate frequency of responses and horizontal axes indicate response options where 1 = strongly disagree, 2 = disagree, 3 = neither agree nor disagree, 4 = agree, and 5 = strongly agree

likely through secondary means. However, just as organic certifiers face pressures and incentives that stem from sources other than the USDA and National Organic Program, inspectors operate with obligations and pressures from more than their employing certifiers. The following section reports on research examining the way in which inspectors balance the multiple, and sometimes competing, pressures that they face.

HOW ORGANIC INSPECTORS' ROLE PERCEPTIONS SHAPE ATTITUDES TOWARDS DISCRETION

In any regulatory context, from building regulations to food safety assurance programs, inspectors experience pressures from at least two entities: the regulatory agencies that they are accountable to and the individuals or firms that they inspect. Even this relatively simple arrangement can create divergent expectations and obligations. For example, in instances where inspectors come to identify with the regulatees they monitor, they may find their allegiances align more with regulatees' concerns than regulatory program objectives (Evans 2010, Nielsen 2006, 2007, Pautz and Rinfret 2013). Such shifts in allegiance constitute the central concern in some conceptions of regulatory capture (Dal Bó 2006) and are a chief motivation for the discretionary controls regulators exercise over inspector personnel.

Consistent with the theme of this book, the design of USDA organic certification creates a more complex environment for organic inspectors. As organic certification street-level bureaucrats they are, by definition, the frontline extension of National Organic Program regulatory authority. Inspectors are more immediately accountable, however, to the certification agents with which they are contracted and employed. Accountability to certifiers could align with National Organic Program provisions and objectives, as is suggested above by the majority of inspectors that indicated they faced consequences from their employing certifiers for deviating from Program regulations. Alternatively, it could incentivize inspectors to prioritize regulatee-client concerns in the name of customer service (Coglianese and Lazer 2003). The data presented earlier regarding inspectors' backgrounds suggest that some inspectors might be predisposed to regulatee concerns, as almost half of the organic inspectors surveyed indicated that they were organic operators at some point in time.

I think of the manner in which organic inspectors navigate these multiple pressures as reflected in their role perceptions—the primary responsibilities that inspectors ascribe to their function and the individuals or entities to which they feel most responsible (Fineman 1998, Schuler 1975, Selden, Brewer, and Brudney 1999). Conceptualized in this way, roles are similar to what Evans (2010, 2016) refers to as street-level bureaucrat "alliances" in an implementation structure. Following role theory (Biddle 1986, Selden, Brewer, and Brudney 1999), I assume that the role perceptions that organic inspectors adopt shape the manners in which they carry out their regulatory duties. In the sections that follow, I draw on the organic inspector survey and interview data describe how organic inspectors perceive their roles, their attitudes towards the application of discretion, and the relationship between the two.

Organic Inspector Role Perceptions

A baseline expectation regarding a decentralized regulatory arrangement such as USDA organic certification is that rather than develop a single uniform understanding of their regulatory function, inspectors perceive multiple role orientations simultaneously, resulting in a "web of obligations, relationships, and meanings" that inspectors regularly navigate (Musheno and Maynard-Moody 2015, 169). Sometimes inspector role responsibilities might converge, for example, when regulatory program goals and the objectives of third-party administrators align. At other times, inspectors might perceive themselves to be caught between divergent obligations, such as when program directives and regulatee concerns compete for favorable consequences stemming from inspector decision making. In these instances, it is likely that an inspector will resolve conflicting role orientations by prioritizing certain obligations over others (Evans and Harris 2004).

I first examined organic inspectors' role orientations through a survey question battery that measured the extent to which inspectors identified with three roles: a regulatory monitor for the National Organic Program, and employee and representative for the certifier(s) that they work for, and a service provider to the operation under inspection. Reponses were measured via respondents' relative agreement with each role orientation, where 1 = "strongly disagree" and 5 = "strongly agree." The results are presented in Table 7.1. On average, respondents most strongly identified as regulatory monitors for the National Organic Program (mean = 3.9/5), followed by representatives of certification employers (3.5/5). Survey respondents were least likely to identify as service providers to regulated operations (2.5/5). Collectively, the results suggest that the average organic inspector perceives themselves as performing two of the three roles queried: National Organic Program regulatory monitor and certifier employee/representative.

All three role orientations were expressed at some point across our interviews with organic inspectors. For example, representing a regulatory monitor role orientation, one interviewee commented "First and foremost, I am there to regulate and assess—are you complying with a national set of standards?" Another stated: ". . . we are providing a service to the producer, obviously, but our responsibility, if you like, is to uphold the [National Organic Program]. That's what we are doing." Quotes reflecting a certifier employee and representative role orientation included: "I am definitely also an employee of the [certifier] as an inspector, so unless I was asked to do something clearly unethical I am responsible to them" and "I provide a service to the certifier so that they can in turn—can perform their regulatory role." Finally, indications of a service provider role orientation were exhibited in statements such as "I think we are providing a service to organic farmers . . . so they can keep their organic certifications." Similarly, a public sector certifier-affiliated inspector commented: "I see it as a service to the people we inspect because we are a state organization with education involved and that we really do focus—we go to a lot of meetings and outreach to make sure people understand what is required to be certified."

When quantified, however, the prominence of different role orientations across the interviews mirrored survey findings. National Organic Program monitor was the most frequently cited role, referenced in all ten interviews. Certifier employee and representative was the second most frequently cited role (seven interviews), and service provider was the least frequently cited (five interviews). The comments of one interviewee seemed to summarize the average inspector's role orientation succinctly, as "a kind of nested egg thing"—the inspector first saw her role as a regulatory monitor; within the regulatory monitor role, she was secondarily a certifier's employee, and within that role she provided a service to organic operations.

As expected, inspectors readily reported experiencing role tensions that at times required them to negotiate competing obligations and expectations. Across all examples raised, however, the responsibility that inspectors ascribed to their role as regulatory monitors appeared to supersede conflicting pressures. For example, one contract inspector described encountering a

Table 7.1. Inspector role perceptions and attitudes towards discretion

Construct	*Definitions or measure*ȣ	*Mean (SD)*
Role perceptions		
Regulatory monitor	Regulatory monitor for the National Organic Program	3.9 (1.1)
Employee/representative	Employee and representative of the certifier(s) the inspector works for	3.5 (1.2)
Service provider	Service provider to the operation under inspection	2.5 (1.2)
Attitudes towards discretion		
Interpretive discretion†	Organic inspectors should follow the National Organic Program regulations to the letter.	4.0 (0.8)
Reporting discretion; recordkeeping	An operation's inconsistent documentation should not be reported by the organic inspector if organic integrity is not threatened.	1.9 (0.9)
Reporting discretion; noncompliances†	Every potential noncompliance issue should be reported by organic inspectors without exception.	3.9 (1.0)

SOURCE: Adapted from findings tables in Carter (2017c)
NOTE: Mean values represent respondents' agreement, where 1 = "strongly disagree" and 5 = "strongly agree"; Standard deviations in parentheses; ȣ = second column contains definitions in the case of role perceptions and survey measures in the case of attitudes towards discretion; † = survey response scale reversed in correlation analysis to represent a measure of favorable attitude towards discretion; table reports non-transmuted values

situation in which the inspector's judgment of a noncompliance issue differed from that of their employing certifier's:

> This is what the certifier said: "this is a dilemma between service and regulatory." I had a notion to tell him, well I think your first job is regulatory service, I mean be polite and all that stuff and give them timeliness, but you are not going to give in and call it customer service. If they are not doing something right, you have to be stern.

Notably, during the course of the interviews an additional organic inspector role dimension emerged that was not directly incorporated in our survey. A number of interviewees highlighted that organic inspections are consumer protection. One governmental certifier inspector commented: "We are also working to protect the . . . consumer. If they buy organic, it is organic, and is certified organic under the same set of standards, whether [the operation] is Starbucks or a half acre lavender grower who is a hobby farmer." As these inspectors pointed out, consumer confidence in the organic label is an essential element of the organic industry, and the work of inspectors is fundamental to consumers' trust in "the system." For example, a contract inspector reflected on the role of inspectors by stating: "[inspectors] are really the only ones . . . out there, that have direct contact with most producers . . . I represent the consumer, ultimately."

Organic Inspectors' Attitudes towards Discretion

As noted earlier, discretion is a central focus of much scholarship on regulatory inspectors (Buffat 2015). My examination focused on organic inspectors' attitudes towards the use of discretion, or "discretionary attitudes" (Carter 2017c). I conceptualize discretionary attitudes as reflecting inspectors' comfort or aversion to the application of individual judgment in the execution of program requirements. In other words, the extent to which inspectors perceive what Hupe and colleagues (2015, 17) call "discretion-as-used" to be an appropriate element of inspectors' responsibilities.

I measured organic inspectors' discretionary attitudes through survey respondents' relative agreement with three prompts. The first, which I label "interpretive discretion," pertained to inspectors' adherence to the National Organic Program regulations "to the letter." The second, which I label "recordkeeping reporting discretion," pertained to whether inspectors should report recordkeeping inconsistencies even when organic integrity is not threatened. The third, which I label "noncompliance reporting discretion," pertained to whether every potential instance of noncompliance should be reported.

As seen in the bottom half of Table 7.1, the findings can be summed up as indicating general opposition to the use of discretion among organic inspectors. The average respondent agreed that organic inspectors should follow National Organic Program regulations to the letter and that every potential instance of noncompliance should be reported. Similarly, the average respondent disagreed with the idea that recordkeeping inconsistencies could be overlooked if organic integrity is not threatened. These results were corroborated by interview findings, represented through comments such as: "I go through the points and mark everything on the report, if there were any issues of concern" and "I write up everything."

Explaining Discretionary Attitudes through Organic Inspectors' Role Perceptions

A central premise in my examination of organic inspectors' role orientations was that how inspectors perceive their roles likely shapes their attitude towards the use of discretion (Carter 2017c). Role theory indicates that individual attitudes and behavior can be anticipated by the roles that individuals internalize (Biddle 1986). I therefore expected organic inspectors that perceived themselves first and foremost as regulatory monitors would be most likely to adhere to the "discretionary space" formally constructed by the National Organic Program (Buffat 2015). Whether it be the result of internalization of policy goals or a sense of public service duty, I assumed such inspectors are likely to exhibit more "rule-bound" (May and Winter 2000) and less accommodating (Pautz and Rinfret 2013) inspection practices, reflected in a relative aversion to the use of discretion.

As can be seen in Table 7.2, the expectation was held up in the case of only one of the three discretion types. The table shows the bi-variate correlations between each of the three inspector role orientations and their attitudes towards each of the discretion types. Supporting the expectation, the more an inspector identified with a regulatory monitor role, the less likely he or she was to favor discretion when it came to reporting recordkeeping inconsistencies. The relationship between the regulatory monitor role and the other two types of discretion, while negative in direction, were statistically nonsignificant.

I proposed that inspectors that exhibited a high employee and representative role orientation would be more likely to favor the use of discretion. The expectation was based on the logic that in a context where regulatees pay for program services, greater inspector discretion translates into a more accommodative regulatory approach, giving certifiers a competitive advantage; an

Table 7.2. Associations between inspector role perceptions and attitudes towards discretion

	Interpretive discretion†	*Reporting discretion—recordkeeping*	*Reporting discretion—noncompliances*†
Regulatory monitor	–0.16	–0.21**	–0.09
Employee/representative	0.01	0.04	0.17
Service provider	0.18*	0.24**	0.38***

SOURCE: Replicated from Carter (2017c)
NOTE: *$p<0.10$, **$p<0.05$, ***$p<0.01$; † = survey response scale reversed such that higher values reflect a favorable attitude towards discretion

extension of the Chapter 6 hypothesis that competitive pressures compel certifiers to alter their regulatory practices to attract and retain regulatee-clients. There was a caveat, however, that the expectation might not hold where organizational incentives are aligned with a strict adherence to program rules (Brown, Potoski, and Van Slyke 2006, Considine 2000). The survey data presented earlier in this chapter, particularly data indicating certifiers sanction for deviations from the National Organic Program regulations and enforce ethical inspection standards, suggests that many certifiers indeed align organizational incentives with Program compliance.

The findings of the correlation analysis suggest no relationship between inspectors' employee/representative role orientation and their discretionary attitudes. Although null findings are difficult to interpret, the findings suggest that certifiers may not align organizational incentives with greater discretion, and if they do, organic inspectors' tendency to prioritize their role as a regulatory monitor overrides the influence such incentives might have. Additionally, qualitative interview data provide some evidence that the lack of a relationship may be due, in part, to the clear distinction that the National Organic Program regulations make between certification decisions and inspections. This point is returned to below.

Finally, drawing on regulatory literature showing that inspectors favor cooperative interactions with regulatees over more adversarial relationships, particularly when trust and interdependence between inspectors and regulatees are high (Pautz and Rinfret 2013), I anticipated that inspectors that perceive themselves to be service providers to regulatory clients are more likely to sympathize with regulatee interests and concerns. Such inspectors are therefore more likely to be comfortable exercising judgment, and perhaps flexibility, in the application of regulatory standards. This may be even more expected in the context of organic certification, where many inspectors have been subject to the National Organic Program regulations *themselves* as organic operators and therefore understand the consequences that unfavorable inspection reports can have (Nielsen 2015).

The findings suggest that inspectors inclined to see themselves as assuming a service provide role are more likely to be comfortable with reporting discretion, as the service provider role orientation was positively related with both recordkeeping reporting discretion and noncompliance reporting discretion. The relationships were statistically significant at the $p < 0.05$ level. A relationship between the service provider role orientation and interpretive discretion, although positive in direction, was less robust, as the association was only statistically significant at the $p < 0.10$ level.

Interview data provide additional insight into the findings reported above, as well as evidence of how institutional provisions of the National Organic Program regulations likely shape organic inspectors' perspectives on the use of discretion. First, as noted above, several interviewees followed the regulations in drawing a clear distinction between the role of inspectors in reporting inspection findings and the responsibility of certification personnel to make certification decisions. According to these interviewees, inspectors do not decide whether an issue actually constitutes a noncompliance; rather, they report *potential* issues to certifiers, leaving judgement over whether a noncompliance has occurred up to the certifiers. For example, one inspector stated: "As inspectors we are instructed to report findings rather than make decisions or express opinions." Similarly, another commented: "As an inspector it is important to understand what our role is and what our scope is—I don't make certification decisions."

Second, several inspectors cited the impact of National Organic Program regulation conflict of interest provisions on their inspection responsibilities. Although it was clear that the provisions curtailed the interviewees' willingness to exercise discretion, inspectors raised frustrations that the provisions unnecessarily constrained inspectors' ability to offer information that would aid regulatees' efforts to comply with the regulations. A governmental certifier-employed inspector contrasted his experience conducting organic inspections with that of other types of inspections: "I always feel rather constrained, you know . . . in our other roles, we are allowed to help people, to problem solve, but we can't do that as inspectors for the [National Organic Program]." Another referred to the conflict of interest provisions as a "misfortune" for smaller operations, as inspectors are the "only people that [smaller operations] would ever see from the organic industry," and without inspectors' assistance "they are completely out there on their own." The comments contribute additional evidence to the conflict of interest provisions downsides reported elsewhere in this book.

CONCLUSIONS: ORGANIC INSPECTORS AS INSPECTION INTERMEDIARIES

This chapter examined organic inspectors as the street-level inspection intermediaries of USDA organic certification. Although accredited certifier personnel review organic system plans for compliance with National Organic Program regulations, with the exception of the smallest certifiers, they are rarely the individuals that visit organic farms and handling facilities to ensure plan adherence. Instead, certifiers employ or contract with inspectors with training and expertise in conducting on-site organic standards monitoring. USDA organic certification offers a particularly interesting context for understanding inspectors as the front line of regulatory activity, as it creates a number of conflicting pressures for inspectors to navigate.

Organic Regulation Research Project data provided a rare perspective on organic inspectors' employment arrangements and relationships with employing certifiers. Our survey of 92 organic inspectors found that the majority worked for nongovernmental certifiers; more than three quarters of whom did so on a contract basis. As might be expected, inspectors that worked for governmental and nongovernmental certifiers more-or-less equally mostly did so as contractors, and those that worked for governmental certifiers tended to be employed either full or part time. As contract inspectors tend to work for multiple certifiers, less than half of survey respondents reported working for a single certifier in the preceding year.

Project data also provided valuable insight into the certifier-inspector relationship. Regulatory scholarship suggests that inspection oversight should balance ensuring fidelity in inspectors discretion with overly controlling supervision that handicaps inspectors' ability to attend to unforeseen or unusual conditions (Pires 2011, Scholz 1991)—a balance which may be particularly challenging in a context where many inspectors work for a number of certifiers on a contract basis. Inspector survey findings indicate that most certifiers enforce ethical standards, impose sanctions for deviations from the National Organic Program regulations, and track the practices of their inspectors. The findings further suggest that the most certifiers track their inspectors primarily through reporting paperwork, as survey respondents were split on the extent to which they have contact with certification personnel during the course of inspections and few reported having personnel accompany them during inspections.

Beyond organic inspectors' various employment arrangements and certifier-inspector relationships, the chapter drew on published research to assess how organic inspectors understand their roles and perceive the use of discretion in monitoring USDA organic standards compliance (Carter

2017c). The organic certification context is one in which organic inspectors face a web of obligations and pressures—from their employing certifiers, to the National Organic Program, and the owners of the farms and facilities that they inspect. How inspectors balance those obligations and apply discretion have direct implications for USDA organic certification regulatory fidelity and integrity. Perhaps most evidently, excessive discretion on the part of inspectors may create inconsistencies in how regulatory compliance is monitored and enforced. Furthermore, the manner in which organic inspectors prioritize the potentially conflicting obligations with which they are faced may determine their attitude towards the application of discretion, and therefore, the likelihood that they exercise it.

My analysis found some relationships between organic inspectors' role orientations and their attitudes towards the use of discretion (Carter 2017c). Inspectors that identified more strongly as National Organic Program regulatory monitors were less likely to favor the use of discretion when it comes to reporting recordkeeping problems. In contrast, inspectors that identified more strongly as service providers to organic certification applicants were more open to the use of such reporting discretion and also looked more favorably on the use of discretion when it came to reporting noncompliances.

These relationships notwithstanding, analysis findings by in large suggest inspectors' role orientations and discretionary attitudes likely support organic standards monitoring fidelity and integrity. First, descriptive findings showed that most organic inspectors think of themselves first and foremost as regulatory monitors for the National Organic Program and second as representatives of certifying agents. The role orientation they identified least strongly with was as service providers to organic operations. As importantly, organic inspectors tended to disapprove of the use of discretion, instead favoring a strict interpretation of the National Organic Program regulations and the reporting of all recordkeeping inconsistencies and noncompliance issues. Finally, my analysis indicated no relationship between organic inspectors' identification as representatives to employing certifiers and their attitudes towards discretion—suggesting that even where inspectors feel a greater obligation to their employer than the National Organic Program, the allegiance is not associated with a less stringent approach to their monitoring responsibilities.

This chapters findings thus position organic inspectors as a robust link in the organic certification chain of regulatory authority; one that builds off of prior links' strengths reported in preceding chapters. For example, although the previous chapter's analysis of accredited certifying agents documented apparent inconsistencies in their enforcement actions, I found no evidence that certifiers adjust their regulatory behaviors to attract and retain certification clients. The organic inspector findings recounted in this chapter paint a similarly encouraging picture: certifiers appear to demand ethical behavior from the inspectors they hire and are willing to issue penalties if they deviate from it. Moreover, rather than think of themselves as service providers, most inspectors consider themselves National Organic Program regulatory monitors and oppose deviations from Program regulations. To the extent that the role of organic inspectors is overlooked, as I argued at this chapter's outset, these findings suggest that it may attributable (in part) to the fact that inspectors seem to execute their responsibilities dependably and within the bounds of their professional obligations.

Chapter Eight

A State-Level Enforcement Intermediary

The California State Organic Program

Agricultural and food policy scholar Julie Guthman has observed "California is the birthplace of organic regulation and currently the center of world growth in organic production and consumption" (1998, 137). Of the first part of Guthman's statement there is no doubt: the California–based Rodale Press certification, launched in 1972, was the inspiration and model for other organic certification programs that quickly followed. The accuracy of the latter half is more difficult to assess, given rapidly rising consumer demand beyond U.S. borders in the years since Guthman's statement (PMA Research 2017). Nonetheless, California remains the dominant organic industry and market force in the U.S.: the state accounts for over 20 percent of the domestic certified organic land and almost 40 percent of organic production sales in 2016 (NASS 2017b).

In addition to representing an organic market and industry outlier, California constitutes an unusual regulatory context for organic operations, due in no small part to the California State Organic Program. The State Program is an additional layer of organic standards monitoring and enforcement, situated somewhere in between the National Organic Program and accredited certifying agents. Although several states administer organic certification under state department programs—sometimes under the title of "organic programs"—their authority, responsibilities, and functions are no different than those held by nonprofit and for-profit certifying agents. In contrast, National Organic Program regulation provisions allow for the creation of a state-administered *program* that oversees *all* organic production and handling operations in a state. California is the only state with such a program.

A state program may contain more restrictive organic standards than those outlined by the USDA but is precluded from establishing less restrictive ones.

Importantly, any state program recognized as such (as opposed to simply assuming the role of an accredited certifying agent) *must* assume enforcement responsibility for the National Organic Program regulations; in essence, state organic programs fulfill what, in the terminology of this book, can be thought of as an "enforcement intermediary" role. Utah's Department of Food and Agriculture once operated an approved State Organic Program, however, it terminated the Program in 2009, leaving the California State Organic Program as something of an anomaly within the USDA organic certification regulatory arrangement.

In many ways, the California State Organic Program's history mirrors that of the National Organic Program. For example, the State Program's early years were characterized by oversight and enforcement deficiencies reminiscent of the National Organic Program shortcomings discussed in Chapter 5. Similar to the National Organic Program, the State Program has struggled to balance stringent standards enforcement with the administrative burdens its requirements impose on organic producers and processors. Despite historical shortcomings and challenges, however, the State Program *may* fill important regulatory gaps created by USDA organic certification's administratively decentralized design, thereby supporting National Organic Program regulatory fidelity and integrity.

This chapter first describes the unique function that the California State Organic Program assumes in USDA organic certification, as well as the challenges the Program faced in its early years. Then, because no systematic research has been conducted on the Program to date, I draw on existing publications to discuss the Program's verified burdens and potential benefits. The State Program offers a promising line of inquiry for better understanding the benefits and limitations of state organic programs. It also has the potential to offer theoretical insights regarding multi-layered regulation and the trade-offs of enforcement intermediaries in regulatory administration—a point that is returned to at the end of the chapter.

THE CALIFORNIA STATE ORGANIC PROGRAM: OVERVIEW AND BACKGROUND

The California State Organic Program's origins date back to 1979, when the state passed the California Organic Food Act and became one of the first states to regulate organic food production and sales. The law was amended under the California Organic Products Act of 2003 to comply with the Organic Foods Production Act and National Organic Program regulations. That same year, the California Department of Food and Agriculture (CDFA) petitioned the USDA for recognition of a state program to oversee organic production and handling operations in California. The application was approved in 2004, and California became the first state to assume enforcement of USDA organic standards.

The State Program is administered by the CDFA's Inspection Services Division, which shares oversight responsibilities with the California Department of Public Health (CDPH). The CDFA is charged with regulating fresh organic products, while the CDPH regulates processed organic products. In addition to dedicated staff composed of special investigators and office administrators, the State Program contracts with county agricultural commissioners to conduct county-level inspection and enforcement. Exceptions are made for Marin, Monterey, and Yolo counties due to conflict of interest concerns stemming from the counties' certification programs. The State Program is advised by the California Organic Products Advisory Committee, a fifteen-member advisory board analogous to a state-level NOSB. Advisory Committee members are appointed by the California Secretary of Food and Agriculture and advise the State Program on a range of functions, from reserve fund amounts to Program registration forms (Damewood and Sooby 2015).

The State Program requires that any producer or processor wishing to market and sell products as organic in California register and pay registration fees (in addition to being certified by an accredited certifying agent). The registration requirement extends to operations exempt from certification by the National Organic Program because they made less than $5,000 a year in organic product sales (Damewood, 2018), meaning that even exempt organic operations fall under standards-enforcement oversight in California. State Program registration requirements create an additional layer of administrative burden for California organic operators, a point that until recently attracted considerable discontentment, as discussed later in this section.

With limited exceptions, organic standards enforcement in California is carried out by the State Program or by county-level inspectors contracted by the Program (Damewood and Sooby 2015). This includes managing Program registrations, carrying out unscheduled on-site "spot" inspections of organic operations, conducting inspections at farmers' markets, taking samples for chemical residue testing, and investigating fraudulent organic sales investigations. Enforcement actions carried out under the State Program mirror those of the National Organic Program. Minor noncompliance issues are responded to with notices of noncompliance and unresolved or more serious noncompliances may warrant certification suspension or revocation. Any of these actions may be initiated by a certifier, a county agricultural commissioner's office, or the State Program. Civil penalties might be assessed in the case of non-certified produce fraudulently represented as organic.

Early Deficiencies in State Program Regulatory Oversight

Although the California State Organic Program has operated continuously since its approval in 2004, for several years it failed to do so in compliance with National Organic Program requirements. The 2004 OIG review of National Organic Program oversight (discussed in Chapter 5) found that the State Program was approved despite lacking the required compliance and enforcement procedures because the National Organic Program "wanted to allow California the opportunity to operate and develop procedures as they progressed" (2005, 14). A subsequent 2005 on-site review found required procedures still lacking, including those related to handling complaints of fraudulent organic products, initiating complaint investigations, conducting regulatory compliance surveillance, issuing noncompliances, and referring disputes to mediation and appeals proceedings. The National Organic Program neglected to issue the report to the CDFA, however, meaning that the State Program was never administered a corrective action mandate. The OIG Report cited the National Organic Program's then-director as crediting the omission to "other priorities," including a lawsuit that had been filed against the National Organic Program.

According to a follow-up 2009 OIG review, it was not until 2008 that the State Program initiated efforts to address the missing required procedures in the form concerted moves to standardize enforcement communications and procedures. A major component in these efforts was the Program's *Quality Systems Manual*—a policy document outlining uniform procedures for processing registrations, conducting investigations and residue sampling, and carrying out enforcement actions, among other administrative tasks. At the time of the OIG review, the changes had yet to be fully implemented. For example, a key finding of the OIG's 2009 Report was that the State Program had failed to track the number of organic-related complaints received by the CDFA since 2004. As stated in the Report (2010, 15):

> This problem, which the [National Organic Program] had been aware of since the 2005 review, makes it impossible for either [the OIG] or the [National Organic Program] to evaluate how CDFA is tracking and resolving complaints—a key component in evaluating the overall effectiveness of the [State Organic Program].

The State Program continued its efforts to address regulatory inadequacies after the 2009 follow-up OIG Report, including full implementation of the *Quality Systems Manual.* In 2013 the Program launched an online database to automate and consolidate Program registrations, complaints investigations, inspections and sampling, and noncompliance enforcement actions. A subsequent 2015 review of the State Program by the National Organic Program found that the more glaring procedural deficiencies had been addressed. In September of 2016 National Organic Program Deputy Administrator Miles McEvoy issued a letter reauthorizing the California State Organic Program. That same year witnessed a major Program update initiated by state legislation, intended to address long-standing complaints that the program imposed unnecessarily onerous burdens on California organic producers and processors, as described in the following section.

THE BURDENS AND BENEFITS OF THE CALIFORNIA STATE ORGANIC PROGRAM

In September of 2016, California Governor Jerry Brown signed the California Organic Food and Farming Act into law, representing the first update to California organic law in over a decade. Among the contributing authors and major proponents of the Act was prominent California-based accredited certifier CCOF, a long-time critic of the additional burdens that State Program registration requirements and fees impose upon California organic producers and processors. These criticisms were most clearly spelled out in the 2015 *Review of the California State Organic Program,* co-authored by CCOF Policy Director Kelly Damewood and CCOF Policy Specialist Jane Sooby. In the next subsection I summarize *Review*'s central complaints and subsequent State Program changes adopted by passage of the California Organic Food and Farming Act. A discussion of State Program benefits follows.

Regulatory Layering and the Challenge of State Program Administrative Burden

The CCOF *Review* outlined three central concerns (Damewood and Sooby 2015). The first was that State Program imposed duplicate fees on California organic operations. For example, producer registration fees ranged from $25 for an operation with up to $3,000 in annual organic product sales to $5,000 for those with $25 million or more. The fees were considered duplicative in the sense that organic operations pay them in addition to certification fees charged by accredited certifiers. The second concern was that the State Program imposed unnecessary reporting and verification burdens on California organic operations. Among the requirements that the *Review* highlighted as problematic are operational details, such as acreage, yield, and sales data, which are not required by the National Organic Program, but can translate to considerable costs for operations to compile. Furthermore, the *Review* points out that other Program reporting requirements reflect information already collected by certifiers. The reporting requirements were particularly burdensome for smaller diversified organic operations (those selling a range of organically produced product types), according to the *Review.*

Finally, the *Review* claimed that the State Program's fee-based enforcement activities were unjustified under the regulatory framework of USDA organic certification, citing overlap between State Program functions and those of accredited certifiers and the National Organic Program, as well as other California state regulatory bodies. As one example, the *Review* pointed out that residue testing constituted a significant State Program expenditure but was already carried out by certifiers under National Organic Program requirements, in addition to the testing routinely conducted by the California Department of Pesticide Regulation. Another example was the fact that the State Program fulfilled responsibilities that were mandated of the National Organic Program, such as fraudulent sales investigations.

It appears that the 2016 California Organic Food and Farming Act sought to address the first two concerns, but not the third. First, the Act allows accredited certifier to forward their clients' information, rather than requiring the operations to compile and submit paperwork to the State Program. Second, the Act caps the Program's fees and reduces the fees of some smaller operations that gross less than $250,000 annually in organic sales. In addition, the Act amends the State Program role to allow the California Secretary of Food and Agriculture and California Organic Products Advisory Committee to support organic agriculture in the state through programs such as education and outreach. It's likely that the Act omitted revisions to the State Program's enforcement role (the *Review*'s third concern) due to the National Organic Program regulation requirement that approved state programs assume USDA standards enforcement responsibility. Furthermore, the State Program's enforcement activities are held up by some as important benefits, as discussed below.

As is the case with the National Organic Program's Sound and Sensible initiative, it is too early to tell the extent to which the recent legislative changes have addressed critics' concerns with the California State Organic Program. Unsurprisingly, CCOF celebrated passage of the California Organic Food and Farming Act as "[reducing] unnecessary burdens for organic producers while ensuring a sensible regulatory framework to support the integrity of organic production in California" (CCOF 2018a). Others echoed the sentiment. For example, on the food journalism blog *The New Food Economy,* Lara McCaffrey (2016) claimed it would allow California agriculture to "free itself from this bureaucratic remnant and resume its rightful place as reliably one step ahead." The change has seemed to have calmed criticisms of the State Program, as least for time being, and strengthened claims regarding the Program's benefits.

California State Organic Program Benefits

Although the California State Organic Program's administrative burdens long drew criticisms from the California organic community, some community members are quick to highlight the Program's benefits. Among the clearer articulations of Program benefits is a 2018 *Journal of Food Law & Policy* article entitled "Strengthening the National Organic Program with State Organic Programs," written by CCOF Policy Director Kelly Damewood—a co-author on the aforementioned 2015 *Review of the California State Organic Program.* The premise of the article is that while the California State Organic Program has its drawbacks, these costs are outweighed by the Program's benefits.

Importantly, Damewood's (2018) argument is backed by assertions, rather than evidence, leaving the argument's empirical validity unsubstantiated. The argument also extends well beyond the scope of any existing data against which it could be empirically tested. Nonetheless, among the benefits that Damewood attributes to the State Program are a number of theoretically significant factors that suggest the California State Organic Program may contribute to USDA organic certification regulatory fidelity and integrity—at least within California's geographic boundaries. These factors include State Program funding stability, local enforcement personnel and legal authority, and regulatory enforcement depth and scope that extend beyond that exercised by the National Organic Program in important manners.

Damewood's claimed benefit of State Program funding rests on the relative stability it represents and the that it can be dedicated entirely to USDA standards enforcement. Congressional budget appropriations funding of the National Organic Program have proven unreliable and consistently fall short of the demands reflected in the Program's many responsibilities, ranging from carrying out investigations, to USDA organic standards enforcement actions and accreditation oversight of certifiers. The California State Organic Program, in contrast, funds the majority of its operations through registration fees. In addition to not being subject to the political forces that shape National Organic Program funding (thereby creating a more reliable funding stream), State Program revenue has proved more than adequate for Program functions, as the Program has historically carried a sizeable surplus for years at a time. For example, the CCOF *Review* indicates that the Program took in over \$2.22 million in fiscal year 2013–2014, while reporting \$1.96 million in expenditures, resulting in a surplus of over \$250,000 (Damewood and Sooby 2015). In 2017 the Program's reserve fund held about \$3 million (Damewood 2018, 136).

A second State Program benefit Damewood outlines comprises "localized" regulatory activity in the form of state-level enforcement personnel and legal authority. National Organic Program enforcement requires Washington, DC-based personnel to investigate potential regulatory violations remotely, travel to a complaint location, or coordinate with state department of agriculture staff. Enforcement under the California State Organic Program, in contrast, is carried out by trained State Program investigators or contracted county-based regulatory personnel, offering "boots on the ground enforcement to quickly investigate and resolve compliance issues or complaints of fraud" (Damewood 2018, 125). When it comes to legal action, such as appeals and mediation proceedings, Damewood claims state-level authority allows for greater efficiency when compared to the "backlogged federal system."

Finally, Damewood claims that USDA standards enforcement by the California State Organic Program is more stringent in nature and broader in scope than that carried out by the National Organic Program. Among the stronger elements of the claim is the fact that State Program USDA organic standards enforcement extends to noncertified California operations. According to the National Organic Program regulations, any operation that earns less than $5,000 a year in organic product sales is exempt from certification requirements, meaning that they are not subject to certifier oversight or regular monitoring and enforcement. The State Program, however, maintains a database of noncertified organic operations and their production information, and includes them in State Program-administered oversight in the form of investigations and residue testing.

The State Program also carries out what Damewood refers to as "organic marketplace surveillance," in the form of unannounced spot inspections and residue sampling. For example, according to the CCOF *Review* the State Program conducted 228 residue sample tests in 2015, 34 (15%) of which came back positive for pesticide residues (Damewood and Sooby 2015, 24). To reduce the regulatory overlap between the State Program and accredited certifiers, the Program prioritizes surveillance of noncertified operations, such as through farmers' market inspections. The Program's authority, however, extends to certified operations. Determining the extent of the Program's market surveillance activity beyond the aforementioned residue testing is precluded by a lack of available data—a point discussed further in the following consideration of State Program implications.

CONCLUSION: THE CALIFORNIA STATE ORGANIC PROGRAM AS ENFORCEMENT INTERMEDIARY

On the basis of the preceding discussion, the California State Organic Program holds the potential to both compound challenges of USDA organic certification's already complex regulatory design *and* address some of its limitations. The State Program creates added barriers to effective regulatory enforcement coordination through responsibilities and functions that overlap with those of the National Organic Program and accredited certifiers—the layers of authority between which the State Program is sandwiched. Furthermore, the State Program saddles California organic producers and processors with the added costs that stem from a state-level layer of regulatory oversight.

As discussed in Chapter 5, quasi-voluntary programs such as organic certification face the challenge of balancing standards enforcement stringency, on one hand, with the costs that program requirement impose on program participants, on the other. Without stringent standards and enforcement, program participation loses its value. However, overly burdensome costs due to program stringency detract from the benefits that firms derive from program participation—and in the worst-case scenario, may drive away potential participants. In California, the challenge is compounded by the State Program. Chapter 5 documented National Organic Program efforts to reduce the administrative burdens associated with USDA organic certification through the Sound and Sensible initiative. As discussed above, a similar progression has taken place at the California State Organic Program, although through different mechanisms; whereas National Organic Program efforts are reflected in a Program-led administrative initiative, administrative burdens reductions at the California State Organic Program were spurred by the local organic community and enacted through legislation.

While it is impossible to determine from existing data the extent to which the State Program's additional burdens have impeded USDA organic certification uptake, the costs have not stopped California from consistently ranking as the most productive state organic industry in the country. Indeed, California led the country with $2.9 billion in organic sales in 2016, accounting for 38 percent of the U.S. organic market (NASS 2017a). The state also exhibits the largest share of the nation's certified organic acreage and farms. Taking into account the state's robust organic industry, it seems safe to say that if the California State Organic Program has impeded organic production or certification, the impact has most likely been born by smaller operations that make up a narrow slice of the state's overall organic products and sales volume. Future research should seek to determine the extent to which the 2016 California Organic Food and Farming Act has facilitated more organic operations obtaining USDA organic certification, and in particular, whether the changes brought about by the Act have lowered the barrier for small-scale operations.

The State Program's added layer of regulatory oversight may constitute a net-benefit for USDA organic standards enforcement, especially if the

2016 California Organic Food and Farming Act changes are successful at reducing Program–imposed administrative burdens. Stable and dedicated enforcement funding, localized enforcement personnel and legal authority, and enforcement activities that fill in some of the regulatory gaps created by USDA organic certification's decentralized design likely contribute to National Organic Program regulatory fidelity and integrity. The extent to which this is the case, however, is an open question and one that offers regulatory scholars a promising opportunity for future research. As with the National Organic Program's failure to compile and publish notice of noncompliance data, transparent reporting of California State Organic Program enforcement activities, actions, and determinations would facilitate research regarding the Program's impact on USDA organic standards enforcement—thereby providing an empirical assessment of Damewood's (2018) claim that the State Program benefits the organic sector, as a whole.

Regardless of the increased fidelity and integrity that the California State Organic Program *might* bring to organic standards enforcement in California, an obvious limitation of the Program's impact is that its actions are confined to within state boundaries. While making up a significant portion of U.S. organic food market, as noted earlier, it is still only covers a fraction of the organic products produced in the country. Damewood (2015) argues that other states should develop their own state organic programs. Considering the political and administrative capital this would undoubtedly entail, as well as the conflict-of-interest complications that would arise in states that already operate state certification programs, it seems unlikely many will.

A central theme of this book is the variety of organizations involved in the administration and enforcement of USDA organic certification. The State Program adds another actor category to entities introduced in preceding chapters, including rule-making intermediaries, third-party administrator intermediaries, and inspection intermediaries. The chapter's discussion illustrates that enforcement intermediaries such as the State Program cannot be assumed to play either a constructive or detrimental role in decentralized regulatory administration. Rather, a deeper understanding of enforcement intermediary influence will need to systematically weigh their costs and benefits to determine their net impacts. Such research promises productive lines of inquiry aimed at better understanding regulation in multi-level arrangements characterized by delegated authority. Still other entities work to support the integrity of USDA organic standards enforcement; the following chapter discusses two supporting actor types—professional association coordination intermediaries and organic materials review information intermediaries—and the integral roles they play in U.S. organic certification.

Chapter Nine

Coordinating and Information Intermediaries

Professional Associations and Materials Review Organizations

Organic certification grew from roots of informal association and nongovernmental coordination. As recounted in this book's chapter chronicling the history of U.S. organic certification, beginning with the organic farmers associations that organized to self-regulate in the 1970s, collective action characterized many of the certification programs that predated federal-level intervention. In the words of Brian Obach (2015, 56): "A key factor at this stage of organic's development is that organic farmers themselves were setting the standards through their associations." David and Rebecca Nowacek (2008, 411) find the term "associations" to be more than descriptive in the organic certification context, citing Schmitter and Streeck (1985, 17) on the sociological concept of associations:

> [A]rrangements under which an attempt is made to make associative, self-interested collective action contribute to the achievement of public policy objectives. In generic terms, this is the case where it is in the interest of an organized group to strive for a "categoric good" which is partially compatible or identical with a "collective good" for the society as a whole.

Given these foundations, it is perhaps unsurprising that associations and nongovernmental organizations continue to play pivotal roles in organic food governance. For, although the regulation of organic food has fallen under the National Organic Program's purview for over a decade and a half, the Program nonetheless relies on independent nongovernmental coordination that falls outside of its formal scope of authority. In organizing for the "categorical" goals of addressing critical gaps in the National Organic Program's institutional design, self-coordinated associations serve the "collective good" of buttressing USDA organic certification fidelity.

A first example of National Organic Program reliance on external, "unauthorized" nongovernmental action is found in the IOIA and ACA—voluntary professional associations of organic inspector and accredited certifier cohorts, respectively. Just as early organic farmers coordinated to share information, harmonize early organic standards, and advocate shared interests, organic inspectors and accredited certifying agents coordinate to work across individual and organizational boundaries. The second example of National Organic Program reliance on external, unauthorized nongovernmental action is found in entities generally referred to in the organic industry as "material review organizations." Material review organizations, including the Organic Materials Review Institute (OMRI), the WSDA Materials Review Program, and the CDFA Organic Input Materials Program, emerged to fill what one author refers to as a "fundamental flaw" (Stemwedel 2009) in USDA organic certification: the National Organic Program's inability to regulate organic input materials.

Professional associations and materials review organizations are not incorporated in the 1990 Organic Foods Production Act nor the National Organic Program regulations, and thus hold no formal USDA-delegated regulatory authority. Nonetheless, the functions that they perform bring them well within the definition of regulatory intermediaries, as actors that act in conjunction with regulatory authorities to achieve regulatory goals. When considered within a regulator-intermediary-target conceptualization of USDA organic certification, professional associations are best thought of as "coordinating intermediaries"—their missions reflect attempts to facilitate information sharing, relationships, and interactions that support the effectiveness of the organic regulation system. Materials review organizations, in turn, are "information intermediaries"; their missions are narrower in scope and their functions consist of providing uniform and credible information to organic certification regulatory actors and certified organic operations, alike.

This chapter examines the roles of USDA organic certification coordinating and information intermediaries. The first section centers on the IOIA and ACA. Drawing on published research (Carter and Mahallati 2017) it assesses the scope of professional association coordination, suggesting that while the IOIA and ACA contribute to the fidelity of USDA organic standards administration, they likely have less direct impact on regulatory integrity. The second section centers on organic materials review organizations. The topic of organic input materials review—the process of determining whether an agricultural input product complies with the USDA organic standards and thus can be used in organic food production or processing—has yet to be subjected to systematic empirical research. Nonetheless, available evidence suggests that the effectiveness and impact of materials review organizations has been handicapped by elements of USDA organic certification regulatory design. The chapter closes with an assessment of coordinating and information intermediary impacts and limitations, and a discussion of opportunities for future research.

PROFESSIONAL ASSOCIATIONS AS ORGANIC CERTIFICATION COORDINATING INTERMEDIARIES

Professional associations are nongovernmental groups, usually taking the form of 501(c) nonprofit organizations under the U.S. tax code, initiated to support a specific industry or profession (Gazley 2014, Montagna 1968). Although professional association services vary, they typically focus on facilitating some sort of collective action, from compiling and disseminating industry-relevant information to enforcing professional codes of conduct (Greenwood, Suddaby, and Hinings 2002, Rusaw 1995). In realm of public administration, professional associations have been highlighted as key "implementation resources," helping public service administrators and personal develop a shared vision regarding the goals, priorities, and directives of the program in question. As stated by Hill (2003, 269): "When implementers ask, 'What does policy X say? What does it want?' . . . they might turn to a professional association or newsletter for relevant information."

As discussed throughout this book, aligning the objectives and actions of diverse intermediary bodies towards regulatory fidelity and integrity is an inherent challenge created by USDA organic certification's administratively decentralized design. Organic certification professional associations are among the key entities that have emerged to help meet this challenge. The IOIA has long been considered the authoritative organic inspector professional association and the ACA is the only recognized professional association for accredited organic certifiers.

I have hinted at the integral roles that the IOIA and ACA play in USDA organic certification throughout some of the preceding chapters. For example, Chapter 8 foreshadowed the IOIA's central contributions to organic inspector preparation and training. Similarly, the ACA's response to charges of USDA organic standards development and enforcement inadequacies was recounted in Chapter 4. In this chapter, I look directly at organic certification professional association roles and functions, drawing on a study I published with Nadia Mahallati (2017), in which we examined the extent to which the IOIA and ACA contribute to organic standards regulatory fidelity, program feedback, and regulatory integrity. We posited a spectrum of potential professional association contributions in an administratively decentralized regulatory context, characterized as four function categories. Listed from less- to more-influential, these included:

- providing education and training, disseminating National Organic Program-relevant information, and fostering knowledge sharing within organic certifier and inspector cohorts;
- establishing and encouraging shared understandings of National Organic Program aims and directives;
- serving as collective representation bodies through which organic certifiers and inspectors can convey information to the National Organic Program regarding regulatory performance and challenges, and;
- enforcing standards for appropriate organic certifier and inspector behavior through professional codes of conduct.

In the mode of case study research, our analysis reviewed evidence from several sources. First, we gathered materials regarding the IOIA's and ACA's missions and histories from their websites and publicly available documents. Second, we analyzed interviews from the Organic Regulation Research Project for their relevance to IOIA and ACA activities and impacts, ultimately drawing on eighteen interviews. Interviewees included a National Organic Program representative, an organic certification consultant, a representative of the ACA, three organic inspectors, and twelve accredited certifier representatives. Finally, we drew relevant survey data from two Organic Regulation Research Project surveys: the inspector survey introduced in Chapter 7 and a survey of accredited certifier representatives (see the Methodological Appendix for details).

Our findings suggested that the IOIA and ACA are both essential information and education resources for organic certification intermediaries and the ACA serves as key feedback mechanisms by which information is conveyed to the National Organic Program. We concluded, however, that their roles likely have a greater impact on regulatory fidelity—the consistency with which USDA organic standards are administered—than the integrity of organic standards enforcement. A discussion of our analysis leading to these conclusions is presented below, following descriptive overviews of the IOIA and ACA.

The International Organic Inspectors Association

Founded in 1991 by a group of organic inspectors "who recognized the need for uniform inspector processes and protocols to build inspector skills and promote public confidence" (IOIA n.d.), the IOIA is a voluntary professional association of 243 organic livestock, crop, and processing inspectors, 172 of which are based in the U.S. (as of August 2018). The IOIA welcomes supporting members from individuals and organizations from across the organic industry, including accredited certifiers, organic production consultants, and organic product businesses. Supported by a small staff and volunteer Board of Directors, the IOIA's mission is "to address issues and concerns relevant to organic inspectors, to provide quality inspector training, and to promote consistency and integrity in the organic certification process" (IOIA n.d.).

The IOIA's primary function is to provide training for both new and experienced organic inspectors. This is realized through the IOIA Training Institute's domestic and international inspector training, webinars, and other online resources. Each year, hundreds of new and working inspectors are trained through basic, intermediate, advanced, and custom training courses. Non-members are allowed to participate in IOIA training; however, only members are listed in the member directory and have access to the IOIA's online discussion forum (IOIA 2016b). The IOIA offers inspector accreditation, a credential that can be considered a step above training certificates, for qualified inspectors with at least two years of experience. According to the IOIA's database, twenty inspectors were accredited as of 2018.

The IOIA publishes a newsletter, *The Inspectors' Report*, four times a year. The *Report* offers regulator IOIA updates, training announcements, articles on changes in the organic sector and regulations, and features a regular column on genetic engineering in agriculture. For example, the fall 2016 issue of the Report included updates regarding online resources released by the National Organic Program for organic producers and processors, a notice regarding a Program call for comments on draft regulatory guidance documents, and advanced livestock inspection training, co-sponsored with the organic certifying agent Midwest Organic Services Association (IOIA 2016a). The issue's genetic engineering column commented on how the recently passed National Bioengineered Food Disclosure Law was expected to intersect with organic regulations, clarifying that USDA certified organic products were not expected to carry any additional labeling to comply with the new Law.

Finally, the IOIA requires members adhere to the IOIA Code of Ethics and Code of Conduct and has a procedure in place for investigating possible violations (IOIA 2001). Compliance with these Codes is necessary for IOIA membership, and a complaint procedure is in place to investigate allegations of misconduct (IOIA 2003). According to the procedure, potential punishments from the Ethics Committee and approved by the Executive Committee range from a letter of reprimand to membership revocation.

The Accredited Certifiers Association

Established in 2005, the ACA is a voluntary professional association of fifty-three accredited certifier members, forty-three of which are headquartered in the U.S. (as of August 2018). Another nineteen supporting members are entities involved in other aspects of the organic industry, from organic consultant agencies to materials review organizations. Under the guidance of the ACA Coordinator and volunteer Board of Directors, the ACA's mission is:

> [T]o ensure consistent implementation of USDA Organic Regulations through collaboration and education of accredited certification agencies. Purposes include, developing uniform criteria for implementation of the USDA National Organic Program, certifier training, support and networking opportunities and being a forum for discussion of issues impacting organic certification. (ACA 2018)

The ACA offers a number of services in support of its mission and purposes. It convenes working groups to address regulatory and certification challenges, such as by resolving contested regulatory gray areas or developing preferred practices for certification procedures not expressly detailed in NOP regulations. Working group determinations are offered to ACA members in the form of Guidance Documents or ACA Best Practices White Papers. For example, 2017 working group topics included best practices for GMO sampling, verifying supply chain traceability, assessment of natural resources and biodiversity, and guidance on inspector qualifications. Working group determinations also often provide the basis for ACA comments to the National Organic Program and NOSB. The 2014 letter of support to Secretary of Agriculture Thomas Vilsack is one example (see Chapter 4), although comments often pertain to more specific topics, such as providing feedback on National Organic Program draft guidance, from organic–conventional product comingling and contamination to the use of chlorine in organic practices.

Perhaps the most visible of the ACA's activities is a combined annual meeting held in conjunction with the National Organic Program's annual staff training, during which members receive education regarding changes in the organic sector and the latest guidance on administering USDA organic standards. The ACA also produces a bimonthly newsletter, *The ACA Guidewire*, that compiles information regarding ongoing National Organic Program activities and initiatives, alerts members to NOSB deliberations (e.g., regarding suggested amendments to the National List of Allowed and Prohibited Substances), and outlines ACA policy positions and associated interactions with the National Organic Program. For example, the December 2016 *Guidewire* featured a summary of Program updates and regulatory change recommendations issued at the fall 2016 meeting of the NOSB (ACA 2016b).

Finally, the ACA maintains a Code of Conduct, which is expressly concerned with matters such as consistent implementation of national organic standards, information exchange, and the reporting of regulatory noncompliance and suspected fraud issues (ACA 2011). However, there does not appear to be an established procedure for filing potential Code violation complaints, as discussed in greater detail later in this section.

The Prospects and Limitations of Professional Associations in USDA Organic Certification

Our examination found the scope of the ACA's influence on USDA organic standards administration to extend beyond that of the IOIA (Carter and Mahallati 2017). While both associations appear essential for their respective cohorts' education and training, we concluded that the ACA also actively helped to generate a shared understanding regarding National Organic Program implementation and constitutes a key collective-representation body and feedback channel to the Program. Our analysis suggested that differences in the associations' scopes of influence are likely due to the responsibilities and limitations placed on their respective member bodies: certifiers are responsible for translating NOP regulations into operational procedures and regulatory practices, setting subsequent organizational policies, and making regulatory decisions; inspectors, in contrast, are constrained by National Organic Program regulations to documenting and reporting possible regulatory violations to certifiers (as discussed in Chapter 7).

Study findings suggested that the IOIA's function, albeit limited, is essential for the effective administration of USDA organic standards, as organic inspector training is limited to two sources: employing certifier organizations and the IOIA (Scoles 2013). In other words, the IOIA is the only credible source of training for contract inspectors (the majority of organic inspectors in the data presented in Chapter 7). As stated by one contract inspector interviewee: "I don't have the resources available to me that someone that is an in-house inspector or staff inspector. The only real choice for me was to learn the [National Organic Program] rule was to take IOIA courses." Certifier personnel interviewees were quick to recognize the IOIA's value and most attested to sending inspector employees to the IOIA. One inspector interviewee summed up general sentiments towards the IOIA when he referred to IOIA training as the industry "gold standard." In addition, IOIA materials are a valuable tool for inspectors in the field; 46 percent of surveyed inspectors reported "usually" or "always" relying on them during inspections.

Just as the IOIA is an essential resource for organic inspectors seeking education and training, the ACA appears to be a key resource for certifiers pursuing education, organic standards information, and the knowledge and experiences of other certifiers. In the process, the ACA seems to foster a collective interpretation and vision for USDA organic standards administration. For example, when queried on the effectiveness of the ACA's training regarding the National Organic Program regulations, 90 percent of certifier representative survey respondents indicated that the training is either "effective" or "very effective." Ninety-three percent of respondents indicated that the ACA is either effective or very effective at "providing a forum for discussion of issues impacting organic certification" and 94 percent indicated that it is either effective or very effective at providing networking opportunities for certifiers. A smaller percentage, although still a majority at 77 percent, indicated that the ACA is either effective or very effective at "developing uniform criteria for National Organic Program implementation."

Among the ACA services identified in interviews with certifier personnel, one stood out as especially valuable: an interactive online Listserv through which certifiers would pose and answer questions to one-another regarding the certification process. For example, an interviewee from a smaller nongovernmental certifier commented: "[the Listserv] helps keep you, I think, sharp, and up to date." Reflecting on the utility of reviewing the Listserv archive, a representative from a large nongovernmental certifier remarked: "sometimes you know I don't have time to read the emails in depth, but I can remember—oh yeah, there was something on maple syrup so now I can go back and look at it and actually have that information." Yet another interviewee summed up the Listserv's function with the statement:

> What the ACA Listserv does is it really helps to balance the playing field as far as information goes to ensure that each certifier is, on a daily basis, implementing the same protocols or judgment calls regarding the regulations as the other certifiers. What you see a lot of times is larger certifiers advising the smaller certifiers.

On the Listserv's ability to foster a shared understanding of organic standards administration, an administrator from a smaller state department certifier commented:

> There's [sic] things I have been doing for 15 or 20 years—I've been looking at the rule, and I'll see a post and think 'Oh, here's something I have never thought of' and it might change my whole interpretation and how I am looking at the issue. So it's really, really helpful in generating consensus.

The ACA's program feedback function is illustrated in the previously-referenced communications from the ACA to the USDA, National Organic Program, and the NOSB. Certifier representative interviewees were quick to note the utility of ACA-to-National Organic Program feedback, and one explicitly characterized the ACA as a "feedback channel" to the Program. Another commented that a single certifier is unlikely to catch the Program's attention, but "if there's five or six certifiers our size or larger, that absolutely is going to carry some weight, by going through the ACA." In addition to channeling program feedback, the ACA serves as collective representation to certifiers in political and policy matters, as articulated by a long-time administrator of a mid-sized governmental certifier:

> I went to all the early meetings of the ACA when it formed, and I saw it as a way for certifiers, especially the private certifiers, to make sure that their interests were represented when the [National Organic Program] actually implemented the certification and accreditation systems.

The preceding evidence offers strong indication that the IOIA and ACA fulfill critical functions that support consistency in USDA organic standards administration, therefore contributing to National Organic Program fidelity. Our research found only limited evidence, however, that the professional associations *directly* buttresses the Program's regulatory integrity.[1] For example, although 75 percent of surveyed certifier representatives indicated that the ACA is either effective or very effective at ensuring the integrity of U.S. organic certification, no qualitative interviewee data corroborated the statistic beyond the ACA's collective understanding function described above. Neither Associations' Codes of Conducts were referenced in the interviews, nor were monitoring and sanctioning for unethical behavior.

The extent to which the education and information sharing functions of the IOIA and ACA, as well as the ACA's shared understanding development and program feedback functions, *indirectly* support the regulatory integrity of USDA organic certification is difficult to tell from the evidence presented here. The survey data referenced immediately above suggests that they do, to an unknown extent. Regardless of the IOIA's and ACA's ethical standards reach, providing credible education and training, disseminating National Organic Program–relevant information, and facilitating knowledge transfer within certifier and inspector cohorts are vital functions in the realm of regulatory administration, where "expertise and operational capacities . . . are of paramount importance" (Abbott, Levi-Faur, and Snidal 2017b, 22).

The role of supplying credible information, while clearly performed by the IOIA and ACA as organic certification coordinating intermediaries (Carter and Mahallati 2017), is the express goal of organic materials review organizations. These information intermediaries are the focus of the next section. A chapter summary and conclusion follows.

MATERIALS REVIEW ORGANIZATIONS AS ORGANIC CERTIFICATION INFORMATION INTERMEDIARIES

As outlined in Chapter 4, the materials that go into agricultural production are of central concern when it comes to determining whether a product is produced according to USDA organic standards. For crop production, input materials include fertilizers, soil and soil aids, pesticides, and pest control materials. For livestock production, they include medications and feed supplements and additives. For processing and handling operations, they include processing aids, sanitizers, and facility pest-control materials. Regardless of the operation type, the materials and substances used by a certified organic operation must be approved by the operation's certifier as compliant with the National Organic Program regulations.

According to an ACA white paper (2010), it was widely believed that implementation of the 1990 Organic Foods Production Act would address review of input materials. This was not the case. While National Organic Program regulations contain the National List of Allowed and Prohibited Substances, whether manufactured input products, such as a brand name fertilizer or pesticide, meet National List requirements is left to each individual certifier to decide, resulting in a duplication of material review across certifiers. Furthermore, although many accredited certifiers maintain internal lists of approved input materials, most are not publicly available, contributing to producer and processor uncertainty and resulting in inconsistencies between certifiers' lists. Perhaps most concerning from the perspective of regulatory fidelity, inconsistencies in certifier lists incentivizes certifier shopping, as organic certification applicants may go from certifier to certifier, looking for one that will allow them to use a particular material (ACA 2010, Sircely 2011).

In response to the need for clear and credible review and identification of approved organic input materials and products, organic materials review organizations have emerged as brokers of organic materials advice. The National Organic Program defines materials review organizations as "entit[ies] with expertise in verifying compliance of production and handling materials with the [USDA] organic regulations" (2016b, 1). Two materials review organizations are historically recognized as credible within the organic industry and organic certification system: OMRI and the WSDA Organic Program's Materials Registration Program.[2] A third, the CDFA's Organic Input Material Program, was implemented in 2012. While OMRI, the CDFA, and the WSDA are recognized (to varying degrees), as legitimate USDA organic certification information intermediaries, prominent actors within the organic industry and organic certification community have long called for their institutionalization in the organic certification system and USDA oversight. Such calls notwithstanding, to date they continue to fall outside of the National Organic Program's authority to regulate.

The following section first describes OMRI, the WSDA's Materials Registration Program, and the CDFA Organic Input Material Program. It then discusses the challenges of formal institutionalization of materials review activity. Organic materials review organizations have received little scholarly attention to date; consequently, the little information that is available on them comes primarily from documentation published by the organizations themselves. As is discussed below, this positions materials review organizations as a promising line of future inquiry, both in terms of their empirical influence on U.S. organic certification and regarding the theoretical implications of similar "information intermediaries" in decentralized regulatory arrangements.

OMRI

Of the documentation publicly available, OMRI's website provides the most detailed account of its background and development. The organization's origins date back to the passage of the 1990 Organic Foods Production Act, when certifiers CCOF, Oregon Tilth, and the Organic Crop Improvement Association coordinated with the Organic Trade Association to create an organic input review program. As recounted by OMRI (2018a): "These groups viewed the development of a single resource specializing in input review and materials evaluation as an important step towards implementing a uniform standard." Officially founded in 1997, OMRI developed its first input recommendations under the guidance of an expert advisory council and with funding from a range of entities, including: certifiers CCOF, Oregon Tilth, and the Organic Crop Improvement Association; the Organic Trade Association; the Organic Farming Research Foundation; the Association for Regional Agriculture Building Local Economy; the Human Society, and; private businesses Newman's Own Organics, Whole Foods, and Smuckers. OMRI's first input list, the *OMRI Generic Materials List,* was published in 1998. Several months later, it published its first product-specific list, the *OMRI Brand Name Products List* (later renamed the *OMRI Products List*).

With its foundation predating National Organic Program implementation, OMRI contributed to the development of the USDA organic standards through Technical Advisory Panel reports to the NOSB from 1999 to 2002. It received ISO 65 accreditation (now ISO 17065) from the USDA in 2008, recognizing its conformity with standards for entities involved in certification processes and services. The organization continues to inform the NOSB through Technical Reports guidance under a 2012 agreement with the National Organic Program. These relationships notwithstanding,

OMRI is an independent organization, operating as a recognized 501(c)(3) nonprofit, with the stated mission "to support the growth and trust of the global organic community through expert, independent and transparent verification of input materials, and through education and technical assistance" (OMRI 2018d).

Today, OMRI publishes two lists applicable to U.S. organic certification. The *OMRI Generic Materials List* (2018b) is a catalogue of over 900 input substances and their statuses as allowed, allowed with restrictions, or prohibited for organic production or processing under the USDA organic standards. The *OMRI Products List* (2018c) is a catalogue of over 5,500 branded products and their approved uses. Companies wishing to have their products listed by OMRI are required to apply. Application reviews are informed by OMRI's External Review Panels (crop, livestock, and processing) and may be forwarded to the organization's Internal Review Panel for further vetting. Inspections may be conducted as part of the review process if a Review Panel determines that on-site verification is needed and "random surveillance" inspections are conducted annually for 1 percent of OMRI-listed products.[3] According to OMRI, as of 2018 49 accredited certifiers subscribed to the *Lists*. In addition to the National Organic Program-specific *Lists*, OMRI maintains an *OMRI Canada Standards Manual* and *OMRI Canada Products List*, reflecting Canada Organic Regime standards.

WSDA Organic Material Registration

Little publicly available information exists on the background of the WSDA's Material Registration Program, although the WSDA began registering materials product and brand name well before the National Organic Program's implementation in 2002 (Peroni 2016). Similar to OMRI's *Products List*, the WSDA Program publishes an *Organic Input Material List*—a catalogue of approved organic products, alongside any limitations or required actions that are associated with product use. Manufacturers must submit an application to have a product considered for registration, which is reviewed by the WSDA Program's Review Team. Inspections *may* be required for some product approvals. Listed product registrations must be reviewed annually and the WSDA performs an in-depth re-review of each product after five years.

The CDFA Organic Input Material Program

Development of the CDFA's Organic Input Material Program is documented in a 2012 CDFA *Report to the Legislature* on organic input materials (CDFA 2012). According to the *Report*, motivation for the CDFA Program originated from a 2004 investigation in which the CDFA found that a fertilizer manufacturer was selling organic fertilizer that, although approved by a third-party organic material review organization, contained prohibited synthetic substances. An inability to sanction the manufacturer highlighted the CDFA's lack of authority to regulate organic input materials manufacturers. The CDFA worked with its Fertilizer Inspection Advisory Board to draft a strategic plan for the Fertilizing Materials Inspection Program, an industry-funded program that regulates fertilizer manufacturing and sales in California, to oversee organic fertilizer materials review. The CDFA sponsored the resulting bill (AB 856) which was signed into law in 2010.

The legislation mandates the CDFA Organic Input Material Program to review organic input fertilizers and soil additives that are distributed in California. Any manufacturer wishing to sell organic input fertilizer material in the state must first be registered with the CDFA. The CDFA performs a review of the product and an on-site inspection of the manufacturer to ensure the veracity of nutrient claims and compliance with the National Organic Program regulations. It is illegal to alter approved input materials in a manner that risks their compliance with the regulations and violators are subject to fines and license revocation.

Compared with the wide variety of input materials types found in the OMRI and the WSDA approved input catalogues, the scope of the CDFA's Organic Input Material Program is relatively narrow; because it falls under the purview of the Fertilizing Materials Inspection Program, CDFA review is limited to fertilizer materials. In 2015 the Organic Input Material Program received ISO 17065 accreditation for certification processes and services, meaning that it could be recognized as a "reputable" third-party materials review organization by the USDA, as discussed further below. As of 2015, the Organic Input Material Program had approved over 1,200 fertilizing products for use in organic food production.

The Institutional Challenge of Material Review Independence and Oversight

Although the important role that materials review organizations play in USDA organic certification is widely recognized, their institutional position within the regulatory arrangement has drawn considerable attention and debate over the years. This is due in no small part to what one author has deemed a "fundamental flaw" in USDA organic certification design (Stemwedel 2009): the fact that organic input materials are not required to be certified. Because the manufacturing of organic inputs is not regulated, organic producers and processors are left vulnerable to serious penalties if they are found to have used prohibited substances unknowingly because an input product was marketed and sold as "organic." As indicated earlier, the problem is compounded by the fact that the materials review organizations developed to address the regulatory omission were not anticipated by, nor incorporated in, the 1990 Organic Foods Production Act.

As was the case for the CDFA, the challenge of material review came under national scrutiny after a liquid fertilizer investigation: in 2009, fertilizers approved by several certifiers and OMRI were found to exhibit nitrogen content above that allowed by the USDA organic standards (ACA 2010, Stemwedel 2009). The incident prompted the National Organic Program to issue notice that certifiers' materials review programs would thereafter receive increased scrutiny during accreditation audits. The Program also began requiring liquid fertilizers undergo third-party review and on-site inspections. A majority of certifiers responded by indicating that they would not inspect fertilizer operations, leaving listing through OMRI or another third-party review program as the only viable options for organic liquid fertilizer manufacturers.

The incident prompted debate within the organic community as to how organic input materials review should be carried out, by what entities, and under what authority and oversight. Some argued that materials review organizations, such as OMRI, should be subject to National Organic Program accreditation. Others advocated for a single authoritative review body. A 2010 Materials Review Working Group convened by the ACA argued that the status quo was unsustainable but was unable to come to a consensus on a preferred manner of addressing the issue (ACA 2010).

In early 2011, the National Organic Program requested input from the NOSB on how the Program might go about developing a more uniform and consistent policy for overseeing the materials review procedures of both certifiers and third-party materials review organizations. In December of that year, following the gathering of stakeholder feedback and deliberation through several dedicated meetings, the NOSB Compliance, Accreditation, and Certification Committee responded with a Formal Recommendation. The Recommendation included a tally of the challenges posed by the existing structure of materials review under the National Organic Program. In addition to the aforementioned problems of inconsistencies between certifiers' largely unpublished approved input lists and resulting certifier shopping, these included:

- Situations where the National Organic Program disallowed a material, yet the material remained registered by a material review organization.

- Uncertainty among potential organic operations created by the lack of a universal approved substances list, creating a barrier to organic certification and the organic market.
- Inconsistencies between OMRI and WSDA processes for removing materials from their approved inputs lists,
- A lack of National Organic Program authority to regulate materials manufacturers, meaning that the Program had no way to deter or sanction manufacturers for willful violation of the USDA organic standards or misrepresentation of their products as approved for organic use. Nevertheless, certified organic producers and processors were at risk of sanctions for using such materials.

To address these concerns, NOSB recommended that the National Organic Program actively regulate materials review programs through a new "Materials Review" accreditation scope. Under such an arrangement, certifiers that wished to review input materials would add the scope to their existing accreditations and be subject to the new scope's requirements. Third-party material review organizations, such as OMRI, would be required to pursue and maintain the materials review accreditation. The recommendation further stipulated that there should be equivalency among accredited material review organizations: once accredited, a material review organization's or certifier's material review decision would be recognized by all other accredited entities. The recommendation was met favorably by many. For example, in a letter to the NOSB on behalf of the Organic Trade Association, Associate Director Gwendolyn Wylard (2011) stated:

> We believe every [material review organization] that takes on the responsibility of material review, allowance, and/or certification must operate under uniform standards and requirements, regardless of whether they are a government entity, Accredited Certification Agent (ACA), or third-party reviewer.

Despite the NOSB recommendation and stakeholder support, the National Organic Program determined that it lacked legal authority to regulate third-party materials review organizations, as they were omitted from explicit reference in the 1990 Organic Foods Production Act. Instead, the Program turned to ISO accreditation "to provide adequate oversight and enforcement of [materials review organizations] to ensure consistency of material review by different organizations" (USDA 2016b). Evolution of the Program's policy on materials review requirements is found across the 2011 Policy Memorandum 11-4, which specified material review organization criteria, and a 2013 revision, which added procedures to address inconsistent input materials determinations across certifiers and materials review organizations.

The Program's latest policy revision is outlined in a 2016 Interim Instruction detailing requirements for certifier approval of input materials (USDA 2016b). According to the Interim Instruction, certifiers have several options:

1. perform their own in-house review of materials for compliance with USDA organic standards;
2. consult with another certifier that has already reviewed the product (including the WSDA's publicly available approved substances list) and accept their determination;
3. accept pesticides that have received EPA approval for National Organic Program regulations compliance, or;
4. consult with an ISO 17065-accredited materials review organization, such as OMRI and the CDFA Organic Input Material Program.

Although the Interim Instruction addresses the problem of inconsistent input materials determinations, it does not appear to fully resolve them. If a certifier reviews an input material that had been previously approved by another and finds it does not comply with the National Organic Program regulations, the certifier must notify the Program. If the Program finds that the regulations have been improperly applied, it will instruct the certifier to rescind its approval and communicate the decision to other certifiers and materials review organizations. However, the National Organic Program states its determinations are limited to *generic* materials; it will not "approve or endorse branded (formulated) input products" (USDA 2016b, 4). Furthermore, the Program states that until it has issued a determination regarding a contested material "[a] decision made by certifying agents about the status of a branded (formulated) product remains in effect" (USDA 2016b, 43).

The potential issues with the policy have not gone unnoticed. In public comments on the Interim Instruction, the ACA expressed its support of the National Organic Program's efforts but identified a number of concerns. Among the concerns, the ACA highlighted that Program review of materials is historically slow—taking up to two years—during which time the status of contested input materials remains uncertain. The ACA further urged the Program to consider allowing certifiers to resolve contradictory materials determinations without Program intervention, noting that "in several instances where there were differing determinations, discussions between the [certifiers] identified new information that enabled a resolution" (ACA 2016a, 5). The ACA encouraged the Program to work towards development of a materials review accreditation scope, thereby formally bringing materials review organizations under National Organic Program oversight. Little has changed since the ACA issued these recommendations.

CONCLUSIONS: COORDINATING AND INFORMATION INTERMEDIARIES IN ORGANIC FOOD REGULATION

As described throughout this chapter, USDA organic certification relies on more than the organizations and entities officially incorporated by the 1990 Organic Foods Production Act and National Organic Program regulations. Rather, the efforts of independent nongovernmental organizations are essential to USDA organic standards administration, despite lacking formal authority or institutional roles. The IOIA and ACA fulfill coordinating roles, both within inspector and certifier cohorts and between the cohorts and external actors (most notably, the National Organic Program). OMRI, the WSDA, and the CDFA, in turn, constitute important brokers of organic material input information, attempting to fill an institutional gap in U.S. organic food legislation and regulations.

Through the findings of my published research (Carter and Mahallati 2017), the analysis suggested that the IOIA and ACA both perform important training, information dissemination, and knowledge sharing functions that contribute to USDA organic certification regulatory fidelity by fostering greater consistency in organic inspectors' and certifiers' knowledge and capacities. Furthermore, the analysis indicates that the ACA supports regulatory fidelity by facilitating shared understandings of the USDA organic standards and related regulatory provisions among its certifier members—most notably through an online members-only Listserv. The ACA also enhances organic certification program feedback: by serving as a collective representation and communication channel, the ACA is a mechanism through which certifiers can convey their regulatory experiences and organic standards recommendations to the National Organic Program. ACA feedback thus offers the *potential* for better-informed organic standards and regulatory and policy amendments based on the experiences of those directly responsible for administering them.

The analysis also suggests a limit to organic certification professional association influence. Based on the available evidence, it seems safe to conclude that the IOIA and ACA do not directly shape the regulatory integrity of USDA organic certification. Before one interprets the conclusion as a sign of IOIA or ACA ineffectiveness, however, it's worth considering whether ensuring regulatory integrity *should* be the responsibility of professional associations. The determination and enforcement of appropriate behavior on the part of regulatory intermediaries is the express role of regulatory authorities (such as the National Organic Program). It may be preferable that these functions be carried out by an entity that falls under political and bureaucratic accountability, rather than independent entities with no formal authority or accompanying oversight.

This chapter further identified a key omission in the 1990 Organic Foods Production Act and subsequent National Organic Program regulations: failure to provide the Program authority to regulate organic input products or the organic materials organizations that have emerged to address the policy oversight (Stemwedel 2009). One consequence of the oversight is increased uncertainty and regulatory exposure for organic producers and processors. Other consequences include impaired regulatory fidelity, as a result of input allowance inconsistencies across certifiers, and threats to regulatory fidelity resulting from the potential for certifier shopping on the basis of allowed and prohibited organic input materials.

As of 2018, the National Organic Program's materials review policy, while arguably an improvement on the lack of formal structure or guidance that preceded it, leaves several materials review challenges unresolved. The institutional role of OMRI stands out among these, as does the CDFA's Organic Input Materials program, to a lesser degree. Perhaps most important from a regulatory integrity standpoint—current policy leaves USDA organic certification vulnerable to certifier shopping, as materials approval decisions that are contested between certifiers are likely to remain unresolved until addressed by the National Organic Program—a process that can take years (ACA 2016a). The Program's aversion to issuing determinations on formulated (i.e., branded) products further creates the possibility that discrepancies remain unsettled, even after the Program has weighed in.

This chapter's analysis of materials review organizations as information intermediaries was based on a historical account through secondary documentation and materials. As such, organic materials review organizations represent a promising subject for research examining the emergence, challenges, and institutionalization of information intermediaries in administratively decentralized regulatory arrangements. For example, the USDA organic certification case suggests that information intermediaries may be initiated where regulatory designs exhibit key authority gaps, however, this by no means suggests that they are inevitable. Research can examine when nongovernmental actors respond to such gaps by coordinating to form intermediary bodies, such as OMRI, when they do not, and what helps explain the difference.

My analysis in this book has worked its way "down" the levels of authority characterizing USDA organic certification's decentralized regulatory design, beginning with the NOSB as rulemaking intermediary, to the National Organic Program as regulatory authority, to third-party certification administrators and organic inspection intermediaries, and then to the California State Organic Program as a state-level enforcement intermediary. This chapter's analysis then stepped out of the National Organic Program's formal authoritative structure to adds organic certification professional associations and materials review organizations to the list of organic certification actors. In doing so, it added coordinating and information intermediaries to the catalogue of intermediary types upon which U.S. organic regulation relies. The following chapter concludes my tour through USDA organic certification's regulatory design by turning to central targets of organic food regulation: certified organic producers.

NOTES

1. Interestingly, at the time of our study's publication in 2017, the ACA's mission was to "ensure the integrity of organic certification in the United States." Upon the writing this book in 2018, however, the mission had been revised to "striv[ing] to ensure consistent implementation of USDA Organic Regulations." The reason for the change is not apparent.

2. In addition to OMRI, the WSDA, and the CDFA, some consider the Environmental Protection Agency (EPA) an organic materials review organization, as EPA regulations are pertinent to determining whether certain materials are approved under the USDA organic standards, particularly when it comes to the levels of synthetic substances allowed in organic production, and the EPA identifies some substances as allowed for certified organic production. The discussion in this section is limited to OMRI, the WSDA, and the CDFA, as the purpose of their materials review efforts is to inform USDA organic standards compliance.

3. OMRI also requires high nitrogen liquid fertilizers to undergo two inspections annually as a result of the problematic history of such fertilizers recounted in this section.

Chapter Ten

The Regulatory Targets

Certified Organic Producers

Among the contested aspects of organic agriculture and policy, the changing composition and motivations of organic food producers has arguably drawn the greatest attention. Many organic farming advocates have settled on a general consensus that federal-level organic regulation enabled the contemporary organic food market, as early organic policy proponents intended, but in doing so it also facilitated organic industry cooptation by large-scale corporate agribusinesses. The sentiment is perhaps best captured by what Daniel Buck, Christina Getz, and Julie Guthman (1997) dub the "conventionalization" of the organic sector. Brian Obach (2015, 12) explains organic sector conventionalization and some of its often-cited ramifications:

> "Big Organic," as the corporate organic sector is known by its critics, has superimposed industrial-style agricultural practices onto the organic framework. . . . These growers meet organic standards as defined by the USDA, but they utilize industrial practices such as large-scale monoculture crops, the heavy use of off-farm "organic" inputs, and the intensive confinement of livestock. . . . Critics of the current state of affairs add that as organic production has come to mimic the industrial agriculture system, the health and ecological benefits that motivated many advocates have been lost.

Despite not being the direct focus of preceding chapters, organic producers' motivations are essential factors shaping the incentives and pressures facing each of the aforementioned regulatory actors. As detailed in this book's first chapters, organic producer communities developed organic agriculture as an alternative farming method, eventually giving rise to the organic movement. The support and advocacy of organic farmers was essential to the political will that led to passage of the 1990 Organic Foods Production Act (Guthman

2014, Obach 2015) and farmers made up an important part of public resistance to the USDA's 1997 National Organic Program proposed rule (Henke 2008). Today, organic farmers are key stakeholders in the NOSB's organic standards recommendations, subsequent National Organic Program rulemaking, and the Program's administrative efforts, as most recently reflected in the Program's Sound and Sensible initiative.

Organic producers occupy a valuable vantage point from which USDA organic certification can be assessed (as evidenced in Chapter 6's analysis of accredited certifiers). Organic food consumers typically have limited exposure to and knowledge of organic practices (Yiridoe, Bonti-Ankomah, and Martin 2005), much less an understanding of the National Organic Program or the intermediaries that are essential to Program administration. Organic producers, in contrast, have privileged access to expertise and experiences that inform their perceptions of the National Organic Program and its impacts. Furthermore, the durability of USDA organic certification as U.S. organic food policy depends, in no small part, on favorable producer and processor perceptions of the Program and its benefits.

Of course, from a regulatory perspective, organic operations are a central concern around which much of the activity in this book revolves. Regulatory integrity—a key element of regulatory effectiveness that is central to this book's analysis—hinges in large part on the behavior of organic producers. Preventing opportunistic behavior on the part of agricultural and commercial operations, such as the anecdotal accounts of certifier shopping referenced in earlier chapters, is a key rational for many of the institutional and administrative elements discussed in preceding pages—from the National Organic Program's Age of Enforcement to regulatory conflict of interest provisions that prevent organic inspectors from offering guidance. Furthermore, consumer confidence in organic certification's regulatory integrity is essential for maintaining organic market viability. Stemwedel (2009, 199) states the situation succinctly:

> With organic products, regulation is important because the label is usually the only way for a consumer to tell if the product they are purchasing is truly organic. Sadly, trust alone is not enough to ensure that every person in the supply chain, from grower, to packer, to processor, to retailer will comply with the rules to maintain a product's organic integrity.

This chapter therefore focuses on the USDA organic certification regulatory targets that comprise the foundation of the organic food supply chain: USDA organic certified organic producers. The first section provides an overview of organic production in the U.S. through USDA data. I then draw on Organic Regulation Research Project survey data to offer a producer perspective on U.S. organic regulation. The chapter's second section examines certified organic producers' motivations for practicing organic agriculture and being certified USDA organic. The third section documents organic producers' perceptions of the National Organic Program regulations as organic standards and the Program's environmental, consumer, and market impacts. The fourth section then turns to matters regulatory compliance, looking at producers' experiences in, and motivations for, maintaining compliance with the National Organic Program regulations.

CERTIFIED ORGANIC FOOD PRODUCTION IN THE U.S.

The USDA's National Agricultural Statistics Service's (NASS) 2016 survey of certified organic producers provides the latest snapshot of organic food production in the U.S. (NASS 2017a). The survey was the NASS' fifth organic production survey and third organic-only survey, with the two remaining surveys conducted as Special Studies under the 2007 and 2012 Censuses of Agriculture. NASS surveys focus on certified organic acreage, production, and sales. NASS statistically weights survey findings to account for survey nonresponse bias.[1]

Among the key findings from the 2016 survey highlighted by the USDA (NASS 2017b) is the number of domestic certified organic producers of 14,217, representing an increase of 11 percent between 2015 and 2016. The associated increase in acreage under USDA organic certification was 15 percent, for a total of 5 million acres nationally. The survey found that organic producer sales increased 23 percent from the preceding year to $7.6 billion. $4.2 billion came from crops sales, while $3.4 billion came from livestock and poultry-related products. The top organic commodity in dollar sales was milk ($1.3 billion in sales). Certified organic eggs came in second ($816 million), followed by broiler chickens ($750 million) and apples ($327 million).

Perhaps unsurprising given its role in U.S. agriculture, generally, and organic agriculture, specifically, California leads the country in terms of the number of certified organic producers, certified acreage, and organic product sales. The state boasted 2,713 certified organic producers and 1.1 million acres, with the latter figure representing 21 percent of the certified organic land in the U.S. Organic farm sales in California accounted for almost $2.9 billion in 2016.

The number of certified organic farms and acreage for the remaining states are depicted in the top panel of Figure 10.1. Grey bars indicate the number of organic producers in a state, relative to the left axis. Black markers indicate each state's organic acreage, relative to the right axis. The state organic acreage median of 40,166 acres is indicated by a line. The bottom panel of Figure 10.1 shows the NASS-estimated value in organic production by state and mean per-farm organic production value, calculated by dividing the total organic production value in the state by the number of producers. Grey bars indicate each state's organic production value (in millions of dollars), relative to the left axis. Black markers indicate each state's mean per-farm value, relative to the right axis. The state per-farm organic production value median of $262,568 is indicated by a black line. California is omitted from both panels, as an outlier among the U.S. states, to allow for a better examination of the remaining states.

As seen in Panel 1 of Figure 10.1, Wisconsin followed California in producer prevalence with 1,276 organic farms or ranches and New York comes in third with 1,059. Six additional states are home to more than 500 certified organic producers: Pennsylvania (803), Iowa (732), Washington (677), Ohio (575), Vermont (556), and Minnesota (545). The five states with the lowest numbers of certified producers are Delaware (2), Alaska (8), West Virginia (14), Alabama (18), and Louisiana (21). Not represented in the figure, Alaska follows California in acres under organic certification, but the USDA withholds Alaska acreage data to avoid disclosing information about individual producers.[2]

As seen in Panel 2 of Figure 10.1, Pennsylvania follows California in organic production value with $660 million in organic production sales in 2016. Washington is a close third, at $636 million, followed by Oregon ($351 million) and Texas ($297 million). Alabama, West Virginia, and Rhode Island exhibited the lowest values in organic production sales, with each representing roughly $2 million. Arizona is something of an outlier when it comes to mean per-farm organic production value; the mean per-farm value of over $3 million suggests there is one or two producers in the state with noticeably high sales. The median state per-farm value, in contrast, is $262,568. The USDA withholds sales data for Alaska and Delaware to avoid disclosing information about individual producers in those states.

While this snapshot provides an illustrative overview of USDA certified organic production activity in the U.S., NASS surveys do not collect data that capture the motivations and experiences of certified organic producers, much less their perceptions of the National Organic Program and its impacts. The remainder of this chapter therefore turns to data collected in Organic Regulation Research Project's national survey of certified organic producers. The subsequesnt section examines producers' motivations for using organic practices and pursuing USDA organic certification. Producer's perceptions of the USDA organic standards and National Organic Program follow.

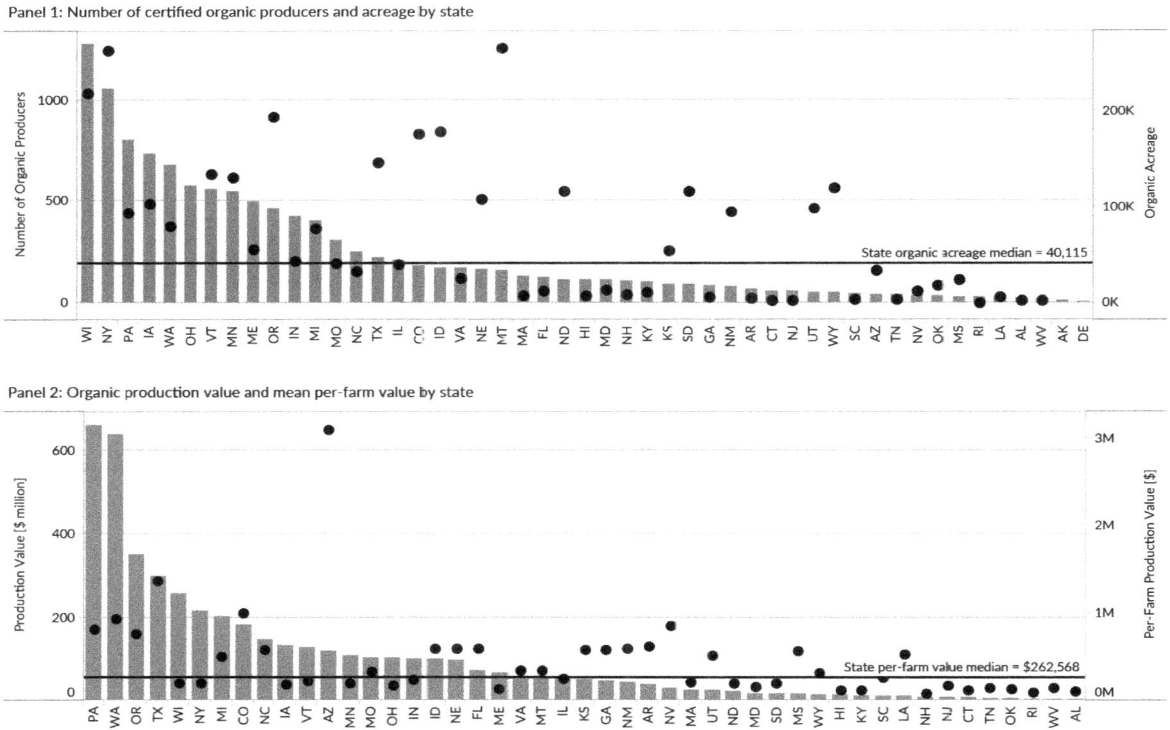

Figure 10.1. Certified organic production statistics from the 2016 NASS organic production survey

SOURCE: Author

NOTE: Grey bars represent left axis measures and black markers represent right axis measures; Figure generated by the author with data from the NASS 2016 Organic Production Survey (NASS 2017a)

CERTIFIED ORGANIC PRODUCERS' MOTIVATIONS

Producers pursue organic practices and opt into certification oversight for a range of reasons that include environmental concerns, a sense of social responsibility, economic incentives, and personal values—among others. An individual producer's motivation likely reflects a multi-dimensional combination of interrelated reasons that include, for example, a concern for the environmental impact of agricultural practices *and* a desire to support their operation's financial success. Furthermore, the relationship between organic methods adoption and organic certification is undoubtedly endogenous; although some farmers may choose to practice organic agriculture as an end in and of itself, many others likely follow organic practices primarily to gain access to organic food markets through USDA organic certification.

Recognizing this endogeneity, the decision to pursue organic methods can be conceptually distinguished from the decision to seek USDA organic certification, and the distinction makes the admittedly interrelated topics easier to analyze and understand (Veldstra, Alexander, and Marshall 2014). This section addresses each topic in turn, beginning with the question of why producers practice organic agriculture.

Motivations for Using Organic Methods

A small literature has developed across several countries regarding why producers practice organic farming over conventional agriculture. Differences in conceptual frameworks and research designs make synthesizing concrete lessons from this research difficult. Comparing study findings is further complicated by the particulars of different country's economic and regulatory contexts. These challenges notwithstanding, some general conclusions can be drawn.

Perhaps somewhat predictably, economists tend to view the choice between organic and conventional agriculture as a financial one, with the decision to pursue organic practices driven by the price premium that they represent in many locations and markets (Chouinard et al. 2008, Musshoff and Hirschauer 2008). Evidence suggests, however, that the prominence of the economic rationale has varied over time, as early organic agriculture adopters were likely less motivated by organic price premiums than those that followed (Läpple and Rensburg 2011). The relative weight of the economic rationale is further conditioned by contextual factors: where organic practices are not socially accepted or organic farmers face technological barriers, they are less likely to be to motivated by economic forces to pursue organic methods (Läpple and Kelley 2013).

Other research supports the prominence of economic considerations in producers' decision making, but suggests that environmental concerns such as resource degradation and biodiversity are also important drivers for many farmers (Mzoughi 2011). Studies further indicate that environmental considerations are entwined with farmers' philosophical orientations towards the role of technology and human-environment relationships (Fairweather 1999, Mzoughi 2011) and personal responsibility regarding consumers' health (Mzoughi 2011). Additional factors that the literature identifies as influencing producers' decision to adopt organic methods include the health of producers and their families, livestock health and welfare, a desire to support soil quality, and the price of synthetic fertilizers and chemicals (Conacher and Conacher 1982, Fairweather 1999).

As part of the Organic Regulation Research Project, we queried certified organic producers regarding five reasons for practicing organic farming by asked producers to indicate their level of agreement or disagreement (measured on a 5-point scale) with each stated reason. The question prompt was "I practice organic farming because, in comparison with conventional practices, it . . ." The reasons included:

- . . . reduces workers' exposure to harmful chemicals
- . . . decreases the environmental impact of agricultural production
- . . . more closely aligns with [the farmer's] personal values
- . . . results in superior products
- . . . is more efficient, and requires less technology, equipment or inputs

The results are depicted in Panel 1 of Figure 10.2. The reason that ranked highest among certified organic producer survey respondents, on average, was reduced exposure to chemicals (mean = 4.5 out of 5), consistent with an early study of Australian organic producers (Conacher and Conacher 1982). Decreased environmental impacts and alignment with producers' personal values—reflecting what Fairweather (1999) refers to as producers' philosophical values—tied for second (mean = 4.4). An assumed superiority of organically produced products came in third (mean = 4.0). Finally, organic agriculture as a more efficient production method ranked last (mean = 3.0).

Survey respondents were given the option to offer their own reasons for using organic practices. The results largely mirrored those cited in the literature, above, with a couple of additions. Among the reasons that they offered were: consumer demand, higher product price in comparison with conventional products, improved animal welfare, improved soil health, and avoidance of genetically modified organisms. In addition, several farmers noted that by producing *some* of their products via organic methods, they were able to

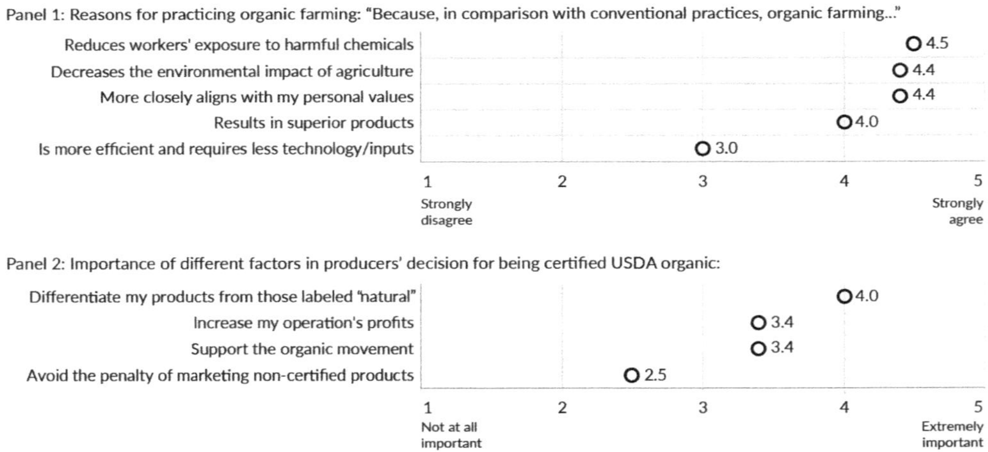

Figure 10.2. Certified organic producer survey respondents' reasons for using organic methods and being certified USDA organic

SOURCE: Author

NOTE: Markers represent survey response means for each associated measure

spread their businesses' exposure to market risks among several markets. Finally, several respondents noted that organic methods were a contract requirement with one or more of their business connections or vendors.

Motivations for Being Certified USDA Organic

As discussed throughout this book, USDA organic certification is a quasi-voluntary program, as producers and processors are only required to adhere to the USDA organic standards if they wish to market and sell their products as organic. The question of why firms opt into regulatory oversight—such as is the case for voluntary or quasi-voluntary programs—has drawn considerable attention from across several relevant literatures, including economics (e.g., Kotchen and van't Veld 2009), private governance (Auld 2014), and public policy (Prakash and Potoski 2007). While the primary driver of voluntary program participation is often assumed to be to gain a competitive advantage, the rationale can be further broken down into at least two reasons. First, firms seek to distinguish their products from those of their competition to signal hard-to-assess qualities such as sustainability and social responsibility (Grunert and Aachmann 2016). A related, yet distinct, motivation is to increase firm profits, for example through the price premium associated with "prestige" products (Carter, Heikkila, and Weible 2018).

Voluntary program participation is not driven by competitive pressures, alone. Individuals may feel compelled to opt into program oversight to support the values that a program embodies—particularly where a voluntary program is borne out of earlier social movement action, as is the case for organic agriculture (see Chapter 3). Finally, some government-sponsored voluntary programs prohibit the use of specified marketing devices for non-participants. In the case of USDA organic certification, producers can only market their products "organic" if they opt into National Organic Program participation or face federally imposed penalties for fraudulent use of the term. A desire to avoid such penalties therefore likely drives some participants to participate in such government-sponsored quasi-voluntary programs.

Drawing from the literature cited above, our survey queried U.S. organic producers regarding the importance of four reasons for being certified USDA organic. The reasons included:

- *Product differentiation*: To distinguish organic products from those of competitors marketed as "natural" or "sustainable."
- *Increased profits*: To secure the market access or price premium associated with USDA organic certification.

- *Organic movement support*: To support the organic movement through participation in the National Organic Program.
- *Punitive deterrence*: To avoid the penalty of selling non-certified products as organic.

As seen in Panel 2 of Figure 10.2, the organic certification reason that survey respondents ranked most important, on average, was product differentiation (mean = 4.0 out of 5). Increased profit and organic movement support tied for second (mean = 3.4). Punitive deterrence ranked as the least important motivation (mean = 2.5). Again, we offered survey respondents the opportunity to list additional reasons for being certified USDA organic. Four additional reasons were identified across the producers that offered a response: import and export sales, to meet contract or purchaser requirements, to support consumer trust in organic products, and to encourage other producers to adopt organic practices.

The Link between Producer Values and the Decision to Be Certified USDA Organic

The preceding discussion provided a window into the various reasons that producers use organic practices and seek USDA organic certification. Although economic factors likely drive many producers' decision to adopt organic practices, other considerations—notably concerns over agricultural impacts on the environment and personal value systems—also play important motivating roles. When it comes to the decision to be certified USDA organic, differentiating one's products from those of competitors is a chief motivating factor, with increasing operational profits and supporting the organic movement closely following in importance.

Chris Weible, Tanya Heikkila, and I (2018) analyzed certification decision data to better understand the factors that shape organic producers' participation in the National Organic Program. Among the questions that our analysis pursued was how producers' personal value alignment with organic practices (measured as a possible reason for their use of organic practices, as discussed above), is related to their reasons for being certified USDA organic. Our findings suggested that the more a producer's personal values align with organic agriculture principles, the more important product differentiation and social movement support are in the producer's decision to be certified organic. In contrast, a closer value alignment with organic practices was negatively associated with the importance producers assigned to increased profits and punitive deterrence. In other words, the more a producer's personal values align with organic agriculture principles, the *less* important increased profits and avoiding penalties are in the producer's decision to be certified organic.

Our findings lend some credence to an intuitive and often-referenced narrative that organic producers can be sorted into different "types" based on their motivations for using organic methods. In the simplest conceptualization, some organic producers are categorized as embracing an organic "ethos," grounded in the philosophical and ethical underpinnings of organic principles, while others are characterized as reflecting an instrumental or productionist ethos, in which organic agriculture and certification are seen as nothing more than a means to a market (Goodman 2000, Vos 2000). While the discussion in this chapter clearly indicates that such a categorization is an oversimplification, the link that we found between producers' organic value alignment and their motivations for pursuing organic certification fits the basic notion that producers that are philosophically motivated to practice organic agriculture are more interested in organic as a *movement* and less motivated by organic profit.

Of course, a central objective of the National Organic Program is to ensure that all organic products are produced according to the USDA organic standards, regardless of producers' motivations. In the process, USDA organic certification is meant to achieve certain policy goals, such as supporting consumer confidence in organic products and a robust organic market. The next section therefore examines producers' perceptions of the USDA organic standards and National Organic Program impact.

CERTIFIED ORGANIC PRODUCERS' PERCEPTIONS OF USDA ORGANIC CERTIFICATION

In this section, I examine Organic Regulation Research Project survey findings regarding certified organic producers' perceptions of USDA organic certification. There are several reasons I focus on certified producers' perceptions. First, although the number of certified organic farms increases year-by-year, the organic sector's continued growth is nonetheless contingent—to some degree—on continued favorable producer sentiments of the USDA organic standards and the National Organic Program. Yet, as identified in Chapter 4, there is growing discontent with USDA organic in some corners of the organic practitioner community, particularly as organic draws evermore interest from conventional producers and corporate agribusinesses (Guthman 2004b, Vogl, Kilcher, and Schmidt 2005). My analysis in this section therefore offers a window into how a national sample of certified producers perceives USDA organic standards and the National Organic Program.

Furthermore, and as discussed in this chapter's introduction, organic producers occupy a distinctive vantage point from which some of the more contested National Organic Program impacts can be assessed. For example, where empirical research findings are mixed regarding the environmental benefits of organic standards versus conventional practices (Reganold and Wachter 2016), organic producers offer an informed perspective on the possible environmental and biodiversity consequences of following National Organic Program regulations. The section therefore reports certified organic producer perceptions of National Organic Program impacts along key dimensions of interest outlined by the 1990 Organic Food Production Act: the environment and biodiversity, organic food consumers, and the organic food market.

Perceptions of the USDA Organic Standards

Chapter 4 of this book discussed the challenges that the National Organic Program faces in establishing regulatory standards that reflect the traditional principles of organic agriculture, while at the same time supporting organic industry growth. One of those challenges is balancing a reliance on general principles, which allows for variation in the way that organic producers meet regulatory requirements, with regulatory prescriptiveness that guards against overly loose standards interpretations. A closely related challenge, as detailed in Chapter 5, is balancing regulatory stringency with the burden that strict standards enforcement imposes on organic certification applicants. To gain producers' perspectives on how the National Organic Program regulations stack up in light of these challenges, the Organic Regulation Research Project survey queried certified organic producers for their perspectives on the regulations.

We measured producers' National Organic Program regulation perceptions by asking survey respondents the extent to which they agreed with four statements. Prefaced by the prompt "the National Organic Program regulations . . ." the statements were:

- . . . establish a minimum standard for organic practices, but my operation goes "above and beyond" the requirements
- . . . should specify allowed and prohibited production practices more precisely
- . . . reflect what I consider to be ideal organic standards
- . . . should allow more synthetic substances

The results are displayed in Panel 1 of Figure 10.3. When asked the extent to which the regulations reflect what producers consider to be "ideal organic

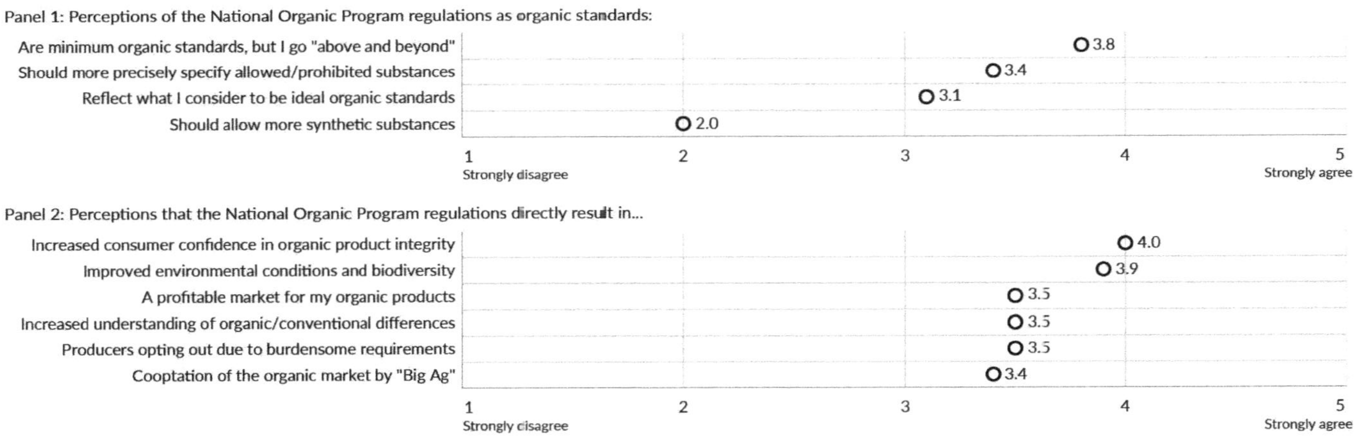

Figure 10.3. Certified organic producer survey respondents' perceptions of the USDA organic standards and National Organic Program impacts

SOURCE: Author

NOTE: Markers represent survey response means for each associated measure

standards," the average response was an ambiguous, translating to neither agreement nor disagreement with the statement (mean = 3.1 out of 5). If anything, the findings suggest that the National Organic Program regulations could be more stringent, as the average respondent indicated that their operations goes "above and beyond" the National Organic Program regulations' minimum standards (mean = 3.8). Furthermore, survey respondents supported more restrictive and prescriptive regulations, as the average respondent tended to *agree* that the regulations should more precisely specify allowed and prohibited practices and *disagreed* that the regulations should allow more synthetic substances (mean = 3.4 and 2.0, respectively).

Perceptions of National Organic Program Impacts

Chapter 4 also introduced debates within organic agriculture stakeholder communities regarding the consequences of USDA organic food policy. Some of the more critical assessment of National Organic Program impacts, for example, include that the Program's minimum standards undermine the environmental benefits of organic agriculture and facilitate the conventionalization of the organic market (Buck, Getz, and Guthman 1997, Guthman 2004b). To understand the extent to which certified organic producers' perceptions mirrored such concerns, our survey queried producers regarding several National Organic Program impacts, modeled after the stated goals of the 1990 Organic Foods Production Act.

We measured producers' perceptions of National Organic Program impacts by asking survey respondents the extent to which they agreed with five prompts prefaced with the statement "The National Organic Program regulations directly result in . . .". The first prompt pertained to the Program's impact on environmental conditions and biodiversity. Two statements pertained to the Program's impact on consumers: the extent to which it increases consumer confidence in organic products and increases their understanding of organic practices. Finally, as the National Organic Program is a marketing program under the Agriculture Marketing Service, three statements related to the Program's market impacts, including whether it results in a profitable organic market, potential organic producers opting out of certification because of Program requirements, and cooptation of the organic market by "Big Ag."

The findings are presented in Panel 2 of Figure 10.3. The two National Organic Program impacts that producer survey respondents expressed the highest support for were increasing consumer confidence in organic products and improving environmental conditions and biodiversity (mean = 4.0 and 3.9 out of 5, respectively). Producers seemed less enthusiastic about the remaining impacts, but the findings nonetheless suggested that producers on average lean towards agreeing that the Program increases consumer understanding of organic products and supports a profitable organic market (mean = 3.5 for both). At the same time, producers also tended to agree on average that Program requirements lead some producers to opt out of USDA organic certification and facilitate Big Ag cooptation of the market (mean = 3.5 and 3.4).

Drawing Lessons from Certified Organic Producer Data

Taken collectively, the findings reported in this section provide a generally positive assessment of USDA organic certification, while at the same time confirming some of the National Organic Program challenges and drawbacks noted elsewhere in this book. Findings related to producers' perceptions of the USDA organic standards suggest many producers likely prefer more stringent and prescriptive regulations that, if anything, allow for fewer allowed synthetic substances over more. These preferences run counter to some of the USDA organic standards developments recounted in Chapter 4; in particular, the USDA's 2013 revision to National List protocols by which allowed synthetic substances remain on the List indefinitely absent a vote of removal and the more recent withdrawal of the 2017 Organic Livestock and Poultry Practices Rule.

The fact that producers appear to feel most strongly about the regulations' support of consumer confidence is encouraging news for the National Organic Program, given that a central rationale for the Organic Foods Production Act was to improve consumer confidence by establishing and enforcing national standards (Guthman 2014, Mosier 2017). Perceptions that the Program results in improved environmental conditions and biodiversity is also promising, particularly in light of criticisms that the principle of sustainability has eroded under the USDA's oversight (Arcuri 2015, Obach 2015). The "lukewarm" nature of producers' assessment that the Program increases consumer understanding of organic practices is less surprising. A considerable body of consumer behavior research documents that while consumers readily distinguish between certified organic and conventional products, they rarely have a good grasp of what organic certification stands for beyond general conceptions of "natural" or "synthetic-free" (Yiridoe, Bonti-Ankomah, and Martin 2005).

Producer's mixed perceptions regarding the National Organic Program's organic market impacts may be reflective of tensions inherent in maintaining and growing an alternative agricultural industry (Obach 2015). It can only be expected that if a USDA organic certification successfully encourages a market, established and even dominant industy players will seek to also benefit from it. The fact that some producers perceive the National Organic

Program as *simultaneously* impeding potential entrants to the organic market and facilitating its cooptation by conventional agribusiness suggests they may be in agreement with criticisms that USDA organic standards favor more powerful conventional agriculture interests at the cost of smaller operations that characterized early organic pioneers (Guthman 2014, Jaffee and Howard 2010, Mosier 2017).

Collectively, this section's findings suggest that certified organic producers credit the National Organic Program for some positive impacts and at the same time may be sympathetic to concerns raised by Program critics, such as the Cornucopia Institute (see Chapter 3). Whether such sympathy extends to the National Organic Program legitimacy concerns discussed in Chapter 4 is beyond the scope of the data presented here. If nothing else, assuming producers seek verification that their operation goes "above and beyond" the USDA organic standards, as the survey data presented above indicates many do, this section's findings suggest that the emergence of supplementary certification programs such as the Rodale Institute's Regenerative Organic Certification may be driven by producer demand as much, or more, than consumer desires.

CERTIFIED ORGANIC PRODUCERS' REGULATORY EXPERIENCES

As with any regulatory program, a basic function of the National Organic Program is to ensure compliance with regulatory standards. Yet, regulatory compliance is rarely, if ever, achieved based on the threat of noncompliance penalties alone. Instead, compliance is the product of a regulatee's capacity to adhere to regulatory requirements and intertwined pressures that are deterrent, social, and normative in origin (May 2004, May 2005, Winter and May 2001a). For example, Peter May (2005) finds that farmers exhibit a higher personal sense of duty to comply with environmental regulations than regulatees in the homebuilding and boatyard sectors. Furthermore, May indicated that the potential for reputational harm was a more important motivator of famers' compliance with environmental regulations than the enforcement practices of regulators.

The Organic Regulation Research Project survey examined certified organic producers' experiences with National Organic Program regulations through two question batteries. We first sought to understand what producers' experiences were in attempting to comply with the regulations by asking for producers' agreement with four statements:

- When my operation is not in compliance, it is for administrative requirements such as paperwork.

- I immediately notify my certifier of noncompliances at my operation.
- Maintaining compliance is extremely difficult.
- I ignore noncompliances at my operation that I consider to be trivial.

The findings are depicted in Panel 1 of Figure 10.4. When asked to respond to the statement that "maintaining compliance [with the regulations] is extremely difficult," the average response hovered between "disagree" and neutral (mean = 2.5 out of 5), suggesting producers do not generally find adhering to the USDA organic standards overly challenging. Respondents reported a tendency to adhere closely to the standards, disagreeing that they ignored even "trivial" noncompliance issues (mean = 1.5). Perhaps predictably, this compliance behavior did not extend to producers' proactively notifying their organic certifiers of noncompliance issues at their operations (mean = 3.0). Finally, seeking to understand the extent to which noncompliances are due to administrative burdens, such as recordkeeping and documentation (as discussed in Chapter 5), we asked producers to indicate whether noncompliances were due to paperwork issues. The findings suggested that this is not likely the case, with the average response reflecting neither agreement nor disagreement with the statement (mean = 3.2).

In the second question battery we sought to gauge what factors are most influential in motivating compliance with the USDA organic standards. Regulatory programs are designed around the assumption that regulatees follow regulatory directives to avoid the penalty that they will incur if caught breaking the rules. Yet, as indicated in this section's introduction, theory and practice suggest other—and sometime more influential—motivations that drive regulatees to comply with regulations. Some motivations are internally derived, such as a personal sense of duty to adhere to program standards (Burby and Paterson 1993, Scholz and Pinney 1995). Others are socially derived. Regulatees may feel pressured to comply by their industry peers or may seek to maintain their business's credibly with consumers and other stakeholders.

Drawing on this range of motivations, we asked producers to indicate the importance of four factors in shaping their regulatory compliance behavior, with the possible responses "not at all important," "moderately important," and "extremely important." The four compliance motivations were:

- Concern for the producer's reputation
- Personal sense of duty
- Fear of penalty from the certifier
- Pressure from other certified organic producers

The findings are presented in Panel 2 of Figure 10.4. A concern for reputation and a personal sense of duty were the highest-ranked organic

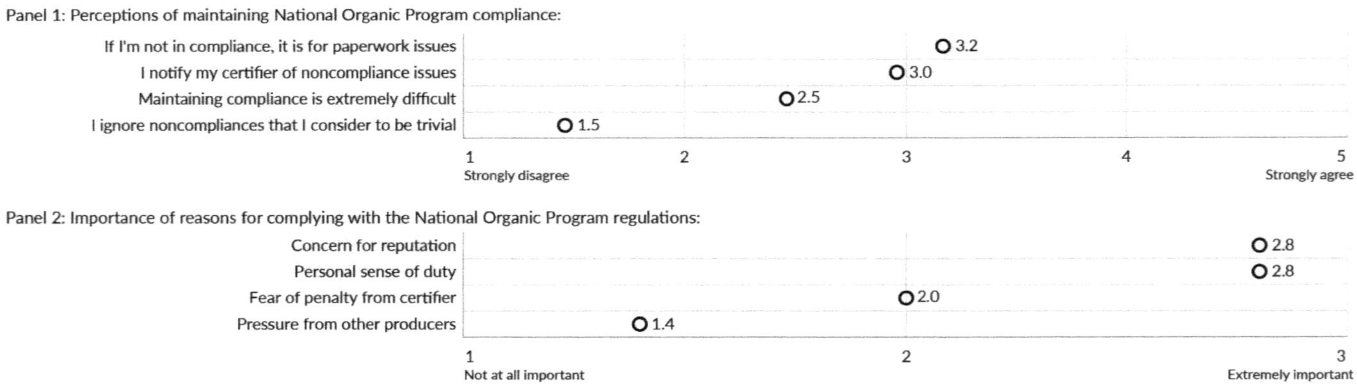

Figure 10.4. Certified organic producer survey respondents' compliance experiences and motivations
SOURCE: Author
NOTE: Markers represent survey response means for each associated measure

regulation compliance motivations, with the average response for each approaching extremely important (mean = 2.8 out of 3 for both). A fear of penalty followed, although the relative importance of the motivation was markedly lower, translating to moderately important (mean = 2.0). Pressure from other producers was the least-important motivation, ranked on-average somewhere in between not at all important and moderately important (mean = 1.4).

Reflecting on Producers' Regulatory Experiences

The data presented in this section provide a window into certified organic producers' regulatory experiences and compliance motivations. Producer-reported experiences suggest that, on average, producers attend to even trivial regulatory requirements and do not experience extreme hardships in doing so. Although far from conclusive, the findings also suggest that the compliance difficulties that producers do experience are not solely related to National Organic Program recordkeeping and documentation requirements. The finding is noteworthy given the concerns discussed earlier in this book regarding the administrative burden of USDA organic certification requirements.

In accordance with prior studies of regulatory compliance, this section's findings indicate that fear of penalty from organic certifiers is not the most important reason that organic producers might feel compelled to follow National Organic Program regulations. On the basis of the data presented here, producers' individual value orientations and reputational concerns are considerably more influential. Peer pressure from organic producer peers, in contrast, seems to have little weight as a motivation to follow the USDA organic standards.

Of course, it is possible that producers rate the threat of penalty as relatively unimportant because they feel like they are unlikely to incur a penalty, rather than the possibility of a penalty simply not weighing as heavily as reputation or duty in producers' minds. When the organic agriculture history and context are considered, however, it seems plausible that reputation and a personal sense of duty indeed constitute the primary drivers of many organic producers' regulatory behaviors. For example, an organic producer's livelihood depends, to some degree, on their business's reputation. A reputation of trying to skirt the regulations may prove more detrimental than the sanctions a certifier is likely to impose, thus producers may view complying with the regulations as much a matter of good business strategy as one of avoiding penalties.

CONCLUSION: LESSONS FROM CERTIFIED PRODUCERS AS REGULATORY TARGETS

This chapter provided a view of USDA organic certification as seen from the "bottom" of the regulatory arrangement—from the perspective of certified organic producers. The chapter began with a snapshot of organic food production in the U.S. through NASS 2016 organic producer survey data. The snapshot depicts a growing sector, in terms of both farm numbers and acres under organic production. It also shows the uneven distribution of certified organic food production, as some states—California in particular—exhibit robust organic food production and markets, while others show minimal organic production activity and sales.

The chapter then turned to survey data colleagues and I collected during the Organic Regulation Research Project to examine the motivations, perceptions, and regulatory experiences of U.S. certified organic producers. When considered collectively, the findings offer several insights that contribute to a better understanding of organic certification under the USDA. The first is in providing further evidence that organic producers' motivations, while certainly influenced by economic considerations, are also grounded in personal values and principles reflective of earlier organic agriculture pioneers, such as a concern for the environmental impact of agricultural practices. Perhaps most notably, supporting the organic movement and increased profits tied as the second most important motivations for seeking USDA organic certification. Both reasons were out ranked by a producers' desire to differentiate their products from competition making "natural" (and similar) marketing claims. One interpretation of the finding is that verification of truly "organic" production practices outranks profit as a certification motivation. In other words, that consumer confidence is more important to many producers than price premiums.

As discussed throughout this book, a central debate regarding USDA organic certification is the extent to which it facilitates the conventionalization of U.S. organic agriculture (Guthman 2004b, Jaffee and Howard 2010). Consistent with the perspective that USDA organic standards reflect a watered-down translation of organic principles, the findings presented above suggest that many producers may prefer more restrictive organic standards and see themselves as going above and beyond those specified by National Organic Program regulations. Nonetheless, and despite measured indication that the National Organic Program facilitates corporate cooptation of the organic market, the findings also indicate that some the hypothesized conventionalization consequences have yet to materialize, as producers maintain that the Program improves environmental conditions and to a lesser degree, a profitable organic market.

The chapter's findings regarding organic producers' regulatory experiences are promising when considered in light of their implications for USDA organic certification regulatory integrity. The data suggest that most producers do not find complying with the National Organic Program regulations excessively challenging and attend to even "trivial" regulatory details. More importantly, the findings suggest that producers experience both internally and externally derived motivations for complying with the regulations that are more important than the threat of certifier sanctions. Regulatory theory indicates that robust compliance is most likely in contexts where regulatory monitoring and enforcement deterrence is buttressed by normative and social pressures (May 2004, Scholz 1991); this chapter's data affirms that such is likely the case for many producers certified USDA organic.

These findings, while offering valuable insights, should be considered within the parameters of the Organic Regulation Research Project survey sample's limitations, including and beyond those discussed in earlier chapters. Aside from the limitations detailed in Chapter 6 and the methodological Appendix, it should be noted that the survey findings are limited to the perspectives of certified producers and thus omit those of producers that have *opted out* of USDA organic certification. Different findings would likely result from incorporating the assessments of non-certified organically inclined producers. For example, assuming some producers opt out of USDA certification because the investment is not worth the payoff, one might expect less supportive findings regarding the National Organic Program's contribution to a profitable organic market. Similarly, assuming some producers forgo organic certification because they consider the USDA standards to be lacking on environmental protections, including noncertified producers' perspectives would likely result in less favorable findings regarding the Program's impact on the environment and biodiversity.

These limitations notwithstanding, this chapter added a producer perspective that, when combined with the analyses of prior chapters, help to further depict USDA organic certification strengths and limitations. Producers' inclination towards more restrictive standards suggests that the supplementary certification programs discussed towards the end of Chapter 4 are likely driven (to some degree) by producer demand, particularly if producers seek verification and credit for the manners in which their operations go "above and beyond" the USDA organic standards. The supportive findings in regard to National Organic Program impacts, however, temper concerns raised in that chapter regarding the durability of USDA organic certification as U.S. organic food policy. Assuming producers continue to see positive environmental, consumer, and market impacts from the Program, it is arguably unlikely that supplemental organic programs signal a threat to the long-run viability of the National Organic Program.

Earlier chapters detailed regulatory concerns that emerge from decentralization and organizational diversity of USDA organic standards administration. For example, Chapter 5 identified a gap in the National Organic Program's accreditation oversight of certifying agents in the Program's failure to track notice of noncompliance sanctions. Chapter 6 noted inconsistencies among certifiers' issuances of certification suspensions and revocations. This chapter's findings, in contrast, suggest that the motivations of producers likely contribute to National Organic Program regulatory integrity. The fact that a majority of surveyed producers tend to see the USDA organic standards as minimum standards and adhere strictly to them suggests that willful violations of the National Organic Program regulations occur among a relatively small producer subset.

Furthermore, personal values and reputational-driven compliance motivations likely encourage adherence with the USDA organic standards where limitations in certifier monitoring and enforcement create regulatory vulnerabilities. Although such findings fall far short of measuring the frequency with which USDA organic standards noncompliances occur, they are helpful reminders that the integrity of a regulatory arrangement rests on more than just the monitoring and enforcement of regulatory agents. Other influences, from a regulatory program's history and evolution, to the values held by regulatees, contribute to the relative robustness of a regulatory design. These considerations are discussed in following chapter, in which I review the central lessons offered by the analysis spanning this book's chapters.

NOTES

1. For specifics on NASS weighting procedures see the 2016 Certified Organic Survey summary report (NASS 2017a).
2. The USDA also withholds certified organic acreage data for Delaware and Ohio to avoid disclosing information about individual producers in those states.

Chapter Eleven

Appraising the Analysis

Institutional Design, Intermediaries, and USDA Organic Certification

The *Washington Post* published a follow-up investigation of Aurora Organic Dairy regulatory violations in September 2017. As recounted in this book's opening paragraphs, *Post* reporter Peter Whoriskey's 2016 investigation documented that Aurora's High Plains complex failed to follow the USDA's organic livestock Pasture Rule. Rather than grazing its 15,000 cows on open pasture as required by the standards, a majority of the High Plains cattle were confined to feedlots. As the accredited certifying agent contracted to administer Aurora's organic certification, the Colorado Department of Agriculture held some blame for the violation. The Department failed to follow USDA guidance that organic livestock inspections be conducted during the grazing season, instead visiting the High Plains context in November when the complex's pasture rule compliance could not be confirmed.

The 2017 follow-up ran under the headline "USDA closes investigation into a massive organic farm—but what did it check?" As indicated by the headline, details of the USDA's investigation were slim. The Agency reported only that Aurora's livestock and pasture management practices complied with National Organic Program regulations and policies, refusing to comment on whether it had confirmed or disproved the *Post* investigation's findings (Whoriskey 2017b). Harkening back to a similar situation in 2007, no regulatory consequences stemmed from Whoriskey's reporting, either for Aurora or for the Colorado Department of Agriculture.

It's difficult to definitively say what enabled the situation—what more critical observers call a case of organic fraud (Mercola 2017) and more generous observers might characterize as Aurora's liberal interpretation of the organic standards. More than likely there are a host of factors. The Colorado Department of Agriculture, facing the tight financial and staffing constraints of a state program, may have simply been too overwhelmed during the busy grazing season to dispatch an inspector at the right time. The systems-based nature of National Organic Program requirements may have imposed barriers to confirming the alleged regulatory violations by affording little weight to evidence such as the *Post*'s milk product analysis findings. The National Organic Program's accreditation requirements may be poorly situated, or insufficiently enforced, to catch regulatory oversights such as the one exhibited by the State Department. Or, in balancing dual mandates of ensuring organic standards enforcement and a robust organic food industry, the USDA may have leaned in the direction of the latter, reluctant to remove a massive dairy producer from the organic market.

Regardless of the precise causes, the apparent regulatory failure reflected in the Aurora Organic Dairy case raises broader questions regarding how organic food is regulated in the U.S.; questions that I outlined in the opening pages of this book and pursued in the chapters that followed. Questions such as: Is the Aurora Organic case an exception to an otherwise robust regulatory system or does it represent systematic flaws in organic food oversight under the USDA? How is "organic integrity" upheld when the causes of regulatory failures are diffuse and varied? What unseen vulnerabilities arise from the USDA's unusual regulatory system and are they justified by corresponding benefits?

This chapter synthesizes the analyses of preceding chapters to shed light on these, and related, questions. I first recap USDA organic certification's decentralized and organizationally diverse regulatory design, reviewing the entities involved in organic standards administration and summarizing my examination of them throughout this book. I then appraise the analysis findings to discuss the policy implications that stem from the design. In the third section, I recount areas where the available evidence was lacking and identify lines of inquiry to be pursued for a yet more comprehensive understanding of U.S. organic food regulation.

RECAPPING THE FINDINGS: USDA ORGANIC INSTITUTIONS AND INTERMEDIARIES

My first objective in this book was to describe how USDA organic certification functions in the U.S. by identifying the entities involved and their contributions to organic standards administration. Drawing on the concept of regulatory intermediaries—actors independent of a regulatory authority that act on behalf of the authority, or in conjunction with it, to achieve regulatory goals (Abbott, Levi-Faur, and Snidal 2017b)—I described how the National Organic Program relies on the efforts of a range of entities to develop and administer organic standards. Put another way, I illustrated how the Program regulates organic food production through a varied assortment of proxies. I also identified key institutional elements of organic certification and how those elements shape organic food regulation under the USDA.

Organic regulation takes place through a web of regulatory action carried out by a actors that are both governmental and nongovernmental, operating both within and outside of the USDA's legislatively authorized chain of authority. The history of organic food governance in the U.S. illustrates how this administratively decentralized and organizationally diverse regulatory design is not the product of imaginative policy designers, but rather a descendent of the institutional legacy that predated federal-level organic food policy. Instead of replacing the organizations and institutional arrangements that preceded the National Organic Program, in many respects the 1990 Organic Foods Production Act made it dependent on them. The organic market's robust growth over the ensuing years indicates the design has been decidedly successful on an economic front. My analysis in the chapters of this book, however, suggests both strengths and vulnerabilities when considered through the design's policy implications.

The USDA organic standards, while modeled after those of nongovernmental programs that preceded them, are a by-product of the National Organic Program's political construction. The process of establishing the standards navigates the distance between different organic policy stakeholders' objectives and interests, with results that some inevitably find less than desirable—particularly when it comes to the standards' limited scope and omitted principles (Guthman 2004b, Obach 2007). The standards' systems-based nature further opens them to overly-liberal regulatee interpretations, prompting revisions towards more prescriptive regulations over time. However, as I showed by tracing the evolution of organic livestock and poultry standards, more prescriptive standards are not inevitable. Although USDA responded to creative regulatee interpretations with more stringent ruminant livestock access to pasture requirements in 2010, it withdrew analogous poultry requirements called for in the 2017 Organic Livestock and Poultry Practices Rule. Even when a majority of stakeholders favor more restrictive regulations, moves towards more stringent standards are vulnerable to the influence of economically and politically powerful opposition.

When U.S. organic certification actors are mapped according to their functional roles (Figure 2.1), the regulatory arrangement begins with the NOSB positioned as rulemaking intermediary. The Board's stakeholder-representative members serve an advisory role, providing the National Organic Program with recommendations on organic standards contents, the National List of Allowed and prohibited substances, and general Program implementation. NOSB processes and decisions are the target of considerable criticism by more vocal corners of the organic community. Critics charge that conventional agribusinesses have outsized representation and influence at the NOSB and that Board decision criteria increasingly skew in the favor of lenient organic standards. The resulting decreased perceived legitimacy with which the USDA organic standards are held has spurred the development of supplementary certification programs, offering added layers of stringency or filling in organic agriculture principles omitted from the natural standards.

Informed by NOSB recommendations, the National Organic Program occupies the top "link" in a chain of organic certification regulatory action. As regulatory authority, the National Organic Program balances a dual mandate of ensuring credible organic standards enforcement, on one hand, and supporting robust growth in the organic market, on the other. By tracing the Program's administrative initiatives, I showed that it has been attentive to both mandates over time. The 2010 Age of Enforcement reflected efforts to implement more robust regulatory enforcement. With the subsequent Sound and Sensible initiative, the Program aimed to reduce the burdens associated with systems-based, quasi-voluntary organic regulations. Through a compilation of USDA records, I demonstrated a track record at the National Organic Program of taking accreditation enforcement actions, for example, by revoking the accreditations of certifying agents. My analysis, however, identified an important gap in Program oversight. Although the program collects documentation of the enforcement actions taken by accredited certifiers in the form of Notice of Noncompliance records, it appears to make no effort to compile or analyze them. In failing to leverage Notice of Noncompliance data, the Program ignores valuable insights into how certifiers apply the regulatory authority delegated to them.

The organic standards are administered by the serial chain of regulatory intermediaries that extends under the National Organic Program. The Program accredits public, nonprofit, and for-profit certifying agents as third-party organic standards administrators; administration intermediaries which are responsible for certifying operations and monitoring their compliance with Program regulations. My analysis of USDA (2018) certification status data showed considerable variation in the enforcement actions of domestic certifiers. Although I noted important caveats with the findings, they nonetheless suggest that certifiers vary in their capacity and/or willingness to take the more consequential enforcement actions. When compiled as a percentage of each certifier's issued organic certificates, suspension rates ranged from 0 to 26 percent. Certificate revocation rates were notably lower, as the clients of only eight certifiers exhibit revocations, and certifiers that are identified as having revoked certifications do so at a rate under 1 percent.

Moving beyond certification status records, a synthesis of my published research sought to explain producer-perceived differences in accredited certifiers' regulatory approach behaviors and services. Analysis findings indicated that sector (public, nonprofit, for-profit) and size explain only limited differences in certifiers' regulatory behaviors. Similarly, the competitiveness of the certification markets were unrelated to their regulatory approaches and services. In contrast, certifiers' services varied systematically according to sector. I found public certifiers limited their services to administration of USDA organic standards, while private-sector and nonprofit certifiers "bundled" peripheral services in distinctive ways, with private-sector certifiers pursuing increased revenues through diversification of certification programs and nonprofits focusing on mission-aligned educational and advocacy services. One interpretation of these findings is that certifiers compete more through their services than through their regulatory behaviors—a point I return to later in this section.

As required by National Organic Program regulations, organic certifying agents separate the certification review process and the on-site inspections that verify operations' organic systems adherence, employing or contracting with inspection intermediaries to carry out inspections. Inspectors thus make up another link in the Program's chain of regulatory action. My analysis of inspector survey and interview data suggested that, generally speaking, certifiers enforce ethical standards on the inspectors they hire, track their practices, and impose sanctions if inspectors deviate from the regulations. Although my research suggests that inspectors experience multiple and sometimes conflicting obligations, they tend to see themselves first-and-foremost as National Organic Program regulatory monitors. Furthermore, organic inspectors tended to reject the use of discretion when performing inspection duties, favoring strict adherence to the regulations and the reporting of noncompliances, including those limited to recordkeeping issues and issues that do not threaten "organic integrity." Taken collectively, the findings suggest that organic inspectors constitute a robust regulatory link in organic certification's chain of authority.

Throughout most of the country, the National Organic Program holds sole authority to respond to regulatory noncompliances through legal action, such as fines or imprisonment. The state of California is an exception, where the California State Organic Program assumes the role of organic standards enforcement intermediary. A synthesis of available State Program documentation showed how state-level organic standards enforcement creates an additional layer of administrative burden for California's organic producers and handlers—burden which the state has sought to reduce through legislation. As CCOF's Kelly Damewood (2018) argues, however, a number of state-level enforcement benefits create a more robust regulatory context for California organic food production, when compared to the rest of the country. These include dedicated funding, local enforcement personnel, and the ability to monitor standards compliance among operations that are otherwise exempt from organic certification requirements. Thus, the State Program is arguably both a hindrance and an asset to California's organic industry.

Stepping outside of the authorized realm of regulatory authority, the National Organic Program depends on the contributions of unofficial, nongovernmental actors that act as parallel regulatory intermediaries. The ACA and IOIA serve as coordinating intermediaries for accredited certifier and organic inspector cohorts, respectively, coordinating activity both within cohorts and between cohorts and external entities. My analysis of the ACA and IOIA found that both professional associations provide critical training and information sharing functions for organic certifiers and inspectors. Furthermore, the ACA serves as a feedback channel by which certifiers can communicate their experiences and recommendations to USDA officials, the NOSB, and National Organic Program staff. There are limitations to the Associations' influence, however, which does not seem to extend to obvious or consistent enforcement of ethical standards.

Material review organizations represent another parallel intermediary type, historically independent of the National Organic Program but more recently recognized by it. The Program lacks authority to regulate commercial organic input materials, such as fertilizers and crop additives, creating challenges for operations attempting to source organic inputs. OMRI, the WSDA Organic Material Registration Program, and the CDFA Organic Input Material Program have emerged as credible suppliers of organic input material guidance, acting as information intermediaries for accredited certifiers, organic operations, and the NOSB, alike. By tracing changes in the National Organic Program's relationship with material review organizations, I documented that the Program has been largely unable to integrate them within organic certification's formal regulatory arrangement. The inability to formally institutionalize material review organizations continues to create obstacles for organic certifiers and the organic operations they monitor.

My investigation ended by shifting the focus from regulatory intermediaries to consider the motivations, experiences, and perspectives of the regulatory targets that constitute the foundation of the organic food supply chain: USDA certified organic producers. Drawing on Organic Regulation Research Project survey data, I first looked at organic producers' reasons for using organic practices, motivations for being certified organic, and their perceptions of the USDA organic standards and National Organic Program impacts. My analysis showed that environmental considerations, such as avoiding harmful chemicals and reducing the environmental impact of agriculture, factor strongly in producers' reasons for using organic practices. Increased profit and a desire to support the organic movement were found to motivate producers' decision to pursue organic certification, however, they were eclipsed by a desire to differentiate organic products from competition marketed as "natural" and "sustainable." When queried on their perceptions of the USDA organic standards, producers tended to favor more restrictive standards. Producers reported relatively favorable perceptions of the National Organic Program's impact on consumer confidence and environmental conditions, while at the same time expressing moderate concern that the Program created a barrier to producers wanting to enter the organic market and market cooptation by corporate agribusinesses.

Finally, I examined certified organic producers' regulatory compliance experiences and motivations. Producers seemed to experience little overall difficulty maintaining compliance and reject the notion that they ignore "trivial" noncompliances at their operations. The findings showed concern for operational reputations and a personal sense of duty are top drivers of producers' regulatory compliance, although fear of penalty was also an important compliance motivation for the average producer. Of course, it is important to note that while survey data regarding producers' experiences and motivations offer valuable regulatee-perspectives on the USDA organic standards, they do not speak to *actual* compliance or the pervasiveness of noncompliant behavior. I discuss the conclusions that *can* be drawn from the findings in the next section. A discussion of analysis limitations and future research follows.

REVIEWING THE EVIDENCE: THE POLICY IMPLICATIONS OF DECENTRALIZED ORGANIC STANDARDS ADMINISTRATION

My second objective with this book's analysis was to understand the policy implications of USDA organic certification's administratively decentralized and organizationally diverse regulatory design. In the discussion that follows, I discuss the implications that I derive from my findings. The discussion is organized around the dimensions of regulatory policy introduced in Chapter 2's framework for analyzing decentralized regulatory administration. The section begins with implications for USDA organic certification regulatory fidelity, and then discusses, in turn, implications for regulatory integrity, program feedback, and policy durability.

I outlined the vulnerabilities of USDA organic certification's decentralized regulatory design in Chapter 2 and I returned to them throughout subsequent chapters where they were most relevant. Before embarking on a review of the evidence, however, it is worth revisiting the theoretical challenges to regulatory fidelity and integrity, program feedback, and policy durability that stem from the regulatory design that characterizes U.S. organic regulation. Each subsection below therefore begins with a synopsis of central theoretical challenges as they pertain to the regulatory policy dimension in question. I then offer assessments of the extent to which the challenges are evident in the U.S. organic regulation, alongside discussion of how the challenges are compounded or ameliorated by USDA organic certification intermediaries and institutions.

Implications for USDA Organic Certification Fidelity

Throughout this book I used the term "regulatory fidelity" in reference to whether the administration of regulatory standards consistently conforms to the intents of policy designers and program administrators. In the case of USDA organic certification, the central obstacle to regulatory fidelity is the feature around which much of this book revolves: its administratively decentralized and organizationally diverse design. In relying on certification agent intermediaries to assume critical monitoring and enforcement functions, the USDA runs the risk that they will do so in a way inconsistent with National Organic Program intents, or that differences in certifiers' organizational capacities, cultures, and objectives translate to inconsistencies in how USDA organic standards are administered. For example, if certifiers vary in how they interpret ambiguous regulatory provisions, some certifiers may allow practices that other certifiers do not (Abbott, Levi-Faur, and Snidal 2017b, Carter 2016).

My findings indicate that such concerns are warranted. The strongest evidence for regulatory fidelity deficiencies came from the variation I found in the rates of certification suspensions and revocations by individual certifiers. Based on the finding, it appears that certifiers vary considerably in either their capacity or willingness to take the more consequential enforcement actions available to them. Plainly stated, whether an organic farm or facility has their organic certificate suspended or revoked because of a serious noncompliance depends, in no small part, on which certifier they've chosen to administer their certification. The findings come with significant caveats, as discussed later in this chapter. Caveats notwithstanding, when combined with anecdotal evidence—such as the Colorado Department of Agriculture's inspection lapses in the Aurora Organic Dairy case—the observed disparities offer considerable evidence that USDA organic standards are administered inconsistently across accredited certifiers.

Of course, it is possible that *greater* disparities would exist between certifiers *without* the National Organic Program's accreditation requirements and enforcement actions. The Program's oversight is a notable institutional feature that distinguishes USDA organic certification from other alternative agriculture certifications, from non-GMO labels to sustainable agriculture programs (Bernstein and Cashore 2007). Nonetheless, the variation I document in certifiers' enforcement actions suggest that the Program is not entirely successful at aligning the practices and decisions of the agents it accredits. As importantly, the Program seems to ignore opportunities to monitor the enforcement actions of certifiers, as it does not track the Notices of Noncompliance certifiers issue in response to "minor" regulatory violations. By compiling the Notice of Noncompliance records that it collects, but currently ignores, the Program has an opportunity to leverage the resulting insights regarding how certifiers apply their delegated regulatory authority towards greater organic standards enforcement fidelity.

The analysis also depicted how regulatory fidelity challenges stem from more than the National Organic Program's reliance on third-party certifying agents. Regulatory fidelity is further threatened by key gaps in the Program's institutional design. The most evident example is the "fundamental flaw" reflected in the Program's inability to regulate organic input materials, which opens the door for considerable inconsistencies not only in organic practices, but in the materials that are allowed or prohibited by organic certifiers (Stemwedel 2009). Another notable omission is found in the National Organic Program's vague requirements for inspector qualifications and training.

My analysis showed that independent, and often nongovernmental, actors have stepped in to attenuate the more pressing concerns created by the National Organic Program's institutional gaps. Material review organizations, including OMRI, the CDFA's Organic Input Material Program, and the WSDA's Material Registration Program, buttress organic certification fidelity by conducting credible organic input material reviews. In the absence of Program guidance, material review organizations offer authoritative (if not formally authorized) information and criteria, encouraging more consistent interpretation and administration of the USDA organic standards. Nonetheless, incorporating materials review organizations within the formal architecture of USDA organic certification has proven problematic. Although more recent USDA policies move in the direction of organic input standardization of by recognizing material review organizations' role, organic input material review remains a regulatory fidelity weakness.

The ACA and IOIA similarly work to generate shared interpretations where regulatory provisions are open to multiple interpretations, although their coordinating roles extend beyond communication and information sharing. The ACA and IOIA effectively set qualifications and training benchmarks for certification personnel and provide educational opportunities through which certifiers and inspectors meet them. Their importance is perhaps best reflected in the fact that the professional associations are the primary training venues for certification personnel and organic inspectors to learn and stay up to date on organic regulations monitoring and enforcement matters (Carter and Mahallati 2017). While the precise impacts of these parallel intermediaries are impossible to discern from this book's analysis, it seems undeniable that these informal parallel regulatory intermediaries contribute to greater fidelity in USDA organic standards administration.

Implications for USDA Organic Certification Integrity

The regulatory fidelity concerns highlighted in the preceding section may, at first glance, appear to undermine the integrity of the USDA's organic certification regulatory arrangement. The term regulatory integrity, however, conveys more than a lack of regulatory coherence. As it is used here, regulatory integrity refers to the extent to which a regulatory arrangement is shielded from undue influences that may threaten the realization of policy goals or the public interest. Classic conceptions of regulatory capture position regulatees' influence over a regulatory agency as the central hazard to regulatory integrity (Dal Bó 2006). With multiple layers of authority, however, decentralized designs feature various junctures at which a regulatory arrangement is vulnerable to such influence. Perhaps more importantly, when enforcement is delegated to third-party administrators in competition with one another for regulatee-derived revenue, third-party intermediaries may face incentives to provide more lax enforcement to attract and maintain regulatee-clients (Abbott, Levi-Faur, and Snidal 2017b, Coglianese and Lazer 2003).

Throughout this book's discussion, anecdotal evidence suggests that USDA organic certification's regulatory integrity is—to some degree—vulnerable to such threats. In particular, several sources (including the ACA (2010) and IOIA (Sircely 2011)) indicate that some operations engage in "certifier shopping" by searching among certifier options for one with more permissive USDA organic standards interpretations. However, my analysis turned up no indication that certifier shopping is widespread, nor did I find systematic evidence of systemic organic regulation intermediary capture.

If certifiers adjusted their enforcement practices in a manner indicative of intermediary capture, one would expect the competitiveness of certification markets to be reflected in their regulatory behaviors. My analysis, however, found no relationship between certification market concentrations (my proxy for competition) and certifiers' producer-perceived regulatory behaviors. Neither were there notable systematic differences between the regulatory approaches of for-profit certifiers, which rely on certification fee revenue, and those of their nonprofit or governmental counterparts. Furthermore, organic inspectors—the primary contact that farmers and handlers have with USDA organic standards enforcement—exhibited a general allegiance to their regulatory role and decidedly stringent approaches to the application of the National Organic Program regulations. Taken collectively, these findings offer considerable evidence that accredited certifiers and the inspectors they employ tend to uphold, or at least do not systematically undermine, organic regulation integrity.

As I noted in the case of regulatory fidelity, National Organic Program oversight *may* play an important role in bolstering organic standards administration's regulatory integrity. After all, the conflict of interest provisions discussed at several points throughout this book were designed to do just that. Furthermore, the National Organic Program is well aware of regulatory integrity threats; as I cited earlier, a Program representative told me that the Program addresses them by auditing certifiers' fee structures, looking out for certifiers "cutting deals with operations," and otherwise monitoring for conflicts of interest.

It's difficult to tell whether the National Organic Program's accreditation oversight and conflict of interest provisions curtail opportunistic behavior on the part of organic operations or organic regulation intermediaries; it's certainly possible, for example, that they encourage certifiers to avoid questionable regulatory actions. There are other explanations, however, for the lack of systematic regulatory fidelity deficiencies indicated by my analysis. First, it's reasonable to believe that many actors feel compelled to contribute to organic regulation integrity, rather than undermine it. Interviews with organic inspectors indicated as much when interviewees referred to their inspections as acts of consumer protection. In the words of one contract inspector: "[inspectors] are really the only ones . . . out there, that have direct contact with most producers . . . I represent the consumer, ultimately" (Research interview, Fall 2012). Certified producer survey data also suggested an inclination towards regulatory fidelity, where the average producer cited reputation and a personal sense of duty as driving their compliance-related behaviors. To the extent such motivations are shared among a wide-enough segment of organic certification actors, attempts to undermine USDA organic certification integrity may be better thought of as exceptions, rather than the rule.

Another explanation is found in broader economic context in which USDA organic certification is embedded. Every associated actor, from organic farmers to certification personnel, depends on consumers' confidence in the USDA organic label. Routinized unscrupulous certification behavior threatens not only National Organic Program regulatory integrity, but the viability of the organic sector as a whole—including the livelihoods of those dependent on a robust organic industry to generate certification-related jobs (Carter 2017c). The explanation is supported by the fact that prior to National Organic Program implementation, some certifiers competed on the basis of offering *more* stringent standards enforcement, rather than less (Marshall and Standifird 2005). Instead of reverting to an enforcement "race to the bottom" with the imposition of national organic standards, my analysis suggests that certifiers turned to the services that they offer as a way to compete for regulatee-clients. The proposition is best stated in the words of an organic certification consultant which I quoted earlier in this book: "It used to be that certifiers would compete on standards, but they cannot do that anymore . . . so now that leaves customer service and types of certification . . . kind of a range of services" (Research interview, Fall 2012).

Implications for National Organic Program Feedback

For regulatory programs to be remain effective over time, program officials must be aware of challenges that are experienced in the interpretation or administration of regulatory standards and how regulations perform "on the ground" (Dale and Gerlak 2007, May 1992). Program feedback refers to officials' ability to access such information. The operational distance that a decentralized regulatory design establishes between regulatory officials and program administration can inhibit program feedback, as challenges experienced by intermediaries must be conveyed to officials across levels of authority (Abbott, Levi-Faur, and Snidal 2017b, Auld and Renckens 2017). Furthermore, where intermediaries take on responsibility for regulatory monitoring and enforcement, program representatives lose the primary contact they would otherwise have with regulatees. The results of such impaired feedback are missed opportunities to make necessary adjustments to regulatory standards or related program guidance, ultimately precipitating unintended consequences or overall regulatory ineffectiveness.

In this book I've described how parallel intermediaries coalesce outside of the National Organic Program's official institutional design to communicate Program-relevant information and experiences across USDA organic certification's multiple layers of authority. First, materials review organizations offer a feedback channel specific to organic input materials information. By tracking commercial organic input developments and vetting new products for compliance with the USDA organic standards, OMRI and the CDFA's Organic Input Material Program (and to a more limited extent, the WSDA's

Organic Material Registration Program) provide timely assessments regarding the input substances being considered and used by organic producers. Although limited in scope, materials review feedback is relevant to more than the NOSB and National Organic Program officials—it is also used by accredited certifiers and their inspectors, not to mention organic operations.

My analysis also identified the ACA as a notable supplier of information regarding the operational reality of USDA organic standards administration—a "feedback channel" to the National Organic Program, in the words of one certification official. This feedback comes in multiple forms, from written comments submitted to the Secretary of Agriculture or National Organic Program officials, to interactions with Program staff at the annual training, and input and guidance on NOSB deliberations. Serving as a collective representation body, the ACA is able to magnify the voices of its certifier members, lending their input greater legitimacy and weight. Furthermore, by cultivating an ongoing relationship with the Program, the ACA ensures its members' feedback is more likely to gain the Program's attention. The ACA thus facilitates the National Organic Program's learning and adaptation—both at the level of USDA organic standards content and how they are administered—resulting in what Auld and Renckens (2017) refer to as "dynamic rule development," in the form of responsive Program policies and guidance.

Although this book's analysis showed that parallel organic certification intermediaries help address the program feedback impediments that result from USDA organic certification's decentralized design, the analysis also highlighted institutional factors that erect still other barriers to program feedback. Most notably, National Organic Program conflict of interest provisions designed to protect organic certification integrity mandate that organic farmers and handlers cannot hold leadership positions in the organizations that they receive organic certifications from. In maintaining the independent, third-party nature of organic standards administration, the provisions exclude organic operators from their most direct avenue for shaping organic policy. While the provisions are thus justifiable from a regulatory rationale, for some they a reflective of how U.S. organic policy effectively "decapitates" organic farmers' voice in organic regulation matters (Hoodes et al. 2010, Obach 2015).

Implications for U.S. Organic Policy Durability

The driving objective of organic food policy in the U.S. is to support a robust market for organic food products. By verifying that foods marketed under the term "organic" are produced according to national organic standards, the USDA organic label is meant to foster consumer confidence in organic product claims, thereby increasing consumer demand for organic products. Thus, any regulatory processes or outcomes that threaten consumer confidence in the label raise concerns regarding the long-run viability of organic food regulation under the USDA—what policy scholars refer to as policy durability (May and Jochim 2013, Patashnik 2014).

Seen from this angle, implications raised in the preceding subsections have both direct and indirect bearing on the durability of USDA organic certification. For example, inadequate or inconsistent organic standards enforcement has the potential to undermine consumer confidence in the organic label, should they gain the public's attention, as do allegations of questionable certification practices, such as certifier shopping (Kindy and Layton 2009). Illustrations of these consumer confidence threats can be readily found in response to the more visible investigative reports into organic food regulation, for instance, claims of "organic fraud" that emerged in response to the Aurora Organic Dairy case that this chapter opened with (Mercola 2017).

While USDA organic standards administration is thus relevant to the National Organic Program's durability, my analysis in this book's earlier chapters highlighted a more acute threat to USDA organic food policy viability: declines in the legitimacy with which the USDA organic standards *themselves* are perceived among key organic policy stakeholders. As cited throughout the book, seemingly isolated disputes over USDA organic standards content can be found throughout the National Organic Program's brief history, beginning with the initial Big Three controversy and more recently visible in the struggle over the 2017 Organic Livestock and Poultry Practices Rule. The unifying theme of such struggles is a belief among some stakeholders that organic standards development by the NOSB and National Organic Program has been effectively coopted by corporate agribusinesses and the conventional agriculture sector (Cornucopia Institute 2016, Jaffee and Howard 2010). The implications of the discontent have not gone unnoticed by policy makers. In the words of Patrick Leahy, the Senator from Vermont who sponsored the 1990 Organic Foods Production Act: "It will unravel everything that we've done if the standards can no longer be trusted. If we don't protect the brand, the organic label, the program is finished. It could disappear overnight" (as cited in Kindy and Layton 2009).

The analysis highlighted a tangible policy implication of stakeholder discontent with the USDA organic standards in the emergence of supplementary certification programs, such as Regenerative Organic Certification and the Real Organic Project. It's too early to know whether the supplementary certification programs will support or undermine USDA organic certification durability; the Rodale Institute claims that the purpose behind its Regenerative Organic Certification is to buttress, rather than subvert, the USDA organic standards. By providing an additional level of standards interpretation stringency, the logic goes, supplementary certification is a value-added proposition to operations already certified under the USDA.

It is possible, however, that by drawing greater attention to perceived USDA organic standards flaws, supplementary certification programs could engender what policy scholars refer to as negative feedback (May and Jochim 2013), in which one-time National Organic Program advocates grow skeptical of USDA organic certification or abandon it altogether. Ultimately, as indicated by the opening paragraph of this section, neither organic advocate discontent nor supplementary organic certification programs are likely to pose grave threats to USDA organic certification durability unless negative feedback reaches the level of organic food consumers. Given the continued double-digit year-over-year growth that the organic market exhibits (OTA 2017c), this has yet to happen.

It should be noted that the concept of policy durability rests on a program's ability to sustain political commitments over time (May and Jochim 2013). As such, my assessment in this section is based on the USDA's narrowly defined role for organic certification as a marketing program, illustrated by the limited political commitments that USDA officials imbued in the National Organic Program from the start. As proclaimed by then-Secretary of Agriculture Dan Glickman in 2000, when the national organic standards were first developed: "Let me be clear about one thing: the organic label is a marketing tool. It is not a statement about food safety. Nor is 'organic' a value judgment about nutrition or quality" (as cited in Miller and Cohrssen 2018). Of course, this limited scope is one of the most fervently condemned aspects of U.S. organic food policy by proponents of traditional organic principles. Whether this limited scope is desirable, and to whom, extend beyond this book's analysis (but see Guthman 2014, Obach 2015). Nonetheless, it's clear that the disconnect between the USDA's goals for U.S. organic policy and the objectives of motivated alternative agriculture advocates means that the institutional landscape governing organic food will continue to evolve.

EXTENDING THE ANALYSIS

I set out in this book to conduct the most thorough analysis possible of the complex regulatory architecture by which organic food is governed in the U.S. Doing so required assembling a range of evidence from a variety of sources. For several of this book's chapters, I was fortunate to leverage primary data collected through the Organic Regulation Research Project. For others, I compiled available secondary evidence, such as government reports and administrative data. And for a couple more, I had to do the best I could with a synthesis of others' writings and accessible "grey" literature. As a result of this amalgamation, I was able to cover some aspects of USDA organic certification in more detail, while only touching on others. Furthermore, even where I was able to marshal considerable evidence, in many respects, my analysis raises as many questions as it answered.

Rather than view limited evidence and unanswered questions as fatal project flaws, I see them as prospects for future inquiry: avenues that curious researchers might probe for a yet more comprehensive understanding of organic food regulation and the theoretical implications of its decentralized regulatory design. Throughout the preceding pages I've attempted to highlight some of the pressing questions that I was left with at the end of each chapter's analysis. These are summarized here in the hopes they spur motivated investigators to continue the search for answers.

The most obvious avenues for extending this book's analysis are the aspects of USDA organic certification which I assessed through the information, analyses, and arguments put forth by others. Of these, the California State Organic Program stands out as a topic urging additional research. My analysis raised, but did not resolve, questions central to the California Program. For example: Has the 2016 California Organic Food and Farming Act successfully reduced the state-level administrative burden associated with organic food production in California? To what extent do the regulatory benefits argued by Kelly Damewood (2018), such as state-level funding and local inspection personnel, have empirical support? An answer to either of these questions will offer valuable insights with implications beyond the borders of California, and, weighing the answers of *both* questions will test Damewood's assertion that similar programs in other states can bolster organic regulation fidelity and integrity writ large.

A second conspicuous research need is found in understanding NOSB processes, recommendations, and how they are weighed by the National Organic Program. My analysis focused largely on charges lodged by some of the Program's most vocal critics, such as the Cornucopia Institute. I asserted that the arguments of such critics are likely as important to the Program's perceived legitimacy, and therefore USDA organic's policy durability, as their veracity. The assertion notwithstanding, systematic and objective analyses examining critics' claims are warranted. Interested researchers will find a logical starting point to be the Cornucopia Institute's NOSB Scorecard and the conclusions the Institute has drawn regarding conventional agribusinesses' influence over NOSB recommendations. More traditional regulatory research will further help unpack the "black box" of National Organic Program rulemaking to determine how USDA officials weigh NOSB recommendations against other forms of stakeholder input when developing national organic standards.

Materials review organizations constitute a third notably opaque aspect of USDA organic certification. My descriptions of OMRI, the CDFA Organic Input Material Program, and the WSDA's Organic Material Registration relied heavily on organizational histories generated by the entities themselves, which are generally thin on details (especially when it comes to the WSDA's program). Furthermore, my analysis was limited to the challenges that the National Organic Program has experienced in attempting to formalize the role of materials review organizations, rather than extending to, for example, discrepancies between material review organizations' criteria or determinations, how these have changed over time, and the extent to which their functions have become more or less important with the National Organic Program's faltering moves at regulating to organic input materials. Research into such topics promises a better understanding of the formal and informal elements that impact USDA organic certification fidelity.

While the aforementioned topics are ones for which this book's evidence could be more readily bolstered, extensions of the analysis would also benefit from data that offers alternative perspectives on some of the more thoroughly covered subjects. For example, although it arguably offered the most complete examination to date, my analysis of organic inspectors relied largely on survey and interview data from inspector personnel. A logical step in further understanding the functions and impact of organic inspectors is an analysis that relies on more objective data, for example, personnel performance records or inspection reports. Such inquiry extends beyond an assessment of biases in study data, such as those that might stem from social desirability bias—it could provide a more in-depth examination of how organic inspections function, the extent to which inspection practices vary across individual inspectors, and how.

Similarly, my analysis of organic producer experiences and perceptions was limited to survey data from USDA-certified organic producers, omitting to the viewpoints of those operations that have chosen to not pursue (or are otherwise impeded from) organic certification. Assuming that those who opt out of organic certification are less likely to hold favorable impressions of the USDA organic standards or National Organic Program, it is likely that incorporating such perspectives would temper some of the more affirmative findings documented in Chapter 10. Furthermore, the analysis was constrained to organic producers and did not speak to the perspectives and experiences of food processors and handlers. Although this is a limitation my analysis arguably shares with food policy research, more generally, it nonetheless precludes the perspectives of integral players in contemporary organic food supply chains. Just about any product on a grocery store shelf has come into contact with a food processor or handler; a comprehensive understanding of

USDA organic certification's dynamics and impacts must therefore incorporate the experiences and perspectives of these less-often recognized food systems actors.

The above opportunities for future research notwithstanding, perhaps the most compelling avenue for extending this book's analysis can be found in further probing some of the central questions that my investigation circled around and poked at from different angles, but ultimately was unable to fully resolve. Chief among these are questions regarding the National Organic Program's ability to effectively address the perverse incentives created by USDA organic certification's competitive third-party design: Does the design of USDA organic certification invite undesirable regulatory behaviors, such as certifier shopping and capture? If so, does the National Organic Program effectively combat these incentives through accreditation requirements and other oversight procedures?

My answer to the first question is both "yes" and "no." Anecdotal accounts of certifier shopping cited in this book affirm that regulatory scholars' warnings regarding the vulnerabilities inherent in the competitive administration of regulatory standards are warranted. The extent to which certifier shopping is endemic is more difficult to examine, however, my findings suggest that most organic certifiers do not modify their regulatory behaviors in response to the competitive certification markets in which they are embedded. On the basis of these findings, I draw the tempered conclusion that certifier capture is not a systemic regulatory malady infecting USDA organic certification.

The answer to the second question is not so clear, for several reasons. My assessment of the National Organic Program relied on secondary evidence compiled and analyzed by the USDA. Although it provided a sketch of the Program's actions over time, it lacked detail regarding the appropriateness, thoroughness, or stringency of Program oversight. As I noted in Chapter 5, a deeper examination of the extent to which the Program's accreditation requirements shape the actions of certifiers will likely necessitate the compilation of accreditation audit findings, determinations, and corrective actions over time. Furthermore, only by linking the Program's oversight with evidence of certifiers' regulatory behaviors will one be able to confidently determine whether accreditation requirements ensure USDA organic certification regulatory integrity.

Such research will likely need to address the critical gap that currently exists in available documentation of certifiers' enforcement action behaviors: the un-compiled Notice of Noncompliance records that have constituted a recurring topic at several points in this book. As demonstrated in Chapter 6, my analysis of the USDA's Organic Integrity records showed considerable variation in suspended and revoked organic certificates across accredited certifiers. Although the finding is telling, it shows only the end result of certifiers' enforcement actions and is further limited to those actions upheld by the National Organic Program. Only by compiling data regarding certifier-issued Notice of Noncompliances alongside certification status data can the full extent of certifiers' regulatory enforcement efforts be understood. Once compiled, however, comparing comprehensive certifier sanctioning data with the National Organic Program's own oversight actions will allow researchers to fully assess the Program's performance as an accreditation body.

Thus, although this book provides the most comprehensive analysis of U.S. organic food regulation to date, many questions await future inquiry. Research opportunities are not limited to the USDA organic certification context, alone. When considered from the perspective of public policy scholarship, the case is just one example of decentralized program design—a phenomena that extends well beyond the regulatory realm. The conclusions drawn in this analysis offer findings, explanations, and propositions ready for the testing in yet other empirical settings. For, although this chapter focused on the study's implications for USDA organic certification, they offer insights applicable to theories of regulatory governance and public administration, more generally. I discuss the broader contributions of the analysis in the concluding chapter.

Chapter Twelve

Final Reflections

The Theoretical Implications of Regulation by Proxy

In the opening pages of this book, I recounted Peter Whoriskey's (2017a) characterization of USDA organic certification as an "unusual" regulatory system. To be sure, the layers of governmental and nongovernmental action operating under both delegated and informal authority bears little resemblance to the typical command-and-control arrangements that the word "regulation" conjures in the minds of many. However, U.S. organic regulation is not a programmatic anomaly. More attentive observers of governmental affairs will recognize in the case an illustration of the transformation that has captured the attention of public administration scholars for decades—a transformation in which independent and nongovernmental actors play increasingly central public policy roles and governmental authorities are challenged to coordinate disparate actors and interests in the pursuit of program goals (Kettl 2000, May 2007).

I set out in this study to sketch the range of intermediaries upon which the National Organic Program depends and examine the policy implications of USDA organic certification's decentralized regulatory design. Along the way, I attached theoretical constructs to substantive topics, from agricultural production standards to materials review organizations, to shed light on the ramifications of how organic food is regulated in the U.S. As this chapter's opening paragraph indicates, the analysis holds more than empirical relevance; it speaks to some of the more pressing concerns facing contemporary public policy scholars and practitioners, alike. In this closing discussion, I focus on the contributions the analysis offers towards a better understanding of institutional design and decentralized administration, in the realms of regulatory policy and beyond.

Although researchers often prioritize theoretical findings over descriptive ones, credible theoretical insights are necessarily preconditioned by thorough descriptive inquiry (Gerring 2012). To this end, my analysis offers an empirically informed catalogue of intermediary positions and roles found in decentralized regulatory contexts. First, the analysis brought advisory committees (long noted in the negotiated rulemaking literature; e.g., Susskind and McMahon 1985) under a regulatory intermediation framework, thereby recognizing stakeholder recommendations as a rulemaking intermediary function. Doing so allowed me to demonstrate that assessing regulatory policy durability, while necessarily influenced by matters of program administration, should account for the legitimacy with which regulatory standards development is regarded. Without credible standards, the long-run viability of a regulatory program is at question, regardless of the rigorousness with which the standards are enforced (Prakash and Potoski 2007).

Second, the analysis added to the emergent literature tackling the multiple "links" involved in decentralized regulatory administration "chains" of authority (Loconto 2017, Lyton 2017, van der Heijden 2017). I showed how delegation of regulatory authority can extend beyond regulatory agencies deputizing third-party administrators with a monitoring and enforcement role; where third-party administrators contract out monitoring responsibilities, inspectors constitute yet another distinct intermediary cohort. The analysis suggests that in decentralized chains of regulatory action, each link constitutes a juncture at which regulatory fidelity and integrity may be buttressed or undermined. The relative variation observed within any given link is shaped by the intermediaries with authority over it, conditioned by the parameters established by a regulatory program's institutional design.

Third, just as the analysis recast the topic of rulemaking advisory councils as an intermediary role, it framed a case of regulatory federalism as one of an enforcement intermediary operating under the oversight of a regulatory authority. The brief investigation raised more questions than it answered. Among them are the extent to which the theoretical benefits of state-level enforcement intermediaries, from local funding to state-level monitoring and legal proceedings, bolster federal-level regulatory integrity. A second is the extent to which the additional burdens imposed by a state-level enforcement intermediary are outweighed by these benefits.

Fourth, I introduced two types of parallel intermediaries in the analysis, although it should be noted that they share conceptual housing with overlapping concepts already found in the literature. I defined coordinating intermediaries as associations developed out of the coordination of intermediary cohorts—a definition which positions them as a variant of what Lee (2010) refers to as information intermediaries. In the context of USDA organic certification, the functions performed by coordinating intermediaries included disseminating information, facilitating communication and shared interpretations of regulatory standards, offering education and training, and serving as a channel for collective representation and feedback to the regulatory authority. Whether coordination intermediaries serve more or fewer, or simply different, roles in other contexts is a promising question for future research.

Finally, I defined information intermediaries as entities independent of regulatory authorities which generate and disseminate critical information to other regulatory actors; in this case, intermediaries, regulatees, and the regulatory authority, alike. Through this characterization, information intermediaries make up a more legitimate and objective type of Kourula and colleagues' (2019) expert intermediaries. In the U.S. organic regulation case, coordinating and information intermediaries take the form of informal and, with a couple of exceptions, nongovernmental, entities. Of course, this need not be the case. Both descriptive and theoretical advancement will come from research in which the characteristics, functions, and roles of coordinating and information intermediaries are compared across empirical contexts to examine what explains the differences, and to what ends.

Perhaps the most prescient theoretical insights this book offers have to do with the consequences of administering regulatory standards through diverse third-party intermediaries. In contexts ranging from building inspection (van der Heijden 2008) to sustainable forestry standards implementation (Meidinger 2006), independent and often nongovernmental entities are called on to perform crucial regulatory functions. Scholars express unease at the idea of such intermediaries assuming important regulatory responsibilities. Peter May, for example, explains the general concern of accountability: "Accountability is a key concept for democratic governance broadly concerned with holding officials responsible for their actions. . . . At issue is how that accountability is achieved when nongovernmental actors assume important roles in regulatory regimes" (2007, 9). Abbott, Levi-Faur, and Snidal outline the more specific concern of intermediary capture: "if the target pays for the intermediary's services . . . then the intermediary may be overly responsive to the target's needs, especially if targets can engage in 'intermediary shopping'" (2017b, 30). Similarly, Coglianese and Lazer speculate: "third-party [intermediaries] probably face incentives to satisfy their clients through at least marginally more lax enforcement" (2003, 718).

My findings substantiate some of these concerns while tempering others. I showed that, in the case of USDA organic certification, relying on multiple third-party administrators to deliver uniform regulatory standards undermines the uniformity of their enforcement—what I call regulatory fidelity and May (2007) refers to as consistency. My findings further corroborate accounts of intermediary shopping found in other contexts, such as Australian build code enforcement (van der Heijden 2017), where regulatees seek favorable regulatory outcomes through strategic intermediary selection. Both findings highlight what Jeroen van der Heijden (2017) dubs the "darker" side of regulatory intermediation, threatening both the effectiveness of regulatory standards and the accountability with which regulatory programs are administered.

The analysis does not, however, support scholars' gravest warnings of systematic intermediary capture. A prediction that third-party regulatory administrators are incentivized towards lax regulatory enforcement assumes that their options for competing for regulatee-clients are limited to the relative stringency of their regulatory behaviors. My analysis suggests another manner in which intermediaries respond to competitive pressures. Third-party intermediaries *may* find it preferable to compete on the basis of ancillary services, rather than run the risk of altering their regulatory practices. While the finding is not likely generalizable to contexts where ancillary services are less desirable or prohibited, it suggests that intermediary capture may be less of a concern in competitive enforcement settings where parallel services are bundled with regulatory ones. The proposition is yet stronger in contexts where regulatory integrity is somehow incentivized—by institutional mechanisms, such as accreditation—or by other contextual factors.

Indeed, regulatory theory posits accreditation as one oversight mechanism with the potential to attenuate perverse incentives established by a competitive third-party design (Abbott, Levi-Faur, and Snidal 2017b). The extent to which accreditation requirements effectively curtail opportunistic intermediary behavior is beyond the scope of this book. Nonetheless, the analysis identified an important manner in which accreditation can fail to ensure full accountability in the delegation of regulatory responsibilities. Accreditation requirements which focus on intermediaries' characteristics and procedures—*but ignore their actions*—leave regulatory authorities blind to how intermediary organizations wield the authority bestowed upon them. Yet, this seems to be precisely the case in the National Organic Program's failure to track how certifiers sanction when they encounter noncompliances that they deem to fall below the threshold of warranting certification suspension or revocation.

To some extent, the National Organic Program's failure to compile Notice of Noncompliance records may be among the more telling findings of this book. Although the cause of the omission is uncertain, the Program's consistently constrained resources and the many responsibilities its small staff juggles point to the central obstacle being one of capacity. As detailed throughout this book, decentralized regulatory designs create complex administrative environments replete with competing incentives and institutional gaps that manifest in challenges for which government agencies, such as the National

Organic Program, are not often equipped to address. The obstacle is not unique to organic certification; nor is it limited to regulatory contexts. Prominent public administration scholar Donald Kettl (2000, 495) refers to this as the "capacity problem" of decentralized governance, which demands government agencies devise new strategies if they are to sustain effective management and accountability in such less traditional governing arrangements.

These challenges notwithstanding, it would be a gross oversimplification to conclude that the decentralized administration of regulatory standards invites nothing but program liabilities. As Abbott, Levi-Faur, and Snidal note: "relying on polycentric enrollment and networks supposes that systems will self-organize in desirable ways" (2017a, 288). The case of USDA organic certification offers powerful examples in support of such a supposition. For example, the ACA and IOIA show that intermediaries can self-organize outside of a regulatory program's authority. In the context of USDA organic certification, these coordinating intermediaries perform a range of vital functions, from facilitating shared interpretations of regulatory standards to providing the widely recognized gold standard for monitoring and enforcement training. Similarly, material review organizations information intermediaries demonstrate how nongovernmental actors can mobilize to address critical gaps in a program's institutional design. Where a regulatory authority is unable or unwilling to generate program-relevant knowledge, capable actors may fill the void by becoming credible information suppliers and brokers.

The self-organization observed among organic certification intermediaries should be considered with an appreciation for the institutional history that predates USDA organic certification. It's likely that the nongovernmental coordination that preceded and ultimately helped realize the 1990 Organic Foods Production Act has carried over, to some extent, to the contemporary organic certification context. Whether the types of intermediary coordination observed in USDA organic certification would exist if were not for a legacy of informal governance and collective action deserves attention. Absent evidence of the counterfactual, it seems safe to conclude that the findings of this analysis are more applicable to regulatory arrangements born out of similar social movement and industry coordination, as is the case for many certification programs (e.g., Auld 2014), and should only be cautiously applied to cases lacking such institutional legacies. Research into yet other decentralized regulatory settings will undoubtedly help identify the extent to which a collaborative history is a precondition for intermediary benefits of the likes observed in the administration of organic standards.

Recognizing these caveats, U.S. organic regulation serves as an example that the success of decentralized regulatory designs does not hinge on formal authority, alone. While the complex administrative landscape created by a decentralization may challenge regulatory agencies inherently structured for hierarchically organized problems and processes, informal and nongovernmental action can help ameliorate the limitations of traditional bureaucratic structure, rather than simply exacerbate them. Assuming an external context conducive to collective action and a motivated cadre of intermediaries, as appear to exist in the National Organic Program's case, the promises offered by government-coordinated cross-sector regulatory standards administration may be fully realized if a regulatory authority is afforded adequate resources and the institutional leeway to effectively leverage intermediary efforts towards policy goals. The proposition is an attractive one, as it combines the coercive authority and associated accountability mechanisms of government with the creativity and popular legitimacy of informal collective action.

This rather optimistic premise rests, of course, on key assumptions that history cautions are uncertain, at best. Just as the National Organic Program tackles a myriad of sometimes incompatible objectives with a lean budget and small staff, agencies across the U.S. government are asked to oversee increasingly complex administrative environments while facing ongoing capacity reductions (Kettl 2000, Rhodes 1997). Assuming political officials remain reluctant to provide agencies with the material and institutional resources sufficient to meet the challenges of less-traditional administrative arrangements, the success of decentralized regulation will continue to rely heavily on intermediaries' internally derived motivations, objectives, and efforts. Sustained scholarly research is therefore needed which probes beyond the causes of regulatory decentralization to examine the many dimensions of regulatory administration which are impacted when governments choose to regulate by proxy.

Methodological Appendix

To conduct the analysis housed in this book, I assembled a variety of data and evidence with elements of sequential and parallel mixed methods, meaning that quantitative and qualitative data were compiled both in stages and concurrently (Leech and Onwuegbuzie 2007, Teddlie and Tashakkori 2009). This appendix outlines the methods by which data were collected and other evidence compiled. As stated in the first chapter, much of the book's evidence is primary data collected in a three-year-long research project carried out by a multi institution research team (the Organic Regulation Research Project; see the Acknowledgments for details). Previously unreleased findings appear alongside published data in some chapters. I also compiled secondary data and conducted reviews of existing documentation and literature where the available primary and secondary data fell short of addressing aspects of the USDA organic certification arrangement.

PRIMARY DATA SOURCES

The Organic Regulation Research Project encompassed qualitative and quantitative data collection involving several populations. This section provides an overview of central data collected during the project; details regarding data collection, construct measurement, and analyses can be found where they are most relevant in the book's analysis. We collected quantitative through three surveys: one of accredited certifiers, a second of organic inspectors, and a third of certified organic producers. We collected qualitative data through in-depth interviews with a range of USDA organic certification actors.

Accredited Certifying Agent Survey

We conducted the survey of accredited organic certifier administrators online during the winter of 2012–2013. Forty-three certifier representatives responded to emailed survey requests, for a response rate of 49 percent. I drew on the survey for data regarding certifiers' coordination through the ACA and associated impacts on USDA organic standards administration.

Organic Inspector Survey

We conducted a survey of organic inspectors in 2014. No publicly available list identifies the individuals that conduct inspections for USDA organic standards compliance. We therefore used organizational affiliations and snowball sampling techniques (Atkinson and Flint 2001) to generate a list of potential organic inspectors. We began by pulling names from the list of IOIA members. We then gathered additional names and contact information through Internet-based searches of accredited certifiers' websites. Finally, we asked verified inspectors that were interviewed during the study (discussed below) to provide the names and contact information for colleagues that we had not already identified through the prior strategies. In total, the names and contact information of 260 individuals thought to be inspectors for the USDA organic standards were collected, 159 of which were IOIA members.

We emailed a request to participate to each of the identified potential organic inspectors, receiving 107 responses. Ten responses indicated that the individuals no longer worked as organic inspectors and another 5 surveys were missing sufficient data to render the results unusable, resulting in 92 serviceable surveys (35 percent of the initial 260 requests sent). Data collected included questions pertaining to inspectors' interactions with their employing certifiers, the roles that inspectors perceive themselves to fulfill in USDA organic certification, inspectors' attitudes towards the use of discretion, and demographic details and employment data. I drew on the organic inspector survey data most heavily in my analysis of organic inspectors. I also pulled in the responses of a question battery for data regarding IOIA impacts.

Certified Organic Producer Survey

We conducted the nation-wide organic producer survey online during the winter of 2013–2014. We sent a survey request to all domestic certified operations holding any combination of crops, wild crops, and livestock certifications for which the USDA listed a valid email address, totaling 6,273 producers and representing approximately half of all certified producers. Responses were received from 1,055 producers for a response rate of 17 percent.

Farmers are a notoriously difficult population to survey and a response rate of 17 percent is consistent with other farmer survey research (Pennings, Irwin, and Good 2002). Nonetheless, the relatively low response rate suggests that the study findings are susceptible to nonresponse bias.

Steps to gauge the survey's vulnerability to nonresponse bias are detailed immediately below. The results of those investigations, while not eliminating the potential for bias in analysis findings, suggest that it is likely small. The most likely source of any such bias is seen in a comparison of respondents' geographic locations with available USDA data (NASS 2014), indicating sample under-representation of Midwest organic farmers and over-representation of those in the Northwest. A more relevant limitation of the producer survey data is that at the email addresses of several certifiers' clients were not listed in the USDA database, constraining the analysis to forty-one domestic certifiers. Despite omitting seven certifiers, it should be noted that the survey data still capture the diversity of the domestic organic certifier cohort, including varying sectoral affiliations, geographic locations, and sizes.

Two of the book chapters relied heavily on the certified organic producer survey. I summarized the findings of several published studies that use the survey data in an analysis of accredited certifiers. I also drew extensively from the survey data to depict certified organic producers' motivations, experiences with the National Organic Program regulations, and perceptions of Program impacts.

Certified Organic Producer Survey: Assessing for Nonresponse Bias

I used three procedures to assess the potential impacts of nonresponse bias on the certified organic producer survey findings: a wave analysis, a nonrespondent survey response comparison, and a comparison of survey sample characteristics with those of the population.

A wave analysis is a comparison of the responses of early survey respondents (an early "wave") with those of later survey respondents (later waves). The underlying assumption of wave analysis is that the answers of late responders are more likely to approximate the answers of nonrespondents than those of individuals that readily respond to survey requests. No statistically significant differences were found between the response means of survey waves. An example is provided in a *Journal of Public Administration Research and Theory* article (Carter 2016), in which I report the mean responses of four survey waves regarding the certifier regulatory approach variables reported in this book:

- Strictness in regulatory interpretation (Means = 1.16, 1.20, 1.30, 1.23; $p = 0.30$)

- Propensity to administer sanctions (Means = 0.88, 0.88, 0.89, 0.91; $p = 0.98$)
- Flexibility (Means = 0.27, 0.46, 0.40, 0.35; $p = 0.32$)
- Willingness to provide assistance (Means = 0.52, 0.72, 0.69, 0.69; $p = 0.24$)

To further assess for nonresponse bias, twenty nonrespondents were contacted by phone and verbally administered seven survey questions. Nonparametric tests (due to the extreme difference in group size) comparing these responses with those of the online sample revealed no statistically significant differences at the $p < .05$ level. The questions/prompts that the follow-up phone sample responded to were:

- I practice organic farming because, compared to conventional practices, it decreases the environmental impact of agricultural production (Online sample mean = 1.36; phone sample mean = 1.10; $p = 0.09$)
- The NOP regulations reflect what I consider to be ideal organic standards (Online sample mean = 0.15; phone sample mean = 0.45; $p = 0.27$)
- The NOP regulations directly result in a profitable market for my products (Online sample mean = 0.49; phone sample mean = 0.45; $p = 0.94$)
- Maintaining compliance with the NOP regulations is extremely difficult (Online sample mean = 0.75; phone sample mean = -0.20; $p = 0.71$)
- How important was the cost of the certifier's services in your selection of certifier? (Online sample mean = 3.17; phone sample mean = 2.29; $p = 0.26$)
- How important was the particular services offered by this certifier in your selection of certifier? (Online sample mean = 3.15; phone sample mean = 2.80; $p = 0.18$)
- How would you rate the quality of your certifier's educational services related to the NOP? (Online sample mean = 3.79; phone sample mean = 3.50; $p = 0.31$)

Finally, a comparison of survey respondents' demographic characteristics with contemporaneous USDA data (NASS 2014) indicated a fair, but not ideal, representation of the USDA certified organic producer population. When survey respondents were asked to report their operation's size relative to the size of operations producing similar products, 51% reported "smallest" or "small." Notably, 17% of respondents classified their operations as "large" or "largest," indicating that the perspectives of larger organic farmers were appropriately incorporated in study findings. While direct comparisons with USDA data are not possible, as the study's operation size measurement does not follow USDA categories, these characteristics are nonetheless consistent with USDA reports that a majority of organic farmers run relatively small operations.

A comparison of reported survey respondent locations with the USDA Organic Integrity (USDA 2018) list indicates fair geographical representation, with sample under-representation of Midwest organic farmers and overrepresentation of those in the Northwest. Midwest producers made up 16% of the survey sample, while accounting for 34% of the population. The highest percentage of survey respondents were from the West (29%; 25% of the population), followed by the Northwest (22%; 12% of the population) and Northeast (18%; 19% of the population). Southeast producers made up 10% of the sample (7% of the population) and Southwest producers made up the remaining 5% (4% of the population).

Of the four certification types, the vast majority held organic crop certification, 17% held organic livestock certification, and less than 4% held certification for wild crops. The most frequently reported commodity types produced by survey respondents were vegetable, grain, fruit, and herb crops. A much smaller percentage of respondents reported eggs, dairy, poultry, or livestock commodities. The breakdown of survey respondents by certification and commodity types roughly mirrors production trends in U.S. organic food production writ large.

Interviews

We collected qualitative data through in-depth, semi-structured interviews with purposive samples from three populations. All interviews were conducted either in person or over the phone by a member of the research team. Most of the interviews were recorded and later transcribed. For the few interviews that were not recorded, the interviewer took detailed notes at the time of the interview. All interviews were conducted under the agreement that interviewee identities would remain confidential.

First, in fall 2012 I held interviews with three key informants selected for their positions in the organic food regulation system and long-term involvement with organic regulation. These included: a representative of the National Organic Program, a representative of the ACA, and an organic certification consultant. Second, we interviewed twelve organic certifier administrators in the winter of 2012/2013. Our sample frame was purposeful, with the intent of capturing the diversity of certifying agents on the basis of organizational form (i.e., public, nonprofit, and private), size, and geographic service area. Finally, a member of the research team interviewed ten organic inspectors in the spring of 2014. Again, the sample frame was purposeful, with the intent of capturing diversity in inspectors' organizational affiliations and employment statuses (i.e., full- or part-time, or contract).

Across this book's chapters I drew selectively on interview data where they best spoke to the topic at hand—often to buttress or compliment secondary evidence or quantitative data. Interview quotes and observations appeared in discussions of the National Organic Program and organic certifiers. I incorporated a systematic analysis of interview data to gain a window into the perceptions of organic inspectors and dew on a separate analysis of interviews with accredited certifier representatives and organic inspectors for qualitative observations regarding the ACA and IOIA. Of course, as is the case with much qualitative research, in addition to providing quotes and systematically-compiled qualitative data, the process of conducting many of the Organic Regulation Research Project's interviews offered me an interpretive perspective on the USDA organic certification system that inevitably shapes this book's analysis and discussion.

SECONDARY DATA, SECONDARY DOCUMENTATION, AND EVIDENCE INTEGRATION

I compiled secondary data from several sources to compliment the primary data described above. The USDA's Organic Integrity Database (USDA 2018) was particularly valuable, as it lists all USDA certified organic operations, their locations and certification statuses (active, surrendered, suspended, or revoked), as well as their certifiers. Several administrative reports from entities that ranged from the USDA, to the U.S. Office of the Inspector General (OIG), to state government agencies, and beyond, were also very useful. These were incorporated in this book's analysis, as cited.

I drew on data and evidence pragmatically according to how well they speak to the topic at hand. Primary or secondary data make up the foundation for analysis and discussion, wherever possible, however, I relied on synthesis of secondary documentation and literature heavily in some chapters to integrate central aspects of the USDA organic certification arrangement that primary and secondary data fail to speak to. As such, the efforts of many scholars and practitioners contributed to the book's analysis (as cited). Of note is the work of authors such as Brian Obach, Julie Guthman, and Samantha Mosier, which feature heavily in my account of the evolution of U.S. organic food governance. Similarly, my examination of the California State Organic Program benefits greatly from publications authored by CCOF's Kally Damewood.

The practice of evidence synthesis is a well-established research approach for examining contemporary phenomena in real-world contexts and carries notable benefits. The research design merges inductive and deductive methods (Van de Ven 2007). In doing so, it combines the strengths of qualitative data, such as nuanced research findings and the identification of considerations not foreseen by a deductive framework (Gerring 2011), with the strengths of quantitative data: greater transparency and replicability, and data collection from a larger sample of participants (Creswell 1994, Teddlie and Tashakkori 2009). Triangulation of multiple data sources further allows a more complete understanding of the topic at hand and integration of primary and secondary evidence increases the validity of study findings by identifying research weaknesses, for example, where evidence is contradictory, and highlighting research strengths, such as where evidence aligns. Not only was the compilation of multiple data types and sources necessary to make this book possible; I believe the analysis is stronger as a result.

References

Abbott, Kenneth W., David Levi-Faur, and Duncan Snidal. 2017a. "Enriching the RIT Framework." *The ANNALS of the American Academy of Political and Social Science,* 670 (1):280–288.

Abbott, Kenneth W., David Levi-Faur, and Duncan Snidal. 2017b. "Theorizing Regulatory Intermediaries: The RIT Model." *The ANNALS of the American Academy of Political and Social Science,* 670 (1):14–35.

Abbott, Kenneth W., and Duncan Snidal. 2009. "Strengthening International Regulation through Transmittal New Governance: Overcoming the Orchestration Deficit." *Vanderbilt Journal of Transnational Law,* 42:501–577.

Accredited Certifiers Associtation (ACA). 2010. *White Paper Regarding Status of Materials Review*. Accredited Certifiers Associtation: Mabel, MN.

Accredited Certifiers Associtation (ACA). 2011. "The Accredited Certifiers Association Code of Conduct." Accredited Certifiers Association. Accessed July 22, 2017. http://www.accreditedcertifiers.org/wp-content/uploads/2013/01/Code_of_Conduct_Final.pdf.

Accredited Certifiers Associtation (ACA). 2016a. *ACA Letter to the National Organic Program Regarding the Interim Instruction on Material Review.* Accredited Certifiers Association: Mabel, MN.

Accredited Certifiers Associtation (ACA). 2016b. "NOSB Meeting Report." *The ACA Guidewire* 12 (2): 1.

Accredited Certifiers Associtation (ACA). 2018. "Accredited Certifiers Association." Accredited Certifiers Association. Accessed September 12, 2018. https://www.accreditedcertifiers.org/.

Agriculture Marketing Service (AMS). 2015a. *Enforcement of the USDA Organic Regulations: Penalty Matrix.* United States Department of Agriculture: Washington, DC.

Agriculture Marketing Service (AMS). 2015b. *National Organic Program Strategic Plan.* U.S. Department of Agriculture: Washington, DC.

Amaditz, Kenneth C. 1997. "The Organic Foods Production Act of 1990 and Its Impending Regulations: A Big Zero for Organic Food." *Food and Drug Law Journal,* 52(4):537–559.

Andrews, Rhys, George A. Boyne, and Richard M. Walker. 2006. "Strategy Content and Organizational Performance: An Empirical Analysis." *Public Administration Review,* 66 (1):52–63.

Arcuri, Alessandra. 2015. "The Transformation of Organic Regulation: The Ambiguous Effects of Publicization." *Regulation and Governance,* 9 (2):144–159.

Atkinson, Rowland, and John Flint. 2001. "Accessing Hidden and Hard-to-Reach Populations: Snowball Research Strategies." *Social Research Update,* 33 (1):1–4.

Auld, Graeme. 2014. *Constructing Private Governance: The Rise and Evolution of Forest, Coffee, and Fisheries Certification*: New Haven, CT: Yale University Press.

Auld, Graeme, and Stefan Renckens. 2017. "Rule-Making Feedbacks through Intermediation and Evaluation in Transnational Private Governance." *The ANNALS of the American Academy of Political and Social Science,* 670 (1):93–111.

Ayres, Ian, and John Braithwaite. 1992. *Responsive Regulation: Transcending the Deregulation Debate*: Oxford, UK: Oxford University Press.

Baker, Brian. 2005. "Brief History of Organic Farming and the National Organic Program." *Organic Farming Compliance Handbook: A Resource Guide for Western Region Agricultural Professionals*. Washington, DC.

Bardach, Eugene, and Robert A. Kagan. 1982. *Going by the Book: The Problem of Regulatory Unreasonableness*. New York, NY: Routledge.

Bartley, Tim. 2007. "Institutional Emergence in an Era of Globalization: The Rise of Transnational Private Regulation of Labor and Environmental Conditions." *American Journal of Sociology,* 113 (2):297–351.

Bartley, Tim. 2011. "Certification as a Mode of Social Regulation." In *Handbook on the Politics of Regulation*, 441–452. Edited by David Levi-Faur. Narthampton, MA: Edward Elgar.

Behar, Harriett. 2014. "Efficiency or Democracy? Nop Changes 'Sunset' Policy without Public Input." *Inside Organics Blog*. Accessed June 7, 2019. https://mosesorganic.org/policywork/inside-organics-blog/nop-changes-sunset-policy-without-public-input/.

Belasco, Warren J. 2014. *Appetite for Change: How the Counterculture Took On the Food Industry*. Ithaca, NY: Cornell University Press.

Bernstein, Steven, and Benjamin Cashore. 2007. "Can Non-state Global Governance Be Legitimate? An Analytical Framework." *Regulation and Governance,* 1 (4):347–371.

Beyl, Caula A. 1992. "Rachel Carson, *Silent Spring*, and the Environmental Movement." *HortTechnology,* 2 (2):272–275.

Biddle, Bruce J. 1986. "Recent Developments in Role Theory." *Annual Review of Sociology,* 12 (1):67–92.

Black, Julia. 2008. "Constructing and Contesting Legitimacy and Accountability in Polycentric Regulatory Regimes." *Regulation and Governance,* 2 (2):137–164.

Bones, Gordon G. 1992. "State and Federal Organic Food Certification Laws: Coming of Age." *North Dakota Law Review,* 68:405–444.

Boyne, George A. 2002. "Public and Private Management: What's the Difference?" *Journal of Management Studies,* 39 (1):97–122.

Bozeman, Barry. 2004. *All Organizations Are Public: Comparing Public and Private Organizations*. Washington, DC: Beard Books.

Bozeman, Barry. 2007. *Public Values and Public Interest: Counterbalancing Economic Individualism*. Washington, DC: Georgetown University Press.

Brown, Trevor L., Matthew Potoski, and David M. Van Slyke. 2006. "Managing Public Service Contracts: Aligning Values, Institutions, and Markets." *Public Administration Review,* 66 (3):323–331.

Buck, Daniel, Christina Getz, and Julie Guthman. 1997. "From Farm to Table: The Organic Vegetable Commodity Chain of Northern California." *Sociologia Ruralis,* 37 (1):3–20.

Buffat, Aurélien. 2015. "When and Why Discretion Is Weak or Strong: The Case of Taxing Officers in a Public Unemployment Fund." In *Understanding Street-Level Bureaucracy*, 79–96. Edited by Peter Hupe, Michael Hill, and Aurélien Buffat. Bristol, UK: Policy Press.

Burby, Raymond J., and Robert G. Paterson. 1993. "Improving Compliance with State Environmental Regulations." *Journal of Policy Analysis and Management,* 12 (4):753–772.

Burros, Marian. 2000. "U.S. Planning Tough Rules for Growing Organic Food." *New York Times*, March 5, 2000: 22.

California Department of Food and Agriculture (CDFA). 2012. *Report to the Legislature: Organic Input Materials.* Edited by California Department of Food and Agriculture. Sacramento, CA: California Department of Food and Agriculture.

Carman, James M., and Eric Langeard. 1980. "Growth Strategies for Service Firms." *Strategic Management Journal,* 1 (1):7–22.

Carpenter, Daniel, and David A. Moss. 2013. *Preventing Regulatory Capture: Special Interest Influence and How to Limit It.* Cambridge, MA: Cambridge University Press.

Carrigan, Christopher. 2017. *Structured to Fail? Regulatory Performance under Competing Mandates*. Cambridge, MA: Cambridge University Press.

Carson, Rachel. 1962. *Silent Spring*. New York, NY: Houghton Mifflin.

Carter, David P. 2016. "Public, Nonprofit, and For-Profit Sector Regulatory Approaches in Third-Party Regulatory Administration." *Journal of Public Administration Research and Theory,* 26 (4):726–744.

Carter, David P. 2017a. "Intermediary Attributes, Regulatee Experiences, and Perceived Expertise in Third-Party Regulation." *Administration and Society.* DOI: 0095399717725350.

Carter, David P. 2017b. "Regulatee Choice in Certification Schemes: Explaining Selection from among Certifier Options." *Public Administration,* 95 (1):232–248.

Carter, David P. 2017c. "Role Perceptions and Attitudes toward Discretion at a Decentralized Regulatory Frontline: The Case of Organic Inspectors." *Regulation and Governance,* 11 (4):353–367.

Carter, David P. 2017d. "Service Diversification and Service Quality Differences in the Third-Party Administration of US Organic Regulations." *Public Management Review,* 19 (6):17.

Carter, David P., and Adrienne Cachelin. 2018. "The Consumer Costs of Food Certification: A Pilot Study and Research Opportunities." *Journal of Consumer Affairs.* DOI: 10.1111/joca.12196.

Carter, David P., Christopher M. Weible, Saba N. Siddiki, John Brett, and Sara Miller Chonaiew. 2015. "Assessing Policy Divergence: How to Investigate the Difference between a Law and Corresponding Regulation." *Public Administration,* 93 (1):159–176.

Carter, David P., Christopher M. Weible, Saba N. Siddiki, and Xavier Basurto. 2016. "Integrating Core Concepts from the Institutional Analysis and Development Framework for the Systematic Analysis of Policy Designs: An Illustration from the US National Organic Program Regulation." *Journal of Theoretical Politics,* 28 (1):159–185.

Carter, David P., and Nadia Mahallati. 2017. "Coordinating Intermediaries: The Prospects and Limitations of Professional Associations in Decentralized Regulation." *Regulation and Governance,* 13(1): 51–69.

Carter, David P., Tanya Heikkila, and Christopher M. Weible. 2018. "How Participant Values Influence Reasons for Pursuing Voluntary Programme Membership." *Public Administration,* 96(4): 787–802.

Carter, David P., Tyler A. Scott, and Nadia Mahallati. 2017. "Balancing Barriers to Entry and Administrative Burden in Voluntary Regulation." *Perspectives on Public Management and Governance,* 1(3), 207–221.

Cashore, Benjamin, Graeme Auld, and Deanna Newsom. 2003. "Forest Certification (Eco-Labeling) Programs and Their Policy-Making Authority: Explaining Divergence among North American and European Case Studies." *Forest Policy and Economics,* 5 (3):225–247.

Caughlan, Goldie. 2010. "Restarting Organic Standards?" *Insights by Goldie*. Accessed July 24, 2018. https://www.pccmarkets.com/sound-consumer/2010-05/goldie/.

CCOF. 2018a. "California Organic Food and Farming Act." CCOF. Accessed July 24, 2018. https://www.ccof.org/policy-advocacy/california-organic-food-and-farming-act.

CCOF. 2018b. "What Is the Organic System Plan (OSP)?" CCOF. Accessed July 24, 2018. https://www.ccof.org/faqs/what-organic-system-plan-osp.

Centers for Disease Control (CDC). 1986. "Epidemiologic Notes and Reports Aldicarb Food Poisoning from Contaminated Melons—California." *Morbidity and Mortality Weekly Report,* 35 (16):254–258.

Century, Jeanne, Mollie Rudnick, and Cassie Freeman. 2010. "A Framework for Measuring Fidelity of Implementation: A Foundation for Shared Language and Accumulation of Knowledge." *American Journal of Evaluation,* 31 (2):199–218.

Chang, Cyril F., and Howard P. Tuckman. 1994. "Revenue Diversification among Non-Profits." *VOLUNTAS: International Journal of Voluntary and Nonprofit Organizations,* 5 (3):273–290.

Charles, Dan. 2014. *USDA Defies Advisers, Allows Carrageenan to Keep Organic Label.* National Public Radio. Accessed June 7, 2019. https://www.npr.org/sections/thesalt/2018/04/04/599550018/usda-sides-with-big-organic-to-allow-emulsifier-to-keep-organic-label

Chouinard, Hayley H., Tobias Paterson, Philip R. Wandschneider, and Adrienne M. Ohler. 2008. "Will Farmers Trade Profits for Stewardship? Heterogeneous Motivations for Farm Practice Selection." *Land Economics,* 84 (1):66–82.

Coglianese, Cary. 2002. "Is Satisfaction Success? Evaluating Public Participation in Regulatory Policymaking." In *KSG Working Paper No. RWP02-038.* Edited by Rosemary O'Leary and Lisa Bingham. Accessed June 7, 2019. http://dx.doi.org/10.2139/ssrn.331420

Coglianese, Cary. 2012. *Measuring Regulatory Performance: Evaluating the Impact of Regulation and Regulatory Policy.* Organization for Economic Co-operation and Development. Accessed June 7, 2019. https://www.oecd.org/gov/regulatory-policy/1_coglianese%20web.pdf

Coglianese, Cary, and David Lazer. 2003. "Management-Based Regulation: Prescribing Private Management to Achieve Public Goals." *Law & Society Review,* 37 (4):691–730.

Coglianese, Cary, Jennifer Nash, and Todd Olmstead. 2003. "Performance-Based Regulation: Prospects and Limitations in Health, Safety, and Environmental Protection." *Administrative Law Review,* 55 (4):705–729.

Conacher, Arthur J., and Jeanette Conacher. 1982. *Organic Farming in Australia.* Peth, Australia: University of Western Australia.

Conford, Philip. 2001. *The Origins of the Organic Movement.* Edinburgh, UK: Floris Books.

Considine, Mark. 2000. "Selling the Unemployed: The Performance of Bureaucracies, Firms and Non-Profits in the New Australian 'Market' for Unemployment Assistance." *Social Policy and Administration,* 34 (3):274–295.

Cook, Jeffrey J., and Sara R. Rinfret. 2013. "A Revised Look: EPA Rulemaking Processes." *Journal of Environmental Studies and Sciences,* 3 (3):279–289.

Cornucopia Institute. 2013. "Fed Shutdown Forces Cease-Fire in Organic War: USDA Louisville Meeting Canceled." *Cornucopia News*, Oct 10, 2013. Accessed July 24, 2018. https://www.cornucopia.org/2013/10/fed-shutdown-forces-cease-fire-organic-war-usda-louisville-meeting-canceled/.

Cornucopia Institute. 2016. *The Organic Watergate-White Paper: Connecting the Dots: Corporate Influence at the USDA's National Organic Program.* Cornucopia, WI: Cornucopia Institute.

Cornucopia Institute. 2018. "Controversial USDA National Organic Standards Board to Meet in Tuscon." *Cornucopia News*, April 22, 2018. Accessed June 7, 2019. https://www.cornucopia.org/2018/04/controversial-usda-national-organic-standards-board-meet-tucson/.

Crandell, Erin M. 2003. "What Is an Organic Inspector?" *Vegetarian Journal.* Accessed June 6, 2019. https://www.vrg.org/journal/vj2003issue1/2003_issue1_organic.php

Creswell, John W. 1994. *Research Design: Qualitative & Quantitative Approaches*. Thousand Oaks, CA: SAGE.

Curry, Lynne. 2017. "Certified 'Organic' Livestock Are Supposed to Have Outdoor Access. In Practice, They Don't." *The New Food Economy*. Accessed June 7, 2019. https://newfoodeconomy.org/usda-organic-animal-welfare-rule-livestock-poultry-practices/.

D'Andrade, Roy. 2006. "Commentary on Searle's 'Social Ontology: Some Basic Principles' Culture and Institutions." *Anthropological Theory,* 6 (1):30–39.

Dahl, Robert A., and Charles E. Lindblom. 1953. *Politics, Economics, and Welfare*. New York: Harper.

Dal Bó, Ernesto. 2006. "Regulatory Capture: A Review." *Oxford Review of Economic Policy,* 22 (2):203–225.

Dale, Lisa, and Andrea K. Gerlak. 2007. "It's All in the Numbers: Acreage Tallies and Environmental Program Evaluation." *Environmental Management,* 39 (2):246–260.

Damewood, Kelly. 2018. "Strengthening the National Organic Program with State Organic Programs." *Journal of Food Law and Policy,* 14 (1):111–153.

Damewood, Kelly, and Jane Sooby. 2015. *Review of the California State Organic Program.* Santa Cruz, CA: CCOF.

De Silva, Nicole. 2017. "Intermediary Complexity in Regulatory Governance: The International Criminal Court's Use of NGOs in Regulating International Crimes." *The ANNALS of the American Academy of Political and Social Science,* 670 (1):170–188.

Deaton, B. James, and John P. Hoehn. 2005. "The Social Construction of Production Externalities in Contemporary Agriculture: Process Versus Product Standards as the Basis for Defining 'Organic.'" *Agriculture and Human Values,* 22 (1):31–38.

Dias, Janice Johnson, and Steven Maynard-Moody. 2006. "For-Profit Welfare: Contracts, Conflicts, and the Performance Paradox." *Journal of Public Administration Research and Theory,* 17 (2):189–211.

Dimitri, Carolyn, and Christina Bronsing. 2015. "US National Organic Standards Board: Does It Preserve the Public Voice amidst USDA and Corporate Interests?" Istanbul, Turkey: ISOFAR Scientific Conference. Accessed June 7, 2019. http://orgprints.org/23696/1/23696_MM.pdf

Dixon, Linley, and Mark Kastel. 2017. "The National Organic Program Is Getting a New Boss, Here's Why That's Long Overdue." The Cornucopia Institute. Accessed June 7, 2019. http://inthesetimes.com/rural-america/entry/20546/usda-national-organic-program-miles-mcevoy-big-ag-corporate-organics.

Eiser, J. Richard, Susan Miles, and Lynn J. Frewer. 2002. "Trust, Perceived Risk, and Attitudes toward Food Technologies 1." *Journal of Applied Social Psychology,* 32 (11):2423–2433.

Evans, Tony. 2010. "Professionals, Managers and Discretion: Critiquing Street-Level Bureaucracy." *The British Journal of Social Work,* 41 (2):368–386.

Evans, Tony. 2016. *Professional Discretion in Welfare Services: Beyond Street-Level Bureaucracy*. New York, NY: Routledge.

Evans, Tony, and John Harris. 2004. "Street-Level Bureaucracy, Social Work and the (Exaggerated) Death of Discretion." *The British Journal of Social Work,* 34 (6):871–895.

Fairweather, John R. 1999. "Understanding How Farmers Choose between Organic and Conventional Production: Results from New Zealand and Policy Implications." *Agriculture and Human Values,* 16 (1):51–63.

Fetter, T. Robert, and Julie A. Caswell. 2002. "Variation in Organic Standards Prior to the National Organic Program." *American Journal of Alternative Agriculture,* 17 (2):55–74.

Fineman, Stephen. 1998. "Street-Level Bureaucrats and the Social Construction of Environmental Control." *Organization Studies,* 19 (6):953–974.

Fountain, Jane E. 2001. "Paradoxes of Public Sector Customer Service." *Governance,* 14 (1):55–73.

Gazley, Beth. 2014. "Good Governance Practices in Professional Associations for Public Employees: Evidence of a Public Service Ethos?" *Public Administration Review,* 74 (6):736–747.

Gerring, John. 2012. *Social Science Methodology: A Unified Framework.* New York: Cambridge University Press.

Goodman, David. 2000. "Organic and Conventional Agriculture: Materializing Discourse and Agro-Ecological Managerialism." *Agriculture and Human Values,* 17 (3):215.

Greenwood, Royston, Roy Suddaby, and C. R. Hinings. 2002. "Theorizing Change: The Role of Professional Associations in the Transformation of Institutionalized Fields." *Academy of Management Journal,* 45 (1):58–80.

Grunert, Klaus G., and Kristina Aachmann. 2016. "Consumer Reactions to the Use of EU Quality Labels on Food Products: A Review of the Literature." *Food Control,* 59:178–187.

Guthman, Julie. 1998. "Regulating Meaning, Appropriating Nature: The Codification of California Organic Agriculture." *Antipode,* 30(2):135–154.

Guthman, Julie. 2004a. *Agrarian Dreams: The Paradox of Organic Farming in California.* Berkeley, CA: University of California Press.

Guthman, Julie. 2004b. "The Trouble with 'Organic Lite' in California: A Rejoinder to the 'Conventionalisation' debate." *Sociologia Ruralis,* 44 (3):301–316.

Guthman, Julie. 2014. *Agrarian Dreams: The Paradox of Organic Farming in California.* Berkeley, CA: University of California Press.

Hannan, Timothy H. 1997. "Market Share Inequality, the Number of Competitors, and the HHI: An Examination of Bank Pricing." *Review of Industrial Organization,* 12 (1):23–35.

Harsch, Jon H. 2010. "Merrigan Promises 'the Age of Enforcement' for Organic Agriculture." *AgriPulse.* Accessed June 7, 2019. http://www.agri-pulse.com/20100415H1asp.

Hattem, Julian. 2013. "Lawmakers Fear New Regulatory Burdens on Organic Farmers." *The Hill.* Accessed June 7, 2019. http://thehill.com/regulation/energy-environment/294781-lawmakers-fear-new-regulatory-burdens-on-organic-farmers.

Heckman, J. 2006. "A History of Organic Farming: Transitions from Sir Albert Howard's *War in the Soil* to USDA National Organic Program." *Renewable Agriculture and Food Systems,* 21(3):143–150.

Hedge, David M., Donald C. Menzel, and George H. Williams. 1988. "Regulatory Attitudes and Behavior: The Case of Surface Mining Regulation." *Western Political Quarterly,* 41(2):323–340.

Heikkila, Tanya, and Andrea K. Gerlak. 2013. "Building a Conceptual Approach to Collective Learning: Lessons for Public Policy Scholars." *Policy Studies Journal,* 41(3):484–512.

Henke, Christopher R. 2008. *Cultivating Science, Harvesting Power: Science and Industrial Agriculture in California.* Cambridge, MA: MIT Press.

Henry, Gary T., and Stephen W. Harms. 1987. "Board Involvement in Policy Making and Administration." *Public Administration Review,* 47(2): 153–159.

Hill, Heather C. 2003. "Understanding Implementation: Street-Level Bureaucrats' Resources for Reform." *Journal of Public Administration Research and Theory,* 13 (3):265–282.

Hoodes, Liana, Michaeal Sligh, Harriet Behar, Roger Blobaum, Lisa J. Bunin, Lynn Coody, Elizabeth Henderson, Faye Jones, Mark Lipson, and Jim Riddle. 2010. *National Organic Action Plan: Advancing Organic Agriculture in the U.S.* Pittsboro, NC: Rural Advancement Foundation International.

Howard, Albert. 1946. *The War in the Soil.* Emmaus, PA: Organic Gardening.

Howard, Philip H., and Patricia Allen. 2006. "Beyond Organic: Consumer Interest in New Labelling Schemes in the Central Coast of California." *International Journal of Consumer Studies,* 30(5):439–451.

Hupe, Peter, Michael Hill, and Aurélien Buffat. 2015. *Understanding Street-Level Bureaucracy.* Bristol, UK: Policy Press.

IFOAM. 2014. *The IFOAM Norms for Organic Production and Processing.* Bonn, Germany: International Federation of Organic Agriculture Movements.

Ikerd, John. 2018. "The Industrialization of Organics." *Journal of Agriculture, Food Systems, and Community Development,* 8(12):9–12.

International Organic Inspectors Association (IOIA). 2001. "Ethics." Accessed July 22, 2017. http://www.ioia.net/ethics.html.

International Organic Inspectors Association (IOIA). 2003. "Complaint Procedures." Accessed July 22, 2017. http://www.ioia.net/complaint_procedures.html.

International Organic Inspectors Association (IOIA). 2009. "McEvoy Takes Helm at NOP." *The Inspector's Report,* 18(4):1–4.

International Organic Inspectors Association (IOIA). 2016a. *The Inspector's Report* 25(4): 1.

International Organic Inspectors Association (IOIA). 2016b. "2017 IOIA Member Dues and a New Benefit." *The Inspector's Report,* 25(3):6.

International Organic Inspectors Association (IOIA). n.d. "International Organic Inspectors Association." International Organic Inspectors Association. Accessed July 22, 2017. http://www.ioia.net/.

Jaffee, Daniel, and Philip H. Howard. 2010. "Corporate Cooptation of Organic and Fair Trade Standards." *Agriculture and Human Values,* 27(4):387–399.

Johnson, Nathanael. 2014. "Showdown at the Organic Standards Board Meeting." *Grist.* Accessed June 7, 2019. https://grist.org/food/showdown-at-the-organic-standards-board-meeting/.

Judge-Lord, Devin, Constance L. McDermott, and Benjamine Cashore. 2018. "Do Private Regulations 'Ratchet Up?' A Comparative Classification Framework." American Politics Workshop, University of Wisconsin-Madison. Accessed June 7, 2019. https://apw.polisci.wisc.edu/APW_Papers/JudgeLord%20APW%20Private%20Regulation.pdf

Kane, Patricia. 2010. *Letter to the National Organic Program on Behalf of the ACA.* Mabel, MN: Accredited Certifiers Association.

Kettl, Donald F. 2000. "The Transformation of Governance: Globalization, Devolution, and the Role of Government." *Public Administration Review,* 60(6):488–497.

Kindy, Kimberly, and Lyndsey Layton. 2009. "Integrity of the Federal 'Organic' Label Questioned." *Washington Post,* July 3, 2009. Accessed June 7, 2019. http://www.washingtonpost.com/wp-dyn/content/article/2009/07/02/AR2009070203365.html.

Kneafsey, Moya, Rosie Cox, Lewis Holloway, Elizabeth Dowler, Laura Venn, and Helena Tuomainen. 2008. *Reconnecting Consumers, Producers and Food: Exploring Alternatives.* New York, NY: Berg.

Kotchen, Matthew J, and Klaas van't Veld. 2009. "An Economics Perspective on Treating Voluntary Programs as Clubs." *Voluntary Programs: A Club Theory Perspective,* 67–86. Edited by Matthew Potoski and Aseem Prakash. Cambridge, MA: MIT Press.

Kourula, Arno, Markus Paukku, Andrew Peterman, and Mikko Koria. 2019. "Intermediary Roles in Regulatory Programs: Toward a Role-Based Framework." *Regulation and Governance,* 13(2): 141–156.

Kuepper, George. 2010. *A Brief Overview of the History and Philosophy of Organic Agriculture.* Poteau, OK: Kerr Center for Sustainable Agriculture.

Läpple, Doris, and Hugh Kelley. 2013. "Understanding the Uptake of Organic Farming: Accounting for Heterogeneities among Irish Farmers." *Ecological Economics,* 88:11–19.

Läpple, Doris, and Tom Van Rensburg. 2011. "Adoption of Organic Farming: Are There Differences between Early and Late Adoption?" *Ecological Economics,* 70(7):1406–1414.

Lathrop, Kyle W. 1991. "Pre-empting with Oranges: Federal Regulation of Organic Food Labeling." *Journal of Corporation Law,* 19:885–930.

Lee, Eungkyoon. 2010. "Information, Interest Intermediaries, and Regulatory Compliance." *Journal of Public Administration Research and Theory,* 21(1):137–157.

Leech, Nancy L., and Anthony J. Onwuegbuzie. 2007. "An Array of Qualitative Data Analysis Tools: A Call for Data Analysis Triangulation." *School Psychology Quarterly,* 22(4):557–584.

Levi-Faur, David. 2011. "Regulation and Regulatory Governance." In *Handbook on the Politics of Regulation,* 3–24. Edited by David Levi-Faur. Northampton, MA: Edward Elgar.

Levi-Faur, David, and Shana M. Starobin. 2014. "Transnational Politics and Policy: From Two-Way to Three-Way Interactions." *Jerusalem Papers in Regulation and Governance.* Jerusalem, Israel: The Hebrew University.

Lipsky, Michael. 1980. *Street-Level Bureaucracy: Dilemmas of the Individual in Public Services*. New York, NY: Russell Sage Foundation.

Loconto, Allison M. 2017. "Models of Assurance: Diversity and Standardization of Modes of Intermediation." *The ANNALS of the American Academy of Political and Social Science*, 670(1):112–132.

Lotter, Donald W. 2003. "Organic Agriculture." *Journal of Sustainable Agriculture,* 21:59–128.

Lyton, Timothy D. 2017. "The Taming of the Stew: Regulatory Intermediaries in Food Safety Governance." *The ANNALS of the American Academy of Political and Social Science,* 670(1):78–92.

Marshall, R. S., and Stephen S. Standifird. 2005. "Organizational Resource Bundles and Institutional Change in the US Organic Food and Agricultural Certification Sector." *Organization and Environment,* 18(3):265–286.

Martin, Andrew. 2005. "Organic Milk Debate: Dairies Dispute 'Organic' Values." *Chicago Tribune*, January 10, 2005. Accessed June 7, 2019. http://articles.chicago tribune.com/2005-01-10/news/0501100142_1_aurora-organic-dairy-organic -industry-national-organic-standards-board.

May, Peter J. 1992. "Policy Learning and Failure." *Journal of Public Policy,* 12(4):331–354.

May, Peter J. 1993. "Mandate Design and Implementation: Enhancing Implementation Efforts and Shaping Regulatory Styles." *Journal of Policy Analysis and Management,* 12(4):634–663.

May, Peter J. 2002. "Social Regulation." In *The Tools of Government,* 156–185. Edited by Lester Salamon. New York, NY: Oxford University Press.

May, Peter J. 2004. "Compliance Motivations: Affirmative and Negative Bases." *Law and Society Review,* 38(1):41–68.

May, Peter J. 2005. "Regulation and Compliance Motivations: Examining Different Approaches." *Public Administration Review,* 65(1):31–44.

May, Peter J. 2007. "Regulatory Regimes and Accountability." *Regulation and Governance,* 1(1):8–26.

May, Peter J., and Ashley E. Jochim. 2013. "Policy Regime Perspectives: Policies, Politics, and Governing." *Policy Studies Journal,* 41(3):426–452.

May, Peter J., and Raymond Burby. 1998. "Making Sense Out of Regulatory Enforcement." *Law and Policy,* 20(2):157–182.

May, Peter J., and Robert S. Wood. 2003. "At the Regulatory Front Lines: Inspectors' Enforcement Styles and Regulatory Compliance." *Journal of Public Administration Research and Theory,* 13(2):117–139.

May, Peter J, and Søren Winter. 1999. "Regulatory Enforcement and Compliance: Examining Danish Agro-Environmental Policy." *Journal of Policy Analysis and Management,* 18(4):625–651.

May, Peter J, and Søren Winter. 2000. "Reconsidering Styles of Regulatory Enforcement: Patterns in Danish Agro-Environmental Inspection." *Law & Policy,* 22(2):143–173.

May, Peter J., and Søren Winter. 2007. "Politicians, Managers, and Street-Level Bureaucrats: Influences on Policy Implementation." *Journal of Public Administration Research and Theory,* 19(3):453–476.

McCaffrey, Lara. 2016. "In California, Ending Double Trouble for Organic Producers." *The New Food Economy*. Accessed June 7, 2019. https://newfoodeconomy.org/organic-farming-bill-california/

McEvoy, Miles. 2012. "Organic 101: Complaints and How They're Handled." *USDA Blog*. Accessed June 7, 2019. http://blogs.usda.gov/2012/04/13/organic-101-complaints-and-how-theyre-handled/.

McEvoy, Miles. 2014. "Ensuring Organic Integrity through Inspections." *Organic 101*. United States Department of Agrictulture. Accessed June 7, 2019. https://www.usda.gov/media/blog/2014/02/26/organic-101-ensuring-organic-integrity-through-inspections.

McEvoy, Miles. 2017. "In Their Words: Miles McEvoy." Organic Produce Network. Accessed June 7, 2019. http://www.organicproducenetwork.com/article/318/in-their-words-miles-mcevoy.

Meidinger, Errol. 2006. "The Administrative Law of Global Private-Public Regulation: The Case of Forestry." *European Journal of International Law*, 17(1): 47–87.

Meier, Kenneth J., and Laurence J. O'Toole Jr. 2011. "Comparing Public and Private Management: Theoretical Expectations." *Journal of Public Administration Research and Theory,* 21(S3): i283–i299.

Mercola, Joseph. 2017. "More Details Emerge in Organic Industry Fraud." Organic Consumers Association. Accessed June 7, 2019. https://www.organicconsumers.org/news/more-details-emerge-organic-dairy-fraud

Miars, Peggy. 2012. "Establishing Consistency: Regulation of Material Review Organizations Is the First Step to a New Era." *Materials Review: News and Information for the Organic Community,* 13(4):3.

Miller, Henry, and John Cohrssen. 2018. "Why Not Genetically Engineered Organic Foods?" *Washington Examiner*, June 3, 2018. Accessed June 7, 2019. https://www.washingtonexaminer.com/opinion/that-organic-label-doesnt-mean-anything-except-marketing-and-higher-prices.

Mitchell, Jerry. 1997. "Representation in Government Boards and Commissions." *Public Administration Review,* 57(2):160–167.

Montagna, Paul D. 1968. "Professionalization and Bureaucratization in Large Professional Organizations." *American Journal of Sociology,* 74(2):138–145.

Mosier, Samantha L. 2017. *Creating Organic Standards in US States: The Diffusion of State Organic Food and Agriculture Legislation, 1976–2010*. Lanham, MD: Lexington Books.

Musheno, Michael, and Steven Maynard-Moody. 2015. "Playing the Rules: Discretion in Social and Policy Context." In *Understanding Street-Level Bureaucracy,* 169–86. Edited by Peter Hupe, Michael Hill, and Aurélien Buffat. Bristol, UK: Policy Press.

Musshoff, Oliver, and Norbert Hirschauer. 2008. "Adoption of Organic Farming in Germany and Austria: An Integrative Dynamic Investment Perspective." *Agricultural Economics,* 39(1):135–145.

Mzoughi, Naoufel. 2011. "Farmers Adoption of Integrated Crop Protection and Organic Farming: Do Moral and Social Concerns Matter?" *Ecological Economics,* 70(8):1536–1545.

National Agricultural Statistics Service (NASS). 2014. *2012 Census of Agriculture: Organic Survey (2014).* Washington, DC: U.S. Department of Agriculture.

National Agricultural Statistics Service (NASS). 2017a. *Certified Organic Survey 2016 Summary.* Washington, DC: U.S. Department of Agriculture.

National Agricultural Statistics Service (NASS). 2017b. *NASS Highlights: 2016 Certified Organic Survey.* Washington, DC: U.S. Department of Agriculture.

Nielsen, Vibeke Lehmann. 2006. "Are Street-Level Bureaucrats Compelled or Enticed to Cope?" *Public Administration,* 84(4):861–889.

Nielsen, Vibeke Lehmann. 2007. "Differential Treatment and Communicative Interactions: Why the Character of Social Interaction Is Important." *Law and Policy,* 29(2):257–283.

Nielsen, Vibeke Lehmann. 2015. "Law Enforcement Behaviour of Regulatory Inspectors." In *Understanding Street-Level Bureaucracy,* 115–131. Edited by Peter Hupe, Michael Hill, and Aurélien Buffat. Bristol, UK: Policy Press.

National Organic Standards Board (NOSB). 2016. *Organic Standards Board Policy and Procedures Manual.* Washington, DC: U.S. Department of Agriculture.

Nowacek, David M., and Rebecca S. Nowacek. 2008. "The Organic Foods System: Its Discursive Achievements and Prospects." *College English,* 70(4):403–420.

Obach, Brian K. 2007. "Theoretical Interpretations of the Growth in Organic Agriculture: Agricultural Modernization or an Organic Treadmill?" *Society and Natural Resources,* 20(3):229–244.

Obach, Brian K. 2015. *Organic Struggle: The Movement for Sustainable Agriculture in the United States.* Cambridge, MA: MIT Press.

Oberholtzer, Lydia, Carolyn Dimitri, and Catherine Greene. 2005. "Price Premiums Hold on as US Organic Produce Market Expands." In *Electronic Outlook Report.* Edited by Economic Research Service. Washington, DC: US Department of Agriculture, Economic Research Service.

Office of the Inspector General (OIG). 2005. *Audit Report: Agricultural Marketing Service's National Organic Program.* Office of the Attorney General: Washington, DC.

Office of the Inspector General (OIG). 2010. *Oversight of the National Organic Program.* Office of the Attorney General: Washington, DC.

Onwuegbuzie, Anthony J., and Nancy L. Leech. 2007. "Sampling Designs in Qualitative Research: Making the Sampling Process More Public." *The Qualitative Report,* 12(2):238–254.

Oregon Tilth. n.d. *Oregon Tilth Guide for Organic Consultants.* Oregon Tilth. Accessed June 7, 2019. https://tilth.org/education/resources/organic-consultants/.

Organic Materials Review Institute (OMRI). 2018a. "History of OMRI." Organic Materials Review Organization. Accessed September 12, 2018. https://www.omri.org/history-omri.

Organic Materials Review Institute (OMRI). 2018b. *OMRI Generic Materials List.* Eugene, OR: Organic Materials Review Organization.

Organic Materials Review Institute (OMRI). 2018c. *OMRI Products List.* Eugene, OR: Organic Materials Review Organization.

Organic Materials Review Institute (OMRI). 2018d. "Organic Materials Review Organization." Organic Materials Review Organization. Accessed June 7, 2019. https://www.omri.org/.

Organic Trade Association (OTA). 2017a. *Comment on Regenerative Organic Certification.* Washington, DC: Organic Trade Association.

Organic Trade Association (OTA). 2017b. *Organic Trade Association Sues USDA over Failure to Advance Organic Livestock Standards*. Washington, DC: Organic Trade Association. Washington, DC: Organic Trade Association.

Organic Trade Association (OTA). 2017c. *Maturing U.S. Organic Sector Sees Steady Growth of 6.4 Percent in 2017.* Washington, DC: Organic Trade Association.

Ostrom, Elinor. 2005. *Understanding Institutional Diversity*. Princeton, NJ: Princeton University Press.

Ostrom, Elinor. 2011. "Background on the Institutional Analysis and Development Framework." *Policy Studies Journal,* 39(1):7–27.

Ostrom, Elinor. 2014. "Do Institutions for Collective Action Evolve?" *Journal of Bioeconomics,* 16(1):3–30.

OTCO. 2018. "About Oregon Tilth." Accessed May 12, 2018. https://tilth.org/certification/start/why/.

Patashnik, Eric M. 2014. *Reforms at Risk: What Happens after Major Policy Changes Are Enacted*. Princeton, NJ: Princeton University Press.

Pautz, Michelle C. 2009. "Trust between Regulators and the Regulated: A Case Study of Environmental Inspectors and Facility Personnel in Virginia." *Politics and Policy,* 37(5):1047–1072.

Pautz, Michelle C., and Sara Rinfret. 2013. *The Lilliputians of Environmental Regulation: The Perspective of State Regulators*. New York, NY: Routledge.

Pennings, Joost M. E., Scott H. Irwin, and Darrel L. Good. 2002. "Surveying Farmers: A Case Study." *Applied Economic Perspectives and Policy,* 24(1):266–277.

Peroni, Heidi. 2016. "Organic Roots: Washington's Extensive History of Organic Agriculture and Certification." *Ag Briefs.* Accessed June 7, 2019. https://wastatedeptag.blogspot.com/2016/09/organic-roots-washingtons-extensive.html.

Pierson, Paul. 1993. "When Effect Becomes Cause: Policy Feedback and Political Change." *World Politics,* 45(4):595–628.

Pires, Roberto R. C. 2011. "Beyond the Fear of Discretion: Flexibility, Performance, and Accountability in the Management of Regulatory Bureaucracies." *Regulation and Governance,* 5(1):43–69.

PMA Research. 2017. "What's Driving Continued Growth in Organic Produce?" *PMA Research.* Accessed June 7, 2019. https://www.pma.com/content/articles/2017/10/whats-driving-continued-growth-in-organic-produce.

Pollan, Michael. 2006. *The Omnivore's Dilemma*. New York, NY: Penguin Press.
Pollitt, Christopher. 2005. "Decentralization." In *The Oxford Handbook of Public Management*, 371–397. Edited by Ewan Ferlie, Laurence E. Lynn Jr., and Christopher Pollitt. New York, NY: Oxford.
Potoski, Matthew, and Aseem Prakash. 2009. *Voluntary Programs: A Club Theory Perspective*. Cambridge, MA: MIT Press.
Power, Michael. 1997. *The Audit Society: Rituals of Verification.* New York, NY: Oxford.
Prakash, Aseem, and Matthew Potoski. 2007. "Collective Action through Voluntary Environmental Programs: A Club Theory Perspective." *Policy Studies Journal,* 35:773–792.
"Protests Prompt Delay on Government's Rules for Organic Food." 1998. *New York Times*, February 6, 1998, 18A.
Rawson, Jean M. 1998. *Organic Foods and the Proposed Federal Certification and Labeling Program.* Washington D.C.: Congressional Research Service.
Raynolds, Laura T. 2004. "The Globalization of Organic Agro-Food Networks." *World Development*, 32(5):725–743.
Read, Richard. 2017. "The Dirt on 'Organic' Food: U.S. System Lets Fakes Get Through." *NerdWallet*. Accessed June 6, 2019. https://www.nerdwallet.com/blog/organic-label-pineapple-investigation-costa-rica/.
Real Organic Project. n.d. "Real Organic Project." Accessed June 7, 2019. https://www.realorganicproject.org/.
Reganold, John P., and Jonathan M. Wachter. 2016. "Organic Agriculture in the Twenty-First Century." *Nature Plants,* 2:15221.
Rhodes, Rod A. W. 1997. *Understanding Governance: Policy Networks, Governance, Reflexivity and Accountability*. Philadelphia, PA: Open University Press.
Rice, Scott. 2014. *ACA letter to U.S. Secretary of Agriculture Thomas Vilsack.* Mabel, MN: Accredited Certifiers Association.
Rinquist, Evan J., Jeffrey Worsham, and Marc A. Eisner. 2000. *Contemporary Regulatory Policy*. Boulder, CO: Lynne Rienner Publishers.
Robichau, Robbie Waters, and Laurence E. Lynn Jr. 2009. "The Implementation of Public Policy: Still the Missing Link." *Policy Studies Journal,* 37(1):21–36.
Rodale Institute. n.d. "Regenerative Organic Certified." Accessed June 14, 2018. https://rodaleinstitute.org/regenerativeorganic/.
Rodale, J.I. 1945. *Pay Dirt*. Emmaus, PA: Rodale Press.
Rodale, J.I. 1971. "Join the Fight against Organic Phonies." *Organic Gardening and Farming*, 18(6):190–112.
Rusaw, Carol A. 1995. "Learning by Association: Professional Associations as Learning Agents." *Human Resource Development Quarterly,* 6(2):215–226.
Schmitter, Philippe C., and Wolfgang Streeck. 1985. *Private Interest Government: Beyond Market and State*. Thousand Oaks, CA: SAGE.
Scholz, John T. 1991. "Cooperative Regulatory Enforcement and the Politics of Administrative Effectiveness." *American Political Science Review,* 85(1):115–136.
Scholz, John T., and Neil Pinney. 1995. "Duty, Fear, and Tax Compliance: The Heuristic Basis of Citizenship Behavior." *American Journal of Political Science,* 39(2):490–512.

Schuler, Randall S. 1975. "Role Perceptions, Satisfaction, and Performance: A Partial Reconciliation." *Journal of Applied Psychology,* 60:683–687.

Scofield, A. M. 1986. "Organic Farming—the Origin of the Name." *Biological Agriculture and Horticulture,* 4(1):1–5.

Scoles, Margaret. 2013. "Margaret Scoles on Organic Inspection." In *Brian Kahn's Home Ground.* Edited by Brian Kahn: Montana Public Radio. Accessed June 7, 2019. https://www.youtube.com/watch?v=xeweR5XFPbs.

Searle, John R. 1964. "How to Derive 'Ought' from 'Is.'" *The Philosophical Review,* 73(1):43–58.

Selden, Sally Coleman, Gene A. Brewer, and Jeffrey L. Brudney. 1999. "Reconciling Competing Values in Public Administration: Understanding the Administrative Role Concept." *Administration and Society,* 31(2):171–204.

Selznick, Philip. 1985. "Focusing Organizational Research on Regulation." In *Regulatory Policy and the Social Sciences*, 363–367. Edited by Roger N. Noll. Berkeley, CA: University of California Press.

Shulman, Stuart W. 2003. "An Experiment in Digital Government at the United States National Organic Program." *Agriculture and Human Values,* 20:253–265.

Sircely, Matt. 2011. "Evaluating Livestock Inputs." *The Inspector's Report,* 20(4):17.

Stemwedel, Daren A. 2009. "A Fundamental Flaw in the National Organic Program: The Case for National Regulation of Organic Input Materials." *San Joaquin Agricultural Law Review,* 19:199–222.

Stoker, Gerry. 1998. "Governance as Theory: Five Propositions." *International Social Science Journal,* 50(155):17–28.

Strom, Stephanie. 2018. "As the Organic Movement Fractures, Farmers and Food Companies Are Redefining the Standards They Built." *The New Food Economy,* June 14, 2018. Accessed June 7, 2019. https://newfoodeconomy.org/farmers-food-companies-regenerative-organic-certification/.

Susskind, Lawrence, and Gerard McMahon. 1985. "The Theory and Practice of Negotiated Rulemaking." *Yale Journal on Regulation,* 3:133–165.

Teddlie, Charles, and Abbas Tashakkori. 2009. *Foundations of Mixed Methods Research.* Thousand Oaks, CA: SAGE.

Temkar, Arvin. 2015. "New Rules on Organic Foods Challenged." *Courthouse News Service*, April 8, 2015. Accessed June 7, 2019. https://www.courthousenews.com/New-Rules-on-Organic-Foods-Challenged/

Thilmany, Dawn. 2006. "The U.S. Organic Industry: Important Trends and Emerging Issues for the USDA." *Agricultural Marketing Report,* 61(1):1–8.

United Stated Department of Agriculture (USDA). 1980. *Report and Recommendations on Organic Farming.* Washington, DC: U.S. Department of Agriculture.

United Stated Department of Agriculture (USDA). 2015a. *Instruction: Accreditation Policies and Procedures.* Washington, DC: U.S. Department of Agriculture.

United Stated Department of Agriculture (USDA). 2015b. *List of Surrendered, Suspended, and Revoked Organic Certifying Agents.* Washington, DC: U.S. Department of Agriculture.

United Stated Department of Agriculture (USDA). 2015c. *Sound & Sensible.* Washington, DC: U.S. Department of Agriculture.

United Stated Department of Agriculture (USDA). 2016a. *Exporting Organic Products from the U.S.* Washington, DC: U.S. Department of Agriculture.

United Stated Department of Agriculture (USDA). 2016b. *Interim Instruction: Material Review Edited by U.S. Department of Agriculture.* Washington, DC: U.S. Department of Agriculture.

United Stated Department of Agriculture (USDA). 2017. *Count of Certified Organic Operations Shows Continued Growth in U.S. Market.* Washington, DC: U.S. Department of Agriculture.

United Stated Department of Agriculture (USDA). 2018. *Organic Integrity Database.* Washington, DC: U.S. Department of Agriculture.

United Stated Department of Agriculture (USDA). n.d. "FAQ: Becoming a Certifying Agent." Accessed September 11, 2018. https://www.ams.usda.gov/services/organic-certification/faq-becoming-certifying-agent.

"USDA Abandons Three Contentious Issues in Proposed Organic Standards." 1998. *American Journal of Alternative Agriculture,* 13(2):95.

Van de Ven, Andrew. 2007. *Engaged Scholarship: A Guide for Organizational and Social Research.* New York, NY: Oxford University Press.

van der Heijden, Jeroen. 2008. *Competitive Enforcement: Comparative Analysis of Australian Building Regulatory Enforcement Regimes.* Amsterdam, The Netherlands: IOS Press.

van der Heijden, Jeroen. 2017. "Brighter and Darker Sides of Intermediation: Target-Oriented and Self-Interested Intermediaries in the Regulatory Governance of Buildings." *The ANNALS of the American Academy of Political and Social Science,* 670(1):207–224.

Veldstra, Michael D., Corinne E. Alexander, and Maria I. Marshall. 2014. "To Certify or Not to Certify? Separating the Organic Production and Certification Decisions." *Food Policy*, 49:429–436.

Vogl, Christian R., Lukas Kilcher, and Hanspeter Schmidt. 2005. "Are Standards and Regulations of Organic Farming Moving Away from Small Farmers' Knowledge?" *Journal of Sustainable Agriculture*, 26(1):5–26.

Vos, Timothy. 2000. "Visions of the Middle Landscape: Organic Farming and the Politics of Nature." *Agriculture and Human Values,* 17(3):245–256.

Walker, Richard M., and Emma Jeanes. 2001. "Innovation in a Regulated Service: The Case of English Housing Associations." *Public Management Review,* 3(4):525–550.

Warner, Melanie. 2010a. "Federal Organic Regulators Discover a Novel Concept—Enforcement." *CBS News*. Accessed June 7, 2019. http://www.cbsnews.com/news/federalorganic-regulators-discover-a-novel-concept-enforcement/.

Warner, Melanie. 2010b. "Trouble in the Henhouse: The Scam of Organic Eggs." *CBS News*, October 19, 2010. Accessed June 7, 2019. https://www.cbsnews.com/news/trouble-in-the-henhouse-the-scam-of-organic-eggs/.

Weible, Christopher M., and David P. Carter. 2017. "Advancing Policy Process Research at Its Overlap with Public Management Scholarship and Nonprofit and Voluntary Action Studies." *Policy Studies Journal,* 45(1):22–49.

Whetsell, Travis A. 2013. "Theory-Pluralism in Public Administration: Epistemology, Legitimacy, and Method." *The American Review of Public Administration,* 43(5):602–618.

Whoriskey, Peter. 2017a. "Flaws in the 'USDA Organic' Certification Can Allow Ordinary Products to Be Labeled as Organic." *The Washington Post*, May 20, 2017. Accessed June 7, 2019. http://www.columbiatribune.com/news/20170520/flaws-in-usda-organic-certification-can-allow-ordinary-products-to-be-labeled-organic.

Whoriskey, Peter. 2017b. "USDA Closes Investigation into a Massive Organic Farm—but What Did It Check?" *The Washington Post*, Wonkblog. Accessed October 16, 2018. https://www.washingtonpost.com/news/wonk/wp/2017/09/28/usda-closes-investigation-into-a-massive-organic-farm-but-what-did-it-check/?utm_term=.ed0bf7851918.

Winter, Søren C., and Peter J. May. 2001. "Motivation for Compliance with Environmental Regulations." *Journal of Policy Analysis and Management,* 20(4):675–698.

Wright, Charles L. 1977. "A Note on the Decision Rules of Public Regulatory Agencies." *Public Choice,* 31(1):151–155.

Wylard, Gwendolyn. 2011. *OTA Comment on the Evaluation of Material Review Organizations.* Washington, DC: Organic Trade Assocation.

Yang, Raymond H. 2014. "Organic Certification Evolution." IFOAM Organic World Congress 2014, Instanbul, Turkey.

Yiridoe, Emmanuel K., Samuel Bonti-Ankomah, and Ralph C. Martin. 2005. "Comparison of Consumer Perceptions and Preference toward Organic versus Conventionally Produced Foods: A Review and Update of the Literature." *Renewable Agriculture and Food Systems,* 20(4):193–205.

Index

About the Author

David P. Carter is an assistant professor of public policy and administration at the Public Affairs Program of the Department of Political Science, University of Utah. His research spans regulatory design and administration in the context of USDA organic certification, institutional innovations in local governance, and collective action between climbers, among other topics.

Lightning Source UK Ltd.
Milton Keynes UK
UKHW020412171019
351750UK00006B/108/P

9 781498 574198